RETHINKING ECCLESIA

Being and Becoming Christ Communities:
Towards a Borderless Church

National and Global Ecumenical Perspectives

RETHINKING ECCLESIA

Being and Becoming Christ Communities: Towards a Borderless Church

National and Global Ecumenical Perspectives

EDITORS

Daniel Rathnakara Sadananda
Solomon Paul J.

CHURCH OF SOUTH INDIA
2021

Rethinking Ecclesia – Being and Becoming Christ Communities: Towards a Borderless Church – National and Global Ecumenical Perspectives - Jointly Published by the Indian Society for Promoting Christian Knowledge (ISPCK), Post Box 1585, Kashmere Gate, Delhi-110006 and The Church of South India (CSI), CSI Centre, No. 5, Whites Road, Royapettah, Chennai – 600 014.

ISBN: 978-93-90569-17-5

Laser typeset by

ISPCK, Post Box 1585, 1654, Madarsa Road, Kashmere Gate, Delhi-110006 • *Tel:* 23866323

e-mail: ashish@ispck.org.in • ella@ispck.org.in
website: www.ispck.org.in

Contents

Acknowledgements

Rethinking Ecclesia publication is a result of well thought and planned series of 8 consultations in the year 2018. These consultations are indeed a historical moment in the history of CSI as we commemorated 70 years of faithful journey and Reformation 500. All the papers presented and the meaningful conversations helped the Church of South India to engage more vigorously in the process of searching new theological directions and visions as CSI steps into a new decade.

The theme "Being and becoming Christ communities – towards a borderless Church" were discussed from a) Biblical perspective, b) theological and ethical perspective, c) liturgical and missiological perspective, d) prophetic and diaconal perspective, e) empowerment and educational perspective, f) healing and reconciliation perspective, g)National and global ecumenical perspective.

The Moderator of the Church of South India, Most Rev Thomas K Oommen, who inaugurated these consultations, remarked that the theological exercise of Rethinking Ecclesia consultations has helped the Church to find new directions in the pilgrim journey of CSI. He said that these explorations should continue to challenge the church and its mission and also make way for newer forms of ministerial engagements with the people at the grassroots.

These consultations has enabled the church to make a theological audit of CSI, create a network of theological educators who are CSI and gave opportunity for the seminary and the church to bridge the existing gaps in working closely with one another for the sake of a united mission.

This book is a compilation of articles presented during the Biblical and Theological perspective consultations held at CSI Synod, Chennai. Biblical scholars and theologians of CSI came and presented their insights on the theme.

At this moment we thank the God of koinoinia who called CWM to partner with CSI from the beginning till the end of this Rethinking Ecclesia consultations helping us to encourage each other and also assuring us of God's accompaniment in our Pilgrim journey.

I also place my thanks to the Youth Department of CSI for their meticulous efforts in planning and implementation of these consultations and coordination in bringing out this publication.

Special thanks to ISPCK for publishing these books and partnering with CSI in continuance of God's mission.

Rathnakara Sadananda

Preface

It is with great joy and contentment that I present the book – **Rethinking Ecclesia: Being and Becoming Christ Communities - Towards a borderless Church**, a series of articles deliberating on the theme from National and Global Ecumenical perspectives.

Borders have become an undeniable reality today. Both the nation-state and the Church are governed by borders. If borders are to offer security and protection, the same borders also exclude or de-mark the other. The Church in India, since many decades now has been struggling to engage with the many identity-markers such as caste, region, denomination, tradition, gender and so on... Though the Church is called to live and profess the liberating Spirit of God which transcends borders yet, she is engaged in grappling with the many challenges imposed by the identity-markers.

These identity-markers which promote intrinsic value to the worth of an individual and betterment of the community have become a strong border/barrier among communities leading to negation of life. It is in this context that the book "Rethinking Ecclesia" tries to find meaning and sense for the existence of the CSI today and tomorrow.

The articles in this book resonate the visions, dreams, aspirations and even frustrations in re-imaging a new community centered on Christ and show the way forward towards a borderless Church. These articles are not ashamed of the grave mistakes the Church has committed in stiffening borders and building walls of animosity, but have rather lamented over them in repentance, waiting for another opportunity to set it right through theological articulations. They reflect on the present context of the Church battling even more greater hurdles as the socio-geo-political climate of the nation is going through a shift towards rightist ideological forces.

"**Rethinking Ecclesia**" is the result of a well-thought and planned series of eight consultations in the year 2018. These consultations were indeed a historical moment in the history of CSI as we commemorated 70 years of faithful journey and Reformation 500. All the papers presented, and the meaningful conversations helped the Church of South India to engage more vigorously in the process of searching for new theological directions and visions as the CSI steps into a new decade.

The theme "**Being and becoming Christ communities – towards a borderless Church**" were discussed from a) Biblical, b) Theological, c) Liturgical and Missiological, d) Prophetic Diaconal, e) Empowerment and Educational, f) Health, Healing and Harmony as well as g) National and Global Ecumenical perspectives. Around 109 papers were presented during these consultations containing voices from within and outside, voices of complement and voices of dissent, voices from the vulnerable and those in responsible positions.

The Moderator of the Church of South India, Most Rev Thomas K. Oommen, who inaugurated these consultations, remarked that the theological exercise of Rethinking Ecclesia consultations has helped the Church to find new directions in the pilgrim journey of CSI. He said that these explorations should continue to challenge the Church and its mission and also make way for newer forms of ministerial engagements with the people at the grassroots, especially in liberating the weak and the oppressed.

These consultations affirmed that the Church is the sign and the sacrament of the reign of God; that as the continuation of the incarnation and an instrument of the reign of God, the Church ventures to live out her commitment and faith as an alternative, that proclaims boldly that another world is possible, right here and now in our midst; and that the Church is the penultimate, subject to change and transformation till she is ultimately absorbed into the very reign of God. And therefore, the consultations were indeed a prophetic call to rethink *ecclesia*, not only its significance, importance and relevance, but also its being and becoming.

These consultations have enabled the Church to make a theological audit of CSI, create a network of theological educators in the CSI and provide opportunity for the theological faculties and the Church to bridge the existing gaps in working closely with one another for the sake of a united mission. Consultations also provided the much-needed space for the Church and the theological fraternity to listen to, have dialogue with one another, and work together to overcome the lacuna that exists between the seminary and the sanctuary.

This book is a compilation of articles presented during the consultations from **National and Global Ecumenical perspectives** held at CSI Synod, Chennai. Theologians from both national and global ecumenical partner churches and organizations of the CSI presented their insights on the theme. The opinions and theological assertions expressed in the articles are of the authors themselves put forth with sincere faith and hope that, they would help the people of God to clearly and relevantly articulate the self-understanding of being and becoming Ecclesia.

Heartfelt thanks to the Moderator of CSI, Rt. Rev. Thomas K. Oommen, Deputy Moderator, Rt. Rev. V. Prasada Rao, and Treasurer, Adv. C. Robert Bruce for their immense solidarity and leadership during all the consultations that took place. Special thanks to the General

Secretary, Rev. Dr. Daniel Rathnakara Sadananda, who was responsible for this theological exploration and exercise, without whose guidance, these consultations and this publication would not have been possible.

We thank the God of *koinoinia* who called the CWM to partner with CSI from the beginning till the end of these "Rethinking Ecclesia" consultations by helping us to encourage each other and also assuring us of God's accompaniment in our pilgrim journey towards becoming a borderless Church.

I also place my thanks to Mrs. Augustina Margaret, staff, Youth Department, CSI for her efforts in planning and implementation of these consultations and for coordinating to bring out this publication. Thanks to Mrs. Jessica Richard and Mrs. Angel Merlin for their help in proof reading and special thanks to ISPCK for publishing these books and partnering with CSI in the continuance of God's mission.

Epiphany, 2020   **Solomon Paul J.**
Chennai, India   **Editor**

Towards a Borderless Church

At the time of independence in August 1947, the colonial masters re-drew the borders of our nation even as it wriggled in pain and tension. People began to move to safer places, many were displaced from their habitats and lives and livelihoods lost. The country paid dearly for its independence. In September 1947, our fore-fathers and mothers decided to overcome the borders of denominational faith, mission allegiance and regionalism to form the Church of South India. Inspired by the Lord's prayer for unity and oneness 'that they all may be one as we are one', our fore-fathers and mothers ventured into a radical discipleship of imitating God's oneness. To a divided India, to the divided church worldwide, the Church of South India became a parable of unity, a beacon of hope, an aroma of the Gospel.

Borders do exist. Each cell in our body has a border. However, each cell communicates and interacts with the other. Every one of us lives within certain borders and ever-widening borders, within the borders of our home, family, congregation, faith communities, village, town, state, and country. At times we share borders, we cross borders, we merge borders, we re-draw borders. We dream of borderless-ness. Thus, we live with borders, yet we yearn for borderless-ness. In our quest to understand borders and borderless-ness, we learn to understand the energy, power, potentials and the possibilities and opportunities that evolve in crossing and going beyond our borders.

A borderless Church calls us to look intently at our borders. Normally, borders are identity markers. Borders do inform us about what we are and what we are becoming. Anglican, Presbyterian, Congregationalist, and Methodist Christians in Southern India decided to redraw their ecclesial borders together to form, very consciously, a united and uniting Church of national and cultural identity. They indeed looked intently on the form of their faith, spiritual expressions, traditions, spiritual practice and how they organised themselves as congregations and churches. The varied faith expressions, spirituality, and liturgical traditions mingled together in their many-ness, yet interwoven into a colourful and powerful expression of oneness. The borders merged, were redrawn, new borders emerged.

In the first creation story, borderless-ness and harmony are evident. The varied, multiple forms and creatures created multitudes of borders that were held together in oneness and wholeness, an intrinsically connected, networked, harmonious blend is seen as good, and very good, culminating in Sabbath, the Shalom. Only the second creation story speaks of the process of self-discovery in relation to the other - in holding the other in respect and dignity, the identity of each is defined, interpreted and enhanced. The concept of identity formation, freedom with responsibility is introduced in the narrative only to affirm that when identity is misrepresented, and when the creature tries to impersonate the Creator, the connections, bonds and networks get destroyed.

The call and election narratives in the Old Testament are an invitation to understand this complex, yet beautiful interrelatedness and intrinsic value. The narratives of Abraham, Sarah and Hagar, Isaac and Rebecca, Esau, Jacob, Leah and Rachel show that they are invited to cross borders, share borders, draw new borders, and understand the mysteries beyond their borders and become a borderless community. For the writers of Genesis, their histories inform us of God's initiative that challenges human community to rediscover, reinvent and remember the borderless creation and be part of God's Shalom.

The story of Exodus is about breaking the borders that exploit and are oppressive. It is a story of empowerment for liberation; crossing the red sea - a baptism in water, is the visual symbol of overcoming borders and becoming a liberated community, a parable of liberation. The liberated community was called to represent the possibility of another world, where the world can hear its breathing and visualise its being. The commandments and the book of the covenant were given in order to make an alternative, another world possible, it was drawing new borders that would negate the borders that exploit, oppress, destroy and threaten life and proclaim the coming of justice and peace, not only within the borders of the liberated community, but beyond its borders and everywhere. Love, faithfulness, peace, justice, and righteousness are to be seen and experienced within the liberated community in order that it becomes the Gospel to the whole world.

The Deuteronomic eucharistic prayer (*anamnesis* - Deut. 26:5-10) holds together the wandering Aramean walking from the margins, crossing borders, the small and insignificant, few and negligible, strangers and aliens becoming empowered, to go through the struggles, pains, and sufferings, getting liberated from the crushing clutches of death and destruction to emerge as a people. It is a narration of resilience and resurrection, a living experience of breaking the chains of bondage and enslavement, to redraw borders that seem to extend and expand unceasingly.

The Prophetic literature which came at the time of exilic and post exilic period clearly depicts the community that was called to be an alternative, liberated community, which by losing its way and its borders emerged from its struggles of being conquered and occupied. The prophetic voice makes it clear that when the community loses its vision of liberation, corruption and injustice extinguish the power to move, connect and be open, when the community loses its dynamism and becomes static; connectivity, networks, and the power to transcend are destroyed and in the process people get marginalised and lose the creative power to overcome the borders and transcend the borders. Therefore, the prophetic call comes first as comforting, then as sowing the vision of a new heaven and new earth, but with a strong inclination to empower the community against corruption, injustice, oppression, and exploitation, so that they may discern and embrace the new that is already there and sprouting. Only in empowering the marginalised, in drawing out the inherent, innate, and immanent potentials, does the community once again regain movement, connectivity, and openness.

In the New Testament, Jesus' understanding of God as is defined in his conversation with the Samaritan woman is very instructive and profound - "God is Spirit; those who worship him must worship him in Spirit and truth" (Jn.4.24). God does not belong to one community, he is not stationary at Jerusalem or in Shechem, on the mount; God cannot be bound to certain traditions and forms of spirituality; he is boundless and borderless.

Jesus was preaching the reign of God, its imminence, and the reign of God, not the Church, was at the centre of his teaching. The reign of God is the safe space, that comforts, cares, heals and reconciles. It is a place where one receives forgiveness, grace, and loving kindness. The reign of God is where one rests powerlessness, vulnerability, frailty, weakness, insufficiency, and gets empowered. The reign of God calls the excluded, rejected, oppressed and outcastes, embraces them into an inclusive solidarity, to offer justice and peace. The reign of God is love, joy and hope, that brings integrity, wholeness, and harmony. It is the space and place where people experience the presence and accompaniment of God. The reign of God that Jesus proclaimed therefore, is not only borderless, but that which also gives assurance of eternity.

To make God's reign felt and experienced by commoners, Jesus' movement was evolved within the borders of Jewish religion. Jesus called out (*ecclesia*) twelve/seventy and created a community within the community. On this rock, I will build my Church (Matt.16.18), a rock-like, solid faith; but unlike the traditional understandings of messianic liberation, redemption was brought about by the suffering servant. Jesus standing firmly on the prophetic traditions of his faith, practiced prophetic *diakonia* as the means and instrument of liberation (Matt.16:21,24,25). Indeed, this was the culmination of a borderless, prophetic diaconal movement that moved from Nazareth to Gennesaret, to Tire Sidon, Samaria and to Jerusalem and back to Galilee. A borderless movement that empowered the margins, resisted the empire, critiqued religion and embraced the marginalised. It was a community called to be salt and light; a new life-giving and life-affirming movement, as flowing water and wind that blows wherever it pleases, a borderless new creation.

The Evangelists interpreted the crucified Christ as the one who draws all people to himself as he is lifted up. The crucified one, broken, crushed, and eliminated signifies the movement of the crucified people, and draws together those who are condemned to margins, denied of space, opportunity, rights and honour, bound because of their innocence and ignorance, excluded, made voiceless and unjustly persecuted. The crucified one in his passion and death enters the crucified communities and releases the power of life. The resurrected one who is boundless, and has overcome the limitations of time and space, inaugurates a new creation, boundless and borderless.

The early Church was indeed borderless, as it understood Jesus' command to go and make disciples of all nations (Matt.29:19), as a mandate to create borderless Christ communities. It also had a clear geographical strategy, 'you will be witnesses, in Jerusalem and in all Judea and Samaria and to the ends of the earth' (Acts 1:8). Peter also is 'converted' to the borderless Church, after the vision and real-life experience at Joppa and Caesarea (Acts 10). Paul, after his world-encircling, missional engagements writes his faith conviction; his *magna carta* "there is neither Jew nor Greek, slave nor free, male or female for you are all one in Christ" (Gal.3:28). It is very consistent with his sacramental theology which envisions a borderless Church, "Do you not know that all of us who have been baptized into Christ Jesus were baptized into his death? Therefore, we have been buried with him by baptism into death, so that, just as Christ was raised from the dead by the glory of the Father, so we too might walk in newness of life" (Rom.6:3,4). Every follower of Christ has been baptized into Christ, and therefore when he writes to Corinthians he clarifies that "The bread that we break, is it not a sharing in the body of Christ? Because there is one bread, we who are many are one body, for we all partake of the one bread" (1 Cor.10:16,17).

The ecclesiological reflections in the letter of Hebrews speaks of the visible and invisible Church. The language that 'we are surrounded by a great cloud of witnesses' (Heb.12:1), connects us with the Church of yesterday, with the Church of today and the future. The language used in the catholic epistles, of being strangers and pilgrims, to reflect the nature and being of the Church, depicts the struggles of living up to the great vision of a people of God. The theological affirmation that the Church is the Household of God (Eph.2:19) compared to the households of the time, and of the Church as God's House inform us about the profound theological affirmation: "Once you were not a people, now you are the people of God" (1Pet.2:10).

The eschatological vision of the book of Revelation depicts the New Jerusalem, the space of peace as an inclusive space, without borders. It speaks about a most valuable, yet fully transparent space, a space without a temple, as the whole space itself has the presence of God, which is light. All the nations of the earth will bring their splendor into it, it has gates that will always remain open, yet nothing impure will enter it (Rev.21:22ff). Even the heavenly space is not static; it is dynamic and transforming. The river of water of life, as clear as crystal flowing from the throne of God, and the trees of life which are for the healing and reconciliation of the nations, clearly affirm the process of being and becoming a Christ community, a borderless Church.

Today, we understand the Church as a sign and sacrament of the reign of God. She is an instrument of the reign of God and alternative that proclaims that another world is possible, that it is here and now in our midst. The Church is the penultimate, subject to change and transformation till she is absorbed into the reign of God. As a sign and sacrament of the reign of God, the Church has distinctive, discernible identity markers and borders, yet calling and exhorting people to the borderless reign of God.

As the Church of South India steps into the eighth decade of her being and becoming, may she be given grace upon grace to understand anew the gift of oneness and unity. May the 70-year celebrations be a sign of prophetic SEVA (*diakonia*), Social Empowerment - a Vision in Action upholding the sacramentality of life, where she, as a borderless Church travels beyond suspicion, fear and hostility in a multi-religious, multi-lingual, multi-cultural society. May she be empowered and emboldened to share, cross and redraw borders in order to set the energy of the margins, the crucified peoples free. May the children and the young be inspired to DARE into a process of Discernment And Radical Engagement, and be change makers and signs of transformation. May she be given grace to be a real MITHRA (friend) - Migrant Intervention Towards Holistic Responsive Action, to understand the beauty and significance of the small, frail and vulnerable, and be a movement of protest and resistance that gives DISHA, a new direction (Disability Intervention for Solidarity and Holistic Accompaniment), for those disabled, excluded, and condemned to margins. May the Church of South India be given grace to be God's instrument that brings dynamism and moves people, to connect not only with the Creator, but also with those around and all of God's creation, to open new possibilities of celebrating and living life in all its fulness. May the Church of South India be a new GEET, song (Gender Equity and Enabling Timetable), harmony that proclaims and practices equality, justice, and peace. In being and becoming a borderless Church, may the Church of South India open herself to God's eschaton, move in her radical engagement in the ever-continuous movement of unity and oneness of all and experience the fullness of Him who fills everything in every way (Eph.1:22), so that God may be all in all (1 Cor.15:28).

Rev. Dr. D. Rathnakara Sadananda
General Secretary, CSI

1

"Mountains shall drip Sweet Wine and they shall drink it."

Borderless Church and its Vision in the 21st century Indian context

K. Jesurathnam

Amos 9:11-15 New Revised Standard Version (NRSV)

The Restoration of David's Kingdom

[11] *On that day I will raise up the booth of David that is fallen, and repair its[a] breaches, and raise up its[b] ruins,and rebuild it as in the days of old;*

[12] *in order that they may possess the remnant of Edom*
and all the nations who are called by my name,
says the LORD who does this.

[13] *The time is surely coming, says the LORD,*
when the one who plows shall overtake the one who reaps,
and the treader of grapes the one who sows the seed;
the mountains shall drip sweet wine,
and all the hills shall flow with it.
[14] *I will restore the fortunes of my people Israel,*
and they shall rebuild the ruined cities and inhabit them;
they shall plant vineyards and drink their wine,

and they shall make gardens and eat their fruit.
¹⁵ I will plant them upon their land,
  and they shall never again be plucked up
  out of the land that I have given them,
says the LORD your God.

The church in the twenty first century India is facing many odds both in terms of its hope and frustrations, many aspirations and agonies than ever before. While on the one hand it stands as a beacon of hope and symbol of un-quenching thirst for yet to be realized but already existing Kingdom of God, on the other hand it is also standing in many odds and contradictions caught up amid corruption and related anomalies than ever before. While the church as a people's movement is ever and always flourishing and progressing well, but the institutional church is getting weaker and at times stand in contradiction to the calling and mission entrusted to her. We have not lost or exhausted in the hope that God called his church and with all its flaws and weakness it is a most visible sign of God's Kingdom present in the word at this kairotic moment. There are number of biblical texts that affirm this fact. We shall reflect on Amos 9:11-15 as a relevant biblical text in the light of our proposal of the vision of borderless church in the paragraphs that follow.

The Context of Amos

Under Jeroboam II (793-753 B.C.E) Israel, the Northern Kingdom, enjoyed military success (2 Kings 14:25), high prosperity (e.g., Am 3:15) and luxurious living (e.g., Amos 6:4-7). But the people no longer recognized their covenant with the LORD. They oppressed the poor among them (e.g., 2:6; 5:11; 8:4-6), perverted justice (e.g., Amos 5:7, 12, 15), and made religious ceremony a hypocritical cover-up for idolatry and godless living (e.g., Amos 5:21-26). Therefore, the Holy One of Israel would punish his covenant people (e.g., 3:2; 6:14). The visions of judgment the Lord showed Amos in chapters 7 through 9 have come to a climax with the fifth and last vision in 9:1-4 (the other four visions are in Amos 7:1-3; 7:4-6; 7:7-9; and 8:1-3). The Lord himself appears at (or even *on*) the altar to call for the destruction of the shrine at Bethel and the death of the unfaithful Israelites. "Not one will get away, none will escape," no matter where he may try to hide from the almighty creator. God will fix his eyes on them for evil and not for good (9:1-4). His own people have become like a heathen nation in his sight, no different from their historic enemies the Philistines or the Arameans. His saving acts, such as the exodus from Egypt, give an impenitent Israel no special claim on his favor (9:7). "I will destroy [the sinful kingdom] from the face of the earth," God thunders (9:8). It was no empty threat. A generation later the kingdom of Israel was no more. While this general gloomy situation was widely discussed by Amos in all through his oracles in all the nine chapters, for a moment, a ray of gospel promise shines through the dark cloud of judgment on Israel's horizon: "Yet I will not totally destroy the house of Jacob" (9:8). Like a farmer sifting grain in a sieve, God will disperse his people among the nations to separate the precious remnant from the waste (9:9). Then the thunder rolls again: all the secure sinners among the Israelites will die by the sword (9:10). Finally, the unconditional gospel promise in 9:11-15 brings the book of Amos to a close, brilliant sunset in the last moments of a stormy day.

Many critical commentators cannot deal with such a radical turnaround from judgment to grace. Julius Wellhausen found here "roses and lavender instead of blood and iron"[1] would not accept Amos as the author of these verses. More recent scholars like Mays also call this passage a later addition: "After the Exile, when the prophetic message of judgment had been fulfilled, the oracles of salvation in 9:11-15 were added to let the broken community hear the full counsel of God."[2] Nothing in the book itself separates these final verses from the other words of Amos. God's law has done his "strange work...his alien task" (Isa 28:21) of condemning sinners. In the last five verses of the book the Lord of faithful grace takes up "his own work" of comforting the condemned and raising the spiritually dead with his promise of salvation (cf. *Apology* XII, 51).

God would personally get involved in the process of restoration and it will be demonstrated in all its abundance and fullness of life (Amos 9:13). What Amos had earlier pronounced a reversal has now been announced by means of rebuilding of the ruins (9:11), and planting of vineyards and gardens (9:13). The earlier threat of futile labor is now transformed into the proclamation of success. Thus, the threat of judgment of destruction and drought is fully cancelled (see Amos 5:11 and 3:11 and 15 and 6:8 and 11). Additionally, Amos announces the reversal of the threat of exile earlier announced in 5:27; 7:11 and 17. Moreover the punishment of the expulsion from the land will never again take place. God, affirms Amos, the land "which I have given them" from which Israel shall never again be taken away. "As in the days of old" (9:11b) says God I will restore their fortunes in the manner we discussed above.[3] But Amos makes it clear that it is only because of God's initiative the new bestowal of restoration transcends the old one. God's action alone effects this intensified renewal of God's salvific gift and not all by any human initiative and effort.

Interpretation of Amos 9:11-15 in the post-biblical context

The rebuilding of the fallen booth of David is later interpreted by the Qumran community and in the New Testament. In the Qumran community in Cairo Damascus Document (CD 7:16) where Amos 9:11 is cited to inform the interpretation of Amos 5:26. Also in 4QFlor 1:12-13 Amos 9:11 is directly interpreted (John M. Allegro, *Qumran Cave 4* Vol 1 4Q 158-4Q 186 Oxford: Clarendon Press, 1968), p. 531: "… just as it is written, 'Then I will raise up the fallen book of David'—that (means) 'the fallen booth of David' who will stand forth to deliver Israel." Wolff, p. 355 comments on this that, here the metaphor of Davidic "booth" must be taken to mean the "Warrior Messiah" or the "Searcher of the Law."

In the New Testament, in Acts 15:16-17, James the brother of the Lord quoted Amos 9:11 at the Council of Jerusalem (Acts 15:16). His purpose was to support the work of Paul and Barnabas with the authority of the prophetic Word. They had been preaching among the Gentiles the good news of pure grace through the blood of Christ. In a unique way the quotation of the prophet's words themselves played an influential part in the fulfillment of the prophecy. Here in the context of Acts the "rebuilding of the booth of David" reflects the rebuilding of the universal church where Jews and Gentiles alike are part of God's universal mission.

The words of Wolff are relevant on Amos 9:11-15 for any contemporary appropriation of the words of Amos. Wolff states:

> *The postexilic theologian, in any case, was asking what new word Yahweh was entrusting to his time. No generation, however, should fail to hear in his words the basic theme that the renewal of fallen community is to be expected only on the basis of God's activity of building and planting. Only in this way will the new life surpass the old. Amos sufficiently drove home the point that, left to its own devices, humanity procures for itself only its demise. The promise which transcends this state of affairs applies only to those who have already been judged and condemned.*[4]

Amos is not just a "prophet of re-union" he is a prophet of eschatological doom and eschatological hope. Amos holds both aspects together; he is the first preacher of eschatology, but not a "popular eschatology." His eschatology is Yahwistic eschatology, in which the divine demands count, and the divine-human relationships are at the center, transforming and shaping all inter-human relationships.[5]

Based on Amos 9:15 we see that the restoration program announced by the prophet are blessed with triad of activities that will be blessed with fruition: first, "they shall rebuild" the desolate cities and inhabit them. Second, "they shall plant vineyards" and drink their wine (for joint blessings of building cities and planting vineyards see

Isa 65:21, Jer 29:5 and Ezek 28:26). Third, "they shall cultivate gardens" and eat their fruits (see Jer 29:5 and verse 28).

The final boon of blessings and restoration is again expressed in agricultural metaphors as follows in verse 15: "I shall plant them" on their own soil and they shall never again be uprooted from the soil. "I shall give" Israel as a tree, permanently planted, never again be uprooted. Once again, the prophet reverses the destiny of Israel (see Amos 5:2 for a contrary situation in the past). Says the Lord your God" is a direct conclusion of the oracle in the second person.[6]

Amos, interestingly, throughout this passage emphatically uses agrarian models where the agricultural metaphors are dominant in order to describe the restoration program of God for the Israelites. God would bring abundance and that abundance is explicated by the overflow of sweet wine dripped from the mountain slopes. While the rulers of ancient Israel in the eighth century BCE boasts about economic boom and development by way of moving from agrarian tribal economy to urban market economy, Amos maintains that it is in the agrarian and egalitarian mode of life that brought abundant blessings to Israel in the past. In this agrarian life the principles of sharing equally among everyone is the real distinct feature. God's restoration program will thus be total, and the transformation will be complete in all respects for the people of Israel. The abundance is also well represented by the way in which people shall plant vineyards and eat their own fruit and this abundance is the sign of God's total restoration program.

Implications of Amos 9:11-15 to the borderless church in the twenty first century Indian context

In the light of the foregoing discussion on the text of Amos 9:11-15 and its various nuanced theological insights we are now able to draw the following appropriate implications for the borderless/universal church of the community of God's people.

First, church as a renewed covenant community: (Covenant of religion and Covenant of society: both as alternate communities). Israelites are obliged to follow the commandments of Yahweh in all possible ways since they are the chosen community set apart for Yahweh. The following verses in Exodus 19:4-6 affirms this idea:

> You have seen what I did to the Egyptians, and how I bore you on eagles' wings and brought to myself. Now therefore, if you obey my voice and keep my covenant, you shall be treasured possession out of all the peoples. Indeed, the whole earth is mine, and you shall be for me a priestly kingdom and a holy nation.

Same is true in today's church as she is chosen by God to be salt and leaven on this earth. The church per se that transcends any denomination and regional and linguistic affiliation can only demonstrate this quality so that it becomes borderless and yet filled with the people of covenant community. As explained above the exiled community of Israel become a covenant community where the religious ideals of justice and holiness will be affirmed and demonstrated would become a distinct yet an inclusive community for all and by all.

For Israelites as a covenant community was the concrete manifestation of special concern towards dispossessed was also at the heart of her identity as God's chosen and people. Prophet Jeremiah affirms the same when he writes:

> *Did not your father eat and drink and do justice and righteousness? Then it was well with him. He judged the cause of the poor and needy; then it was well. Is not this to know me? Says the LORD.*[7]

Second, church as restored community. Just as Amos talks about the restoration program of Yahweh as his visible sign of love towards his people, the borderless church today is a visible expression of God's faithfulness towards his church despite her flaws. God has restored his church by means of the sacrificial death of his son Jesus Christ on the cross. Therefore the restored community is no longer a fallen community but it is a transformed and is in the process of transforming until its perfection to the Kingdom of God realized fully on this earth here and now. In this sense the church is seen as a reformed community where the fallen placed are repaired and renewed.

Third, church as new community: As discussed above in the text of Amos the total restoration and rehabilitation plan of God for Israel had resulted in a new formation of the community in such a way that the old glory of the nation is once again brought back with the grand plan of God's complete restoration. The borderless church that we are envisaging today should show the visible signs of God's Kingdom where there will be no borders in terms of any caste and class discriminations are allowed. In the words of departed Indian Church Dalit leader James Massey this is clearly articulated:

> *I only want to add that the Church in India has to become a community of believers in the Jesus' model. This means that the members of all the Church denominations have to become 'Christian' in the real sense of the word, which will pave way for them to build a 'transformed community' or a 'new community' (world), to which they belong. This dual transformation (according to Moses' model and Jesus' model) automatically will take care of the problem of various subaltern/ oppressed groups (including that of the Dalits), and together they will succeed in forming a new community in which there will be no Dalits or non-Dalits, Tribals or non-Tribals, Adivasi or non-Adivasis. In that community all men and women will be seen as human beings created in the image of God. This is what we are looking for in the future. Towards the fulfillment of this vision both the 'cultural expressions' of Theology and the 'subaltern expressions' of Theology have to play a very crucial role.[8]*

Let this vision of new community/humanity be spread all over based on the biblical principles of equality, justice and truth that God of Judah and Dalits and others held on to.

Fifth, church as eschatological community of Yahweh. The restored and repaired community of Israel as presented in Amos 9:11-15 has been a visible community of demonstration of God's love, peace and justice. Yet it is in the process of transformative change that would be guided by God's love. The borderless church we are proposing is filled with the hall marks of justice, peace and equality and at the same time it is in the process of becoming and moving towards the eschatological transformation. It is already and not yet in this process of transformation. Here the hallmark of this borderless church is that it is guided by divine-human relationship that will guide and shape inter-human relationships in this borderless universal church. Just as Amos' community of Israel is shaped by God's plan alone so too the borderless church of twenty-first century is founded and guided by God alone.

Let the sweet wine that drips from the mountain of borderless church be tasted by all the people of God in many generations yet to come and born!!

Endnotes

[1] Cited by H. W. Wolff, *Joel and Amos: A Commentary* (Philadelphia: Fortress Press, 1977), p. 352

[2] J. L. Mays *Amos: A Commentary, Old Testament Library* (Louisville: Westminster John Knox Press, 1969), p. 165.

[3] H. W. Wolff, *Joel and Amos*, p. 354.

[4] Ibid, p. 355.

[5] Gerhard F. Hasel, "The Alleged "NO" of Amos and Amos' Eschatology," *Andrews University Seminary Studies*, Vol. 29:1 (spring 1991), pp. 3-18, esp. p.18.

[6] Shalom M. Paul, *Amos: A Commentary on the book of Amos* (Minneapolis: Fortress Press, 1991), pp. 294-295.

[7] Jeremiah 22:15-16.

[8] James Massey, "Theology for a New Community: Looking ahead," in *Theology for a New Community: Dalit Consciousness with a symbolic universe and meaning systems* Eds. T. K. John and James Massey (New Delhi: Centre for Dalit and Subaltern Studies, 2013), p. 320.

2

Borderless Church and Beyond:

Where do We Go from Here?

George Zachariah

"Jesus foretold the kingdom, and it was the church that came."
-Alfred Loisy

"Church is a provisional institution, a transitional organization, and the vestibule of the kingdom."
-Vitor Westhelle

I appreciate the office bearers of the Synod, the revered bishops and the Synod Secretariat for their commitment and vision to transform the 70th birthday celebrations of the Church of South India into a spiritual and theological exercise to introspect, interrogate and to envision together what it means to be an *ekklesia* in our times when ideologies and practices of exclusion, legitimized by theologies, continue to perpetuate borders and walls that divide us. Such a context demands from us radical social and political engagement informed by our faith and inspired by the life and witness of Jesus, the Christ. Anniversaries and jubilees are not merely occasions to glorify the past or to dwell in theological nostalgia. Rather it is the Kairos moment for the church to initiate leaps of faith. Our deliberations on the theme "Rethinking Ecclesia: Being and Becoming Christ Communities - Towards a Borderless Church" during the last one year has helped us to re-imagine our vocation informed by our immersion in the realities around us—the tensions, conflicts, violence, suffering, beauty, wonder and the promise of this historic moment—to engage in relevant forms of public witness in India today.

How do we theologically engage with the borders that divide us? How do we live out the prophetic legacy of the Church of South India in the contemporary context of fascism and conformism? How do we become a truly subaltern church? How do we re-imagine our public witness amid economic and ecological injustice? These are some of the questions that we have tried to wrestle with in the various consultations during this year. We celebrate the seventieth birthday of the CSI at a time when the global church celebrates the 500th anniversary of the Protestant Reformation. Reformation is essentially a movement of the unheard. It is a counter-hegemonic movement from below to de-centre the Church. All human initiatives in history, unfortunately, have the potential to become oppressive, thanks to the reality of sin and our inability for self-redemption. When we absolutize our truths and our institutions, we fail to recognize the pervading hegemonic presence of the Empire within us which lure us to internalize and embrace the logic and culture of the very systems that we tried to destroy in our initiatives of ecclesial and social reformation. The history of Christianity testifies that the Church is not immune to the possibility of getting degenerated into life-denying institutions that legitimize and perpetuate injustice and dominant interests. Betrayal of the original vision is therefore a tragic possibility inherent in all human initiatives including the Church and the ecumenical institutions.

Nevertheless, history also teaches us that such situations midwife the emergence of radical movements of renewal and reformation from the margins. Biblical witness to the life-giving Spirit that hovers over chaotic situations and brings about life and meaning further inspires us to believe in the divine project of renewal and transformation. Said differently, the Reformation is the divine project of making all things new, and we are called to continue to participate in this mission in our times. The task before us—as members and ecumenical partners and well-wishers of the CSI, therefore, is not to romanticize the past and to live in the present glorifying the past; rather our vocation is to reclaim the subversive and creative legacy of the *ekklesia*, and to bear witness relevantly and contextually in the public sphere.

"If your church closed its doors tomorrow, would anyone in the neighborhood care?" The Church is facing an existential crisis in our times. It has lost its relevance. If the neighborhood is not concerned about our existence or death, there is something terribly wrong with us. We have lost our saltiness. Rabbi Abraham Joshua Heschel's observation about the eclipse of religion is instructive here:

> It is customary to blame secular science and anti-religious philosophy for the eclipse of religion in modern society. It would be more honest to blame religion for its own defeats. Religion declined not because it was refuted, but because it became irrelevant, dull, oppressive, insipid. When faith is completely replaced by creed, worship by discipline, love by habit; when the crisis of today is ignored because of the splendor of the past; when faith becomes an heirloom rather than a living fountain; when religion speaks only in the name of authority rather than with the voice of compassion--its message becomes meaningless.

This self-reflexive observation should guide us in our attempts to rethink *ekklesia*.

A critical evaluation of the mainline Christian organizations in India including the churches, unfortunately, reveals that we have betrayed our calling to be a transforming presence in the public sphere. We compete each other in providing spiritual legitimization to the powers and principalities. We continue to use the minority rights card carefully and consistently to protect our institutional interests and to engage in collective bargaining. We are yet to become a subaltern church.

It is in this context that we need to reclaim the spirit of reformation. Reformation is nothing but re-forming the Church. As Jurgen Moltmann rightly observes, Reformed theology is a re-forming theology which is not *"grounded in confessional statements laid down once and for all, nor is it based on a tradition of infallible and irreformable doctrinal decisions.... It is grounded in the 'reformation' of the church 'according to the Word of God' attested in Holy Scripture, which is to be confessed anew in each new situation."* Said differently, reformed theology is re-forming theology, and its vocation is to make reformation a permanent experience in the life of the church.

Confessions of the Church are theological statements that articulate the fundamental doctrinal positions of the Church. In many cases confessional statements are fixed in content and form, and non-negotiable as they contain the universal and timeless truth and beliefs of the Church. However, for Moltmann, *"Confessions are meant to express in concrete terms what needs to be said in the name of God concerning matters of faith here and now."* Therefore, it is imperative on us to negotiate our non-negotiable confessions, polity, and practices, informed by our discernment of the signs of the times, to transform them into gospels of transformation and healing in our neighborhoods and communities. In that process, the Church will happen as *ekklesia* in the life of our communities, witnessing the living God by disrupting the prevailing unjust social order through its subversive and therapeutic presence. This presentation is an attempt to envision a church reclaiming the biblical vision of ekklesia.

Rethinking Ekklesia: Church as Event

Ekklesia was the term that the early Christian communities had chosen to represent their gathering and fellowship of faith. It was a term borrowed from the civic and political practices and institutions of their times. *Ekklesia* represented the assembly of the citizens, called away from their routine life to gather together and deliberate upon issues pertaining to civic and political life to re-enter the public life with new vision. So *ekklesia* primarily signifies the fellowships which are engaged in public witnessing with alternative visions, reflections and commitment. In that sense, e*kklesia* categorically affirms a radical discontinuity with the prevailing order by initiating retreats for introspection and re-visioning to return to relevant interventions in the public sphere.

In fact, the adoption of this new name for their fellowship was a faith confession for the early church because they understood Church as a witnessing community which gathered together to re-vision its calling and dispersed into the wider community to become a transforming presence of the Gospel. For the early Christian community "turning the world upside down" was the vocation of the *ekklesia*. Here, the sanctuary was a not an end in itself; rather it was a transit point for life-transforming rituals, reflections, and fellowships, which empowered and enabled the faith community to return to the public sphere to engage in ministries of prophetic witness.

Ekklesia is not a monument that is built on the foundations of traditions and doctrines; rather it is an empowering and transforming experience that happens in the lives of the communities at the margins. Here the church becomes an event. Church happens as fellowship, solidarity, love, care, compassion, justice, and restoration in the lives of people, who go through the tragic experience of utter God-forsakenness. The model of the church here is no more the household with fortified walls and exclusive claims of supremacy and purity. Rather, the alternative model for the church happening is the model of street. In the context of death and destitution, the street represents our availability and accessibility to each other. It is this sense of mutuality and relationality that helps our brothers and sisters on the margins who barely hang on to life to face life with determination and reclaim their God-given humanity. Street is the abode of those who are thrown out from their homes. Street is also the home of those who are denied entry into household because of their caste, and sexual orientation. Hence the street invites us to experience the happening of the church in the most unexpected places. The vision of *ekklesia* is an invitation to get out of the security and comfort of the institutionalized church to become part of the transformative experience of the *ekklesia* that is happening in the street. Church happens in our constant leap from house to street. The witness of the church in the street—our ministries of compassionate justice and care, our actions of solidarity, our struggles, our rituals—provides the community the foretaste of the eschatological banquet.

Ekklesia: A Church that is Maladjusted to the Prevailing Order

"Do not be conformed to this world, but be transformed by the renewing of your minds, so that you may discern what is the will of God—what is good and acceptable and perfect" (Romans 12: 2). How do we understand the meaning of renewal and transformation in our context? For Apostle Paul, the present eon is a state of corruption, and hence being conformed to the present eon is to participate in its corruptness. Non-conformism is not a negative response. Our non-conformism towards the present eon is creative as it leads to resistance and transformation. As Paul Tillich reminds us, "a church in which the divine protest does not find a human voice through which it can speak has become conformed to this eon." Non-conformity is the resistance to idolatry. It is the critique of our attempts to absolutize ourselves, our church, our tradition, our nation, and our community.

Non-conformism was a favorite slogan for Dr. Martin Luther King Jr. For him nonconformity is creative when it is directed by a renewed and transformed life. "There are certain things in our social system to which all of us ought to be maladjusted. I never intend to adjust myself to the evils of segregation and the crippling effects of discrimination. I never intend to adjust myself to the inequalities of an economic system which takes necessities from the masses to give luxuries to the classes. I never intend to adjust myself to religious bigotry. I never intend to become adjusted to the madness of militarism, and the self-defeating method of physical violence… The salvation of the world lies in the hands of the maladjusted." In a sermon based on Romans 12: 1 and 2 Dr. King further elaborated his theology of creative maladjustment. "The saving of our world from pending doom will come, not through the complacent adjustment of the conforming majority but through the creative maladjustment of a nonconforming majority." In the contemporary Indian context, the vocation of the *ekklesia* is to become maladjusted to the prevailing order, and it requires costly commitment.

To be creatively maladjusted is an alternative worldview and behavior, a radical departure from what is usually expected. Creative maladjustment means to be aligned with the gospel imperative to be persistent on reversing any trend toward exclusion and discrimination, and to be engaged in the struggles of the marginalized. Creative maladjustment means to be inclusive and to reject the purity maps and codes of the dominant worldview. Creative maladjustment, as Paul observes, is not to be conformed to this world, but be transformed by the renewing of our minds. Renewal and transformation begin with a new baptismal vow where we denounce conformity to the prevailing order and intend to live a life of creative maladjustment. This requires the courage to identify systemic evils, to name them, to challenge them, and to eradicate them by participating in the ongoing struggles of the subaltern communities. Renewal and transformation challenge us to radical discipleship to incarnate God's power and embodied presence in history through our creative maladjustment for the sake of life. *Ekklesia* is primarily a community of disciples who affirm the lordship of Christ and live out their faith in Christ contesting the lordship of all imperial powers.

Ekklesia: A De-clericalized Church of the Multitude

Clericalism is all about power and how religious power is exercised in centralized and hierarchical structures. "Clergy in general may be good people dedicated to their calling, but clericalism creeps in when they are positioned in structures that facilitate the hierarchical mode of exercising power and they exercise their authority mainly to safeguard their own interests. Because of the clericalized ecclesiastical structures, many churches function as feudal establishments." The culture of clericalism is a cancer in the body of Christ. It is based on a distorted understanding of religious power and authority given to the ordained. We still harp on the Levitical priesthood and internalize the Levitical injunction that "the anointed of the Lord shall not be questioned or critiqued." Pope Francis addresses this issue when he observes that there is a lack of maturity and of Christian freedom among lay people due to the "sinful complicity of clericalism."

Jesus never called himself or his disciples, priests. He vehemently criticized the Jewish structures of priestly domination. Of course, the early church practiced plurality of ministry functions; but without ontological hierarchy. However, Christian ministry got reduced into hierarchical clericalism when the post-Constantine church copied the hierarchical model of governance from the Roman state and temples to gain recognition as a religion. If we are honest in our attempts to reclaim the values and ethos of *ekklesia*, it is imperative on us to be self-reflexive and evaluate our understanding of ministerial offices to see whether we subscribe to clericalism in our understanding and practice of ministry. Protestant Reformation's affirmation of the priesthood of all believers should inspire us to strive together to become a de-clericalized church. As Pope Francis rightly observed, "Clericalism, whether fostered by priests themselves or by lay persons, leads to an excision in the ecclesial body that supports and helps to perpetuate many of the evils that we are condemning today. To say "no" to abuse is to say an emphatic "no" to all forms of clericalism."

The alternative to a clericalized church is the *ekklesia* of the multitude. Yahu Vinayaraj's vision of the communion of the multitude is instructive here. We are all caught up in the reality of Empire which imposes its subjectivity on all living beings. Empire as sovereignty forms our subjectivities. Multitude is the new communion of subjectivity that resists Empire from within, challenging its borders. It is the living alternative that grows within Empire. Multitude is consisted of a host of "irreducible singularities." Multitude is a political subject with radical social consciousness to transform the world. While retaining their differences, multitude strives together for a common alternative life—the Commonwealth. It is a democracy that invites all to share and participate in the commons—the air, the water, the fruits of the soil, all nature's bounty—the habitat of the community of creation. Multitude is, therefore, an anti-imperial communion of diverse communities, practicing the art of resistance and creating alternatives to Empire.

Ekklesia as the communion of the multitude is a communion of de-imperialized subjectivities. It is a community that refuses to be co-opted by Empire to be incorporated into the imperial logic. Cross is the assurance for us to believe in the possibility to become de-imperialized subjectivities. The vocation of the communion of the multitude is to disrupt the culture of domination and exclusion. *Ekklesia* as the communion of the multitude is therefore a communion of the marginalized and it embodies the politics of the Crucified Christ. It is in our communion with the subaltern social movements that we re-imagine the meaning of church and thus become the *ekklesia* of the multitude. *Ekklesia* of the multitude enables and flourishes anti-imperialistic imaginations and subjectivities. It initiates an alternative politics that destabilize pyramidical power structures. It permeates our surroundings with the de-imperializing gospel of the Cross and flourishes the movement of life.

Ekklesia: A Church with Liturgies of Resilience and Reconstruction

Prayer, according to Jewish theologian Rabbi Abraham Joshua Heschel, "is meaningless unless it is subversive, unless it seeks to overthrow and to ruin the pyramids of callousness, hatred, opportunism, and falsehoods." Worship is a subversive activity that contests and overthrows the prevailing sinful order of injustice and inequality. For Moses, the Mount Horeb experience was not only an alternative experience of theophany, it was also a tutorial for an alternative understanding of worship. The alternative experience of theophany enabled Moses to re-imagine God as the vulnerable One, deeply affected by the scars of slavery. In the vision of the burning bush Moses encountered God as a co-sufferer who was embodied in the life-stories of pain-pathos and struggles for freedom and dignity of the enslaved communities. The sacramental and liturgical symbol of fire in the burning bush provided Moses an alternative understanding of worship. Worship should instill in the enslaved community the audacity to believe that the blazing fire of the dominant cannot destroy the beauty of life. The green leaves in the liturgy of the burning bush empowered Moses to believe in the possibility of a beyond of Egypt.

Moses' commissioning into the mission of liberation was also a liturgical act. He was asked to remove his sandals because he was standing on sacred ground. Moses' removing of the sandals was a rite of passage or an initiation ritual to become flesh in the struggles of the colonized people. In fact it was a public denouncement of his privilege and power: a prerequisite to get organically connected with and grounded in the struggles of the underdogs. Worship is therefore a life-changing experience where we are invited to realize and denounce our power and privilege in order to become credible and authentic comrades of the communities at the margins who are engaged in the salvific mission of turning the world upside down.

For *ekklesia*, worship is the resolve to overthrow the pyramids of economic injustice, and social exclusion such as casteism, patriarchy, and heterosexism. God liberated the slaves from their bondage in Egypt. But they ended up creating and worshipping new idols. The story of the Golden Calf is an invitation to critically evaluate our faith and spirituality to see whether we have replaced the God of the oppressed with the ungods of power, prosperity, and status quo. What we find here is the human tendency to reduce the mystery called Divine into idols of certainty. We also see here the institutionalization of a faith movement for liberation into an organized religion with its hierarchy, priesthood, rules and regulations, and the apparatus and paraphernalia of spirituality.

The dominant always uses religious institutions and religious leaders to exploit the religious sentiments of the common people to grab their possessions to create new idols which ensure them prosperity and power. This was precisely the role of Aaron in this story. Idolatry is nothing but the fetishization of our imperial projects, and liturgy in the context of idolatry celebrates the sacrifice of the powerless and the voiceless in the altar of patriotism, progress, family values, and cultural nationalism. The history of Christianity is also the history of the creation of the golden calves. Ungods are created in history to offer spiritual and theological legitimization to the pyramids of injustice and exclusion. For Sebastian Kappen the Christian Ungod "is the god whom Christians fashioned to legitimize their lust for wealth and power. It is the Christian ungod who authorized the Christian kings to colonize and enslave all pagan nations and to exterminate indigenous tribes of the Americas and Australia. It is the Christian ungod who permitted the Trans-Atlantic slave trade involving more than 30 million Africans. In short, the Christian ungod is a god who takes the side of the affluent and powerful against the vulnerable, a god with hands dripping with the blood of the innocent."

The history of Christianity in India is also not different. At critical times in our history, we betrayed our faith in God and worshipped the ungod. Patriotism, progress, development, caste privilege, patriarchy, heteronormativity, regionalism…the list of our golden calves continues. Many a time we become the worshippers of the ungods to protect and safeguard our vested interests. We are more comfortable in depending on the mercy of the ungods who rule us, than in the empowering presence of the liberating God. We have lost the courage of the early church to say boldly; "We must obey God rather than any human authority." Today, in the context of fascism, we have betrayed our calling, and became followers of the golden calves. Here we are surrounded by a cloud of witnesses, and we need to listen to their voices. When the German churches legitimized the fascist tyranny of the Nazi regime, the Confessing Church came out with the Barmen Declaration affirming that, "we reject the false doctrine that the Church could have permission to hand over the form of its message and of its order to whatever it itself might wish or to the vicissitudes of the prevailing ideological and political convictions of the day." The Kairos document from South Africa reminds us that, "State theology is simply the theological justification of the status quo with its racism, capitalism and totalitarianism. It blesses injustice, canonizes the will of the powerful and reduces the poor to passivity, obedience and apathy." Four decades ago, when we as a country encountered fascism in the form of political emergency, our churches and the ecumenical movements in general were competing to worship the ungod. But there was a remnant within the remnant, and they had the audacity to challenge and dismantle the golden calf.

In our times, it is not only illegitimate to speak against the golden calves, it can also cost our life and our job. This challenges us to continue the exodus even in the Promised Land. Egypt is around us and within us, and we need to discern it and gather the prophetic courage to destroy the golden alves of our times. It is our faith imperative to occupy our churches, our spiritual practices, and our institutions, so as to reclaim them from the worship of the ungods. It is in our unending journey towards freedom, dismantling the pyramids of systemic sin and evil, that we worship the God of life in truth and spirit.

African American theologian Yolanda Pierce, on the wake of the fatal shooting of a young black man in Ferguson, MI, USA, wrote these lines: "Even as the disciples of Jesus grieved at the foot of the cross, they understood there was work to be done. The work of justice is deeply political and requires an engagement in this present world. With tears in our eyes, we are called to march, rally, petition, sing, dance, and use whatever gifts and talents we possess for the work of justice. A grieving people need a church for such a time as this, a church that happens their midst." There are grieving people in our midst looking for an *ekklesia* that happens in their everyday life experiences. Liturgies that contest the ungods and celebrate the God of life enable and empower the faith community to become *ekklesia* in the lives of the grieving people.

Ekklesia: A Sacrament for the Sake of the World

As M.M. Thomas rightly observed, *"there cannot be true church with the continuity of existence in the world. It is a contradiction in terms. Die and get resurrected—everyday a new fellowship—a new creation— not the old one continuing. That alone be Christ's Church."* Ekklesia is not a permanent entity. It is a "provisional reality; a transitional organization; and the vestibule of the Reign of God." *Ekklesia* is the wrappings that cover the Divine gift that we await with anticipation.

Jesus' invitation to his followers to take up their cross and follow him was made before he was crucified. That means to his followers, cross was not yet a religious symbol; but the most brutal form of death penalty imposed by the Roman Empire. So, Jesus' invitation to discipleship is to throw our social status and reputation, and to opt for an alternative existence without social legitimacy. "How different would Christianity look like if Christians understood that their basic vocation is to be illegitimate?" This requires from the church the commitment to become illegitimate for the sake of the world, rather than measuring its strength by the size of its membership, finances, buildings and programs. When we show the nerve to become illegitimate to the prevailing order, we become the *ekklesia*. In our times, we need to be saved from the dominant expressions of Christianity to become a true *ekklesia*.

3

"Do not say anything is not pure"

Rethinking Ecclesia from the Perspective of the Youth

Felix Weise

If we talk about new concepts of ecclesia one perspective should not be missing – the perspective of youth. In fact, I would say the voice of the youth is one of the most important ones. The reason behind that is not only that the youth represents the future of the church. This is a fact. But they are not only that, they are already the living presence of the church. Of 7.64 billion people on earth, 26% are aged under 15 years.[1] Another 23% of the world's population, or 1.8 billion in figures, is aged between 15 and 29 years.[2] This means that half of the world's population is under 30 years old. Considering this numbers, it should be self-evident that in the effort of rethinking ecclesia the voice of the youth should be prominently heard. In this essay I want to focus my attention on the question of what must change in the church for it also to be the church of the youth. I want to begin my reflections with a short biblical narrative of human borders and God's destruction of these borders. Following this, the thrust of the biblical message – God's love has come to all the earth, Jews and Gentiles, shall be explicated from the perspective of the New Testament. Based on that thoughts, I want to ask under what circumstances we can create church today, and what challenges we are facing in that effort. Coming to the core of my reflection the crucial questions will be, who is building ecclesia, the places where we are forming ecclesia, and the circumstances under which we are building ecclesia.

Biblical Input: God's love overcomes borders

The narrative that my reflections are based upon is a story about borders and a story about being called out, the literally meaning of 'ec-clesia'. It is written in the book of Acts in chapter 10. Cornelius, a Roman captain, receives a vision from God in which he is told that his prayers and gifts have been heard and accepted by God, and that he shall therefore get in contact with Peter. He sends messengers to Peter, who lives in a nearby town. Peter himself also receives a vision:

> *He saw heaven open. There he saw something that looked like a large sheet. It was being let down to earth by its four corners. It had all kinds of four-footed animals in it. It also had reptiles of the earth and birds of the air. Then a voice told him, 'Get up, Peter. Kill and eat. No, Lord! I will not!' Peter replied. 'I have never eaten anything that is not pure and clean'. The voice spoke to him a second time. 'Do not say anything is not pure that God has made clean', it said. This happened three times. Right away the sheet was taken back up to heaven. Peter was wondering what the vision meant. At that very moment the men sent by Cornelius found Simon's house. They stopped at the gate and called out. They asked if Simon Peter was staying there.*[3] Peter is told by the Holy Spirit to welcome the men and go with them, for they have been sent by the Holy Spirit. He follows his instructions and visits Cornelius with them the next day. After Cornelius told Peter about his vision, he, the Gentile, states: *Now we are all here. And God is here with us. We are ready to listen to everything the Lord has commanded you to tell us. Peter answers him: I now realize how true it is that God treats everyone the same, he accepts people from every nation. He accepts all who have respect for him and do what is right. You know the message God sent to the people of Israel. It is the good news of peace through Jesus Christ. He is Lord of all.* After that, Peter confesses his faith of Christ, who was born, who healed, who was crucified, died and resurrected from the death. Cornelius

> and his companions are filled by the Holy Spirit and finally Peter
> decides to baptize them, although they are not of Jewish believe.
> *Can anyone keep these people from being baptized with water? They*
> *have received the Holy Spirit just as we have.*

In reflecting that story, I want to name a few aspects, that could be
a paradigm for our actions as church. The basic setting of the story
does not have to be explained, but one fact should be recalled: Up to
that point the proclamation of the Good News had only been directed
at Jewish believers.[4] Now the narrative starts to tell about a Gentile,
that receives a heavenly vision and is told to meet one of the most
important protagonists of the Jesus movement. God is not accepting
the borders of human imagination. The holy spirit is dynamic, erratic
and has no regard for human expectations. This is also reflected in the
vision of Peter: Peter refuses to eat the food shown to him, regarding
it as unclean.

Food-laws were some of the crucial identity-markers of Jews.[5]
The observation of the food-laws was, according to New Testament
scholar James D. G. Dunn, in its importance comparable to baptism
in today's church.[6] Even if this comparison is only partially suitable,
it emphasizes well the enormous meaning of Peter's vision. God asks
him to give up central elements of his belief, of his identity. Something
that he was raised with is now pronounced no longer valid. The divine
vision calls Peter out of his space of belief and values that had been
shaping his whole life before. Later Peter is called out again. And
again, he must throw over a large portion of his evolved set of beliefs.
A gentile, sent by the Captain, asks him to meet him. Used to avoid
the Gentile world as to not get in contact with impurity, Peter faces
the challenge and meets the messengers as well as Cornelius on the
next day. He recognizes that the men are filled with the Holy Spirit,
so that he concludes, that God is the God of all. And he should not
exclude someone, who has been given the Holy Spirit, from getting
baptized: „*They have received the Holy Spirit just as we have?* ".

It is not human to decide what is pure and impure. It is not human to decide whom to preach the Good News to. It is not human to decide to whom God gives the Holy Spirit. Through the Holy Spirit God acts in different People and is not restricted to those, who would be chosen by men. God's salvation cannot be restricted to a group that we would like to define. It is – as it is God's gift – open for everyone.[7] Peter tries – not even consciously – to keep up the borders of his tradition. Israel, in the understanding of Peter, is God's chosen people, that defines itself by the maintenance of the covenant of the Sinai, which has been confirmed in the coming of Christ and can be seen e.g. in circumcision and food laws. God tears down the borders. He calls Peter out of his comfort zone. He acts free and unpredictable. He fills him with the Holy Spirit, so that Peter is able to recognize: He is Lord of all.

This fundamental struggle has been the one main-controversial subject in the early Christian movement and runs like a golden thread to church history: The human attempt to limit God's salvation. The New Perspective on Paul had thrown the academic world into turmoil, when STENDHAL and DUNN started to deconstruct pillars of Lutheran doctrine. One of the main points of their research findings was that Paul's intention was not so much the personal salvation, as in Martin Luther's case, but the proclamation of the restoration of this world to its intended purpose under the Lordship of the Creator."[8] This recreation includes Israel and the Gentiles, and the zeal of Paul's life is to deliver this message to the whole world. In his letters we can find information about problems in that enterprise.

Jewish believers in Christ want Gentile believers to observe food laws and to get circumcised to be full members of the community of God.[9] These Jewish believers thought, that it is necessary to bear signs like the observance of food laws or circumcision, to be member of God's people.[10] As it was expressed in the narrative of Peter and Cornelius there has been an early rejection of that position and the issue was clarified later on the Apostle convent (s. Act 15). The Evangelists and the Apostles, as I was able to show, were preaching a gospel, that tries to overcome such borders and not to build new ones. So, after having a short insight on the systematic conditions involved in building a world-wide community of Christ and reflecting the present conditions under which a church has to been build, I want to show what borders can be found in our church today, especially for our Youth, and what has to happen for them to be overcome.

Systematic-theological reflections

In my consideration, I have neglected to reflect the basic assumption that in a Christian understanding ecclesia always has its roots in and draws its orientation from the creative power and the covenant of the father (cf. Gen 1 and Gen 9), the reconciling life and preaching of Jesus Christ and the connecting dynamic of the Holy Spirit (Act 4). The word 'ecclesia', one of the most used term for the assembly of Christ-believing people in the New Testament,[11] reflects that context: coming together in the community of God is not a human effort, but only caused in God's call into that community.[12] The ecclesia is literally the community of those, who are called out by God, and not, those who are coming together in a certain building or have signed church membership. In its use in the New Testament, the word is already quite universal and does not only label a local community but also embraces the entity of all Christ-believers.[13]

As the church is founded in God's revelation through Jesus Christ, its purpose also is rooted in Jesus life and message of the kingdom of god, that has begun in him. The proclamation of this kingdom and the invitation to live in the light of the coming reign of God in word and deed is therefore the central zeal of the called-out.[14] The aim of the ecclesia can therefore never be self-purpose but lies always beyond her itself. The ecclesia, the called out, are part of the new kingdom of God, but they are not the kingdom of God. In the history of church, the ecclesia has constituted itself in different churches, that all claim for themselves to be part of the ecclesia, or even the only one ecclesia. This claim always must be measured in their fulfilment of the sending through Christ. In a Protestant understanding the preaching of Christ is fulfilled in the proclamation of the Gospel and the administration of the sacraments according to the gospel.[15] While the proclamation of the Gospel in word, deeds and sacrament stays the centre of the ecclesia its means are not fixed, as all people shall be reached by the Gospel. That means, that the exterior form of the ecclesia has no unchangeable shape but is dynamic and can be adjusted to changing relations and challenges.[16]

Another circumstance gets more and more important and shall be reflected in the next section as well: Whereas the protagonist of the reformation, especially Luther differentiate between the visible church, to which everyone part of the institution of the constituted church belongs, and the invisible (or hidden) church, that is only consisting of the assembly of the faithful[17], we have to think about a new concept today. Is there may be a third category of those, who define themselves as Christian, but do not belong to a constituted Christian church, or are not even baptized?

Although the message of the church is timeless and universal, its forms and means are not. This means, that the Gospel of the kingdom of God is not variable. But from a Protestant point of view[18] the communication of the Gospel, although interwoven by the Holy Spirit, is human and therefore underlies human conditions and it is changeable. For that reason, we must choose a form of communication, that is understandable for our partners in dialogue.

Summarizing this section, we must stress, a) that ecclesia has its foundation in the triune God and b) that it has its only purpose in spreading the Good News of the coming kingdom of God. As the origin and the purpose of ecclesia are unchangeable its outer forms are not: its constituted form and its communication are human, and should be adjusted in that way, that the kingdom of God can be proclaimed to all people.

Contemporary conditions of being and building ecclesia

As the church in its outer form is part of the temporal world, it is also an agent in the changing relations and conditions in history. In the following I will depict some of the major changes that shape and have already shaped our world today. In that section, it is not possible to claim universal validity of the described aspects. The view presented here is explicitly a German one, based on German scholarly literature and experience. Certainly, it is also influenced by the interaction with people from all over the world, from the international news and images, that can be consumed every day. But still, as Apostle Paul said: "*What I know now is not complete. But someday I will know completely*" (1 Cor 13,12).

The world has undergone a radical and fast change in the last two centuries, with different faces in different times and places in the world. With its beginning in the 18th century the industrial revolution shaped the following two centuries. Nearly every country passes or has passed major changes in their economic system. The age of industrial revolution was and is still more and more replaced by the rising third sector. The worldwide community is developing to a service society.[19] Hand in hand with the industrial revolution came the revolution of traffic. First the development of the railway, later that of air traffic changed the way people were moving. In the 20th century it has become a lot easier to travel around the world.[20] The distances between countries, that had been far away earlier, has shrunk.[21] The world has become smaller through better transportation.

Another development that strengthens that perception, is the super-fast progression in communication technology. In Germany already 85% of the 12-year oldy had a smartphone in the year 2015.[22] Now, only three years later 97% of the youth between 12 and 19 own a smartphone. A large share of them, more than 85% use the smartphone 3 hours a day or more.[23] The world of this generation has been expanded by a completely new dimension. The new media have not only increased the time of usage per day, but also changed our way of communicating. Private and public communication cannot be separated anymore. Topics are discussed on Facebook, that have been dealt with a closer circle of friends before. Now they can be read by anyone. Whereas the youth had been discussing politics in smaller groups before, many people now join the discussion of newspaper articles in the comment section. Presenting holiday pictures, before a matter of a cosy evening with some friends, is now done on Instagram publicly.

Our private life occurs more and more publicly in the internet. At the same time, youth has become more sceptical towards public institutions, a trend that is spreading to whole society.[24] While individuals are perceived more authentic through the new possibilities of the internet (Blogs, YouTube-Clips a.s.o.), institutions are the losers of that development. They have a hard time trying to be perceived as authentic and attractive and mostly that aim is only achieved by the help of charismatic flagships.

But communication has not only changed regarding its place and publicness, but also regarding the relation between sender and receptor.[25] In an analogue situation of communication the sender has most of the power over what he wants to inform about and what he wants to withhold. This situation has changed dramatically: users of the internet can decide what information they want to read, which image video they want to watch and at the same time it is getting more and more difficult to hide information from the public, as the sources of information are almost infinite.

The new age of information and communication has led to a breakdown of certainties and an acceleration of impressions. On television and in the internet, people are confronted with thousands of different opinions and life plans. The perpetual confrontation with the foreign compromises one's own concept of life. This can either lead to complete disorientation, when the feeling prevails that there is no certainty and truth, or to radicalisation of the own worldview. Certain contributors have noted the struggle of the 21st century and offer simple and reduced worldviews, that seem to explain the troubles of an pluralized world, but rarely withstand more exact investigations. As the youth in this new world of uncertainties has little to build a system of concepts on, the new fixpoint of this generation is one's own self.

The youth of the 21st century is a youth of individualism. They no longer value complex ideologies as communism, liberalism or Christian belief offer them, but compile their own set of ideas, that is dynamic and less set-in stone, from different ideologies. Individualism spawns' personalities with multiple identities that are opposed to mono-dimensional identities of radicalized people, who stick to one idea, that permeates their whole life. I do not want to side with one the options, but only note, that this dichotomy exists and a church, that wants to speak in different contexts, must observe that development and to create ways and concepts to deal with it.

A development, that lies more in the future but should already discussed today, is the further possibilities of technology. The formative problems of humanity since its genesis are up to be solved[26]: There is still hunger, war and disease in the world, but there are already regions where they do not afflict people's life anymore. [27]Even if the worldwide solution of these problems is indeed not foreseeable, new issues and goals enter those people's minds, that no longer must hunger, suffer from diseases or fight in war. The new possibilities of a digital world of algorithms combined with developments of biotechnology bear the possibility of creating a long-living, or even immortal human.[28] On the one hand this obviously involves the improvement of many people's life, but on the other hand it also bears two dangers: First the option of an improved and immortal life creates new injustice. The new products and possibilities will be certainly not available for everyone, so that there would be a new class system of the 'normal people' and the 'enhanced people'. Secondly this means a development of the homo sapiens to the homo deus, whose creative power is sheer without limits. This development to homo deus cannot be compared to anything in history. With every technological, social or political upheaval since the genesis of the homo sapiens, its humanity has not been altered. The upcoming changes are now up to re-engineer human minds, so that a completely new history of a new kind of human begins.[29] This possible development of the future would mean a deep crisis of the anthropology and whole theology of Christian ecclesia and has therefore to be anticipated and be critically accompanied.

Building the Community of Christ in the 21ˢᵗ Century Rethink

As shown above the circumstances of the world today differ largely from that of Martin Luther, let alone the ancient world of Jesus and the apostles. New possibilities are opened by this world, but also new borders and obstacles are emerging. In the first part I have shown that the Gospel paints a image of itself, which overcomes borders building the kingdom of God as preached by Jesus Christ and planted into people's hearts by the Holy Spirit. To critically embrace developments of a new age does therefore not mean, to devote oneself to the zeitgeist, but is something quite old-fashioned. Old-fashioned, because we are taught so in the bible: To preach the Gospel to the Gentiles Paul had to become like a Gentile (1 Cor 9).

The mission of the Gospel is stated clearly and indelible: Preaching the Gospel of Jesus Christ, the new life opened through him, the forgiveness of one's debts, the reconciliation of the world, that "all of them may be one" (John 17,21). The means and the frame to bring the Gospel into the world are - in contrast - changeable, indeed they must be, and we must adapt to the circumstances of the time, if we take our mission seriously. Adapt ourselves to new circumstances from a Christian understanding never stands in danger to lose oneself for two reasons: Firstly, through the altering power of the Gospel, we do not have our identities in ourselves anymore, but are centred in Jesus Christ. Our identity has shifted at the cross from a self-centred identity, that cannot accept the otherness of our environment, to the Christ-shaped identity that embraces the otherness of our counterparts.[30] Secondly, the Gospel entails enormous potential of criticism.

By embracing the world of the 21st century out of the position of a Christ-shaped identity, one can never be in danger of losing itself, because it never simply adopts the new, but also influences the embraced by its changing power. The Gospel of Christ is unfailingly a critical corrective of the existing circumstances, because it has the power to reveal injustice, greed and evil and change it through its power of love. Now from that point of view I want to rethink our ecclesia from three perspectives. I want to rethink who is building ecclesia, the places where we are forming ecclesia, and the circumstances under which we are building ecclesia.

a.   Rethinking who is building ecclesia

A friend of mine was recently trying to start a new youth group in one of the parishes in Heidelberg, the town where I live. The group leaders had met before in a team and discussed everything and made up a thoughtful plan, with a very nice concept. They planned to start a trainee-program, where young people can be empowered to be their own youth leaders and start something on their own. Luckily, before they started, they met with some of the future participants, who had already said, that they were interested in a youth program. When they were asking them, how they would like the youth group to be, they found out, that they had quite contrary ideas of the way this youth group should be shaped. They imagined a totally different youth group in comparison to the one, their youth leaders did.

I often experienced youth work and work of the church in general in a similar way. There are a lot of concepts being made, a lot of ideas are collected, and some vision presented. The problem is not, that these ideas are not good, or that they are not driven by the vision of the Gospel. No, the problem is, that the concepts of youth work do not fit the expectations of young people. Offering a Russian course in Germany may be a nice thing and not wrong, but it won't be attended well, as people in Germany rather prefer to learn Spanish now. To reach the youth with the Gospel of Jesus Christ and to build the kingdom of God together with, we must ask them, what they want. This can be more complicated and more challenging, because it sometimes means that we must abandon our well-designed concepts and that we have to get into something, of which we never thought as youth work. But currently, this is maybe the only way to meet the needs of the youth. Especially in a world, in which we and the youth is surrounded by offers between which can be chosen, we cannot allow ourselves just to go on like before.

The new youth is, as described before, highly individualistic and is not just following the ways and habits of their parents. They are searching something, that fits their needs and character. The church can call the individualism of the youth self-centred and condemn it. In contrast I would suggest embracing the youth: take them seriously, ask them, what they need, create offers for them, and let the Gospel change the character of the youth. That also implicates the necessity of giving more responsibility to the youth. To really understand what young people need, we have to put them in charge. Let the them participate on a decision level and decide what to spent money on during the next years, were to focus resources on and how to build the kingdom of God.

b.   Rethinking the places where we build ecclesia

The developments of the 21ˢᵗ century have opened huge new spaces. On the one hand, in a physical way as in the case of the exploration of outer space. But on the other hand, a analogous infinite space was opened by the development of the internet. The cyber space is huge, it is expanding, and people, especially young people spend a lot of time there. Unfortunately, there is not enough time in this essay to reason why cyber space should be considered as 'real' space; a space comparable to material space, that surrounds us. A simple observation has to be sufficient here.

In many respects young people are using cyberspace as space comparable to the material space surrounding us. They communicate, they have friends, they spent money, they express themselves, they play and the have hobbies in that place. This list could go on a lot longer, but central for this argument is, that young people do use the new space extensively and naturally. Again, church can criticise this development and try to get youth back into the analogue world. The prospects for this to succeed seem quite limited. From the view of the youth the analogue nature of the church can be perceived as huge border. Why should young people, who spend their time most of the day on the Internet, who have their second home online, come to the old building of a church? I would emphatically propose to conceive cyber space as a space that can be shaped by the Gospel as well as the material space. One could now argue, that church is already taking up space online, that the church already is promoting projects, that try to communicate the Gospel online. That is true. I know quite a bunch of projects that take place online. Some of them are successful, some of them fail. What is common to them is, that they do not really conceive the cyber space as new space, but only as extension of the material space. For some agents' virtual space only means, that they can stick advertisement and invitations to youth services to an online billboard. For some, it means simply to communicate by WhatsApp instead of the Phone. Or to use the platform of the internet, to collect money for their new project for charity. But there are only few projects that really see cyberspace as an independent space. To embrace this virtual space as church means to explore its nature.

A strong objection to my claim may be that ecclesia is always, to a certain degree, realized through materiality. This argument loses its validity, as Christian ecclesia is, as I have shown above, not only restricted to local community but has been understood as virtual, world-wide community from the beginning on. Paul understands himself as member of God's ecclesia, although he is travelling most of his later life. But the objection gets stronger, when we take into consideration our practice of the Last Supper.

Depending on the confessional background, materiality - tasting, seeing and smelling the bread - is essential to celebrate the Last Supper together. Accepting the virtual space as space where church can grow therefore raises questions and opens opportunities. Church should be open to rethink the significance of the sacraments. Depending on the answers to those questions virtual ecclesia can be an equivalent to material ecclesia, or alternatively only an incomplete form of ecclesia that needs to be supplemented by material ecclesia. As an outlook two chances can be named: First, the virtual space can be a way to meet the needs of a youth, that is increasingly individualized and able to frame their own needs. Through a diverse range and through different agents from the wide spectrum of Christian denominations young people can find forms of Christian community that suits them. Virtual ecclesia can contribute to the community, that can never be offered by regional churches, that locally confined. Secondly, the premises to build a worldwide community in Christ have never been so promising. Virtual space opens the possibility to experience fellowship with people living thousands of miles away. These encounters cannot be overestimated: Knowing to be a member of a huge community is a huge source of strength for one's own faith. Being in contact with other people gives fresh input to one's own religious life. Lastly, a worldwide ecclesia can realise a solidarity between the parishioners, whose dynamic can overcome almost any border.

c.   Rethinking the circumstances under which we are building ecclesia

In my home church, we were starting a local refugee initiative some years ago. The local pastor recognized the need of the people to react to the needs of the increasing number of refugees who came to Germany during that time. So, he decided to help to build up an organising committee to control different projects. When he told the organising committee that he would like to leave the committee after it had been constituted the other members, all between 40 and 50 years old, were shocked: "You cannot leave, we don't know how to proceed, we need you as a pastor." I was irritated because the other members were all adults, who all had more or less responsibility in their jobs. I didn't understand why they should not be able to manage an organising committee for refugees on their own. Today the pastor is still member of the organising committee.

I think this anecdote represents a wide-spread understanding of church, at least in Germany: *"Church is something that can only be done by professionals."* A lot of people are willing to do volunteer work, but the pastor has to be in command. Church in Germany reproduces that view of church. It is highly sophisticated, and its financial assets exceeds those of many corporations.

In contrast to this attitude, we deal with a youth that is, as shown above, increasingly sceptical towards large institutions., that is not willing to just accept reproduced dogma, but to form their own opinions. We are dealing with a youth that is well informed and feels free to take a more attractive offer, if the old one is not convincing anymore. In future, if we still want church to be a place (virtual or material) that is attractive, we have, in my opinion, to change its settings. From a theological point of view, there are not so many objections to make. God's ecclesia is not necessarily realized by the institution of church, but by the communion of saints. Church is one of its possible structures, but not the only one possible. I do not have an elaborated plan how we have to change these structures but want to propose leading questions: How can we come in contact with young people and first listen to them before we tell them what to do? Do we need to cling to the literal form of our confessions, even if they are not understandable for anyone anymore? Is it necessary, that someone is accepting every single of our man-made confessional documents, or can we accept them as someone driven by the love of Jesus? These are the question that refer to the church as spiritual institution. The balancing act consists of choosing the loss of any universal beliefs and coping with individualistic forms of faith.

On an organizing level, we have to ask to what extent the church really needs its structures as they exist today. The weekly Sunday morning service for example is a relic of the agricultural era. Times have changed. The Sunday of today's youth mostly does not start with service but rather with a large breakfast with friends. If we want to keep the service as centre of ecclesia, we have to ask, if it has to take place Sunday morning. We have to ask if its liturgy – as wonderful as it may be – is absolutely necessary, if our traditional songs cannot be replaced by more suitable ones and if ecclesia always has to be organized by a pastor. But an even more fundamental level, we have to ask the question, whether the whole character of church is still suitable or if we cannot create more suitable and dynamic forms of ecclesia without the stiff framework of the institutional church. The example of evangelical free churches in Germany shows that they sometimes seem more attractive to young people, even if the reason probably is not only their less institutional character. My thrust of these questions goes towards the self-destruction of an institutional church. That is in many respects contradictory and I am not sure if this would be the solution to all our problems.

Traditional church in Germany still reaches many people, who find a solid foundation there. But to continue building the kingdom of God, we should not be driven by the spirit of fear and cling to our traditional forms of church, but be ready to destruct some of them, when they form borders to our youth. Then, if we can leave the safety of the familiar behind, we are open to be driven by the Holy Spirit, ask our neighbours what they need, and together with them form an ecclesia, where they feel at home.

Conclusion

My reflection started with the narrative of Peter and Cornelius. If we are discussing and rethinking ecclesia, its central message should lead our thoughts. It is not ours to decide where to set the borders to rethink ecclesia. If we put the Gospel of Christ in the centre of our reflections, if we rethink ecclesia from the basis of the message of Christ, who has overcome the world, we should not restrict our minds when thinking about how a worldwide community of Christ can be erected. So let's be open to discuss the central aspects of the Church with God's word to Peter in our minds: 'Do not say anything is not pure, what I have made pure.' Our task to build ecclesia is founded in the Holy Trinity of God, Jesus Christ and the Holy Spirit and not in the concern to maintain the institution of the church. So, why don't we give more responsibility to the youth? Why don't we ask them, what they want a Church to be a like? Why don't we discuss the central elements of our worship services – even if that means that they would change radically? Why don't we embrace virtual space critically and think of new forms of ecclesia online? Why don't we just try out new forms of ecclesia that don't fit in the form of institutionalized church? The radicality would be maybe similar to Peters decision to expand his mission to the Gentiles. But if we stay in the light of God, there is nothing we should fear. He is the Lord of all.

Endnotes

[1] Stallmeister, Ute. *5 Fragen - 5 Antworten zur Weltbevölkerung.* Deutsche Stiftung Weltbevölkerung.

https://www.dsw.org/5-fragen-5-antworten-zur-weltbevoelkerung/#4.

[2] Henley, Will. *State of the world's youth population.* Commonwealth Secretariat.

http://thecommonwealth.org/media/news/state-worlds-youth-population-new-index-underscores-urgent-need-invest-young.

[3] All bible quotes are cited after *New International Readers Version.*

[4] Although through the mission in Samaria and the episode of Philip and the man from Ethiopia the expansion of the mission was prepared earlier. Schmidthals, Walter, *Die Apostelgeschichte des Lukas,* 102.

[5] James D. G. Dunn, *The New Perspective on Paul,* in: *The new perspective on Paul,* 108.

[6] Ibid., 108.

[7] Gottfried Schille, *Die Apostelgeschichte des Lukas, 244f.*

[8] Mark D. Nanos, *The mystery of Romans,* 60.

[9] James D. G. Dunn, *The New Perspective on Paul,* in: *The new perspective on Paul,* 115.

[10] Ibid.

[11] Gunther Wenz, *Kirche I. Zum Begriff,* in: *Religion in Geschichte und Gegenwart.*

[12] Michael Herbst, *Missionarischer Gemeindeaufbau in der Volkskirche,* 100.

[13] Gunther Wenz, *Kirche I. Zum Begriff,*in *Religion,* in: *Geschichte und Gegenwart.*

[14] Christian Grappe, *Kirche III. Urchristentum,*in: *Religion in Geschichte und Gegenwart.*

[15] Wilfried Härle, *Dogmatik,* 577.

[16] Ibid., 578.

[17] Ibid., 573.

[18] Cf. §7 of Augsburg Confession, Wikisource, https://en.wikisource.org/wiki/Augsburg_Confession.

[19] Christian Grethlein, *Kirchentheorie,* 207.

[20] Ibid., 207.

[21] Of course that development has reached only a smaller share of the world population. There are still a lot of people that have never been abroad, or set a food in an airplane.

[22] dpa. *Fast alle Jugendlichen besitzen ein Handy oder Smartphone.* https://www.sueddeutsche.de/news/leben/familie-fast-alle-jugendlichen-besitzen-ein-handy-oder-smartphone-dpa.urn-newsml-dpa-com-20090101-150112-99-06042.

[23] Lüdemann, Dagny. *Drei Stunden am Tag sind normal.* https://www.zeit.de/digital/internet/2018-03/social-media-dak-studie-instagram-whatsapp-sucht-jugendliche.

[24] Christian Grethlein, *Kirchentheorie*, 216.

[25] Ibid., 217.

[26] Or maybe better to say: We have never been closer to the possibility of solving them

[27] Yuval Noah Harari, *Homo deus, 1.*

[28] Christian Grethlein, *Kirchentheorie*, 226.

[29] Yuval Noah Harari, *Homo Deus*, 52f.

[30] Miroslav Volf, *Exclusion and embrace*, 99f.

4

Prophetic Imagination and Critical Leadership

Mathew Chandran Kunnel

I'm lonely" God felt as God stepped out of the space and then smiled creating light; then the sun and the moon and the blazing heavens were created and the day and the night were formed; then the stars, planets, earth and hills and valleys were formed through divine providence; then the waters on the earth, rivers, plants, beasts and birds were created; then God again looked around and still felt lonely; then God sat down and like a mammy bending over the baby, kneeling down in the dust and tolling over a lump of clay, God shaped and breathed a living soul into it creating man, thus ending God's loneliness.

Deeply expressing the fundamental characteristic of God and human is relationality, as James Weldon Johnson wrote the poem 'Creation'. Feeling lonely, God created man in divine image and feeling that man is again lonely, God created a complimentary being, woman in order to alleviate the loneliness and to be a friend and companion, both responsible to each other. Humanity, therefore imbibes this relationality from God, who is relationality personified, i.e.; as the

Son proceeds from the Father before time existed and from Father and Son, the Holy Spirit proceeds and thus describing the Trinitarian mystery of Christian faith with the underpinning characteristic as relationality, committing everyone towards a sensibility and sensitivity towards sociality and responsibility.

According to the Jewish *Kabbala* mysticism, it is God's contraction of God's holiness that creates the world in and through the *Shekinah*. Again, one can find here, a deep relationality to accommodate the created beings into His own Beingness. In the *Samkhya* Yoga, we find how the *Purusha* and *Prakriti* is united together and how *Purusha* is sacrificing himself induced by the presence of *Prakriti*, to evolve into the twenty-four evolves. When this relationality, community, communion and rhythm and righteousness were or are broken, Prophets appeared in every time and space in order to rededicate this commitment and whenever righteousness is diminished, they came up with alternative views, instilling hope and radical remedial measures. The beginning of *Bhagavat Gita*, this notion of the incarnation of the Lord in order to bring the world back into righteousness and rhythm is again bringing forth the relationality. Through this conference we are appreciating the role of prophets not as soothsayers of gloom, doom and destruction but as pointers of our faults as we made in our pilgrimage towards this goal and the radical ideals, we need to carry out in realizing this goal.

Purpose of God

To the question why prophets were killed incessantly, there is no exact answer except that they challenged the goals and methods of the existing unjust dictatorships and their totalitarian systems. They looked for the governance of God in a covenantal way, in a relational way, accepting the individuality of the creatures and raising them up into the level of sonship and uplifting them in this process to the pedestal as children of God. They imagine the world totally different from the existing paradigms and propose that God is a lively actor, always the cause of abrupt endings and radical new beginnings. This is the nuance of prophetic imagination. Often the prophets challenge the legitimacy of the existing totalitarian systems because they contradict the purpose of God.

As they are challenging the existing systems, the prophets are therefore expected to articulate an alternative world view that God is birthing for us and they are called to be the midwifes in bringing forth this brand-new world. They are thus not only prophets of criticism but also prophets of hope just as Amos, Isaiah and Jeremiah who came up with the extraordinary rhetoric of beating swords into ploughshares and where the lamb and the leopard will lie down with the goat, the calf and lion eat together and a little child who will lead them all invoking an imagery bringing out the importance of innocence, relationality, multiculturalism and purity in any leadership style. This posing of hope comes up to the expression of Martin Luther King's famous metaphor, "I have a dream". It is a dream that expresses that an alternative world is possible which is indeed an exactly opposite to what we are all experiencing at here and now.

Alternate Worldview

In order to have an alternate worldview for our present times, we have to eliminate the prevalent extractive materialistic consumerism, deleting greed and hate, the underpinning foundations of both the philosophy of Capitalism and of Marxism. The futility of the gospel of prosperity and the fragility of the healing propaganda should also to be addressed in order to be a prophet in our times.

Therefore, we need to have a new ecumenism, a wider ecumenism where we embrace all human beings and nature, fusing into an ecological ecumenical continuum. In order to have such a greater openness, we need to come back to the older narratives, to be transformed into an old-fashioned form and to have and to emphasize a preferential option for God. We need to have new confessional statements, making room for all religions and spiritual traditions, and make them allies in our search for justice, wholeness and holiness. In this alternative model, we need to embrace the *anawim* of *Yahweh*, the widows, the orphans, the immigrants, the oppressed, the vulnerable and the poor as shown by Mother Teresa of Kolkata. We need to integrate the divisive matriarchal and the patriarchal styles prevalent in our country into the complimentarily of the love of the neighbour.

The love of the neighbour needs to be reinterpreting the laws and redistributing the belongings and in order to realize these radical measures we need to learn and live with *aprigraha* and *ahimsa*, with non-possessiveness and non-violence and ready to be eternally churned by the search for truth, namely, *satyagraha*. This is the way the father of our nation Mahatma Gandhi became a prophet for all times transcending geography which was being followed up by Martin Luther King Jr and nelson Mandela. Searching for truth and discovering it in all the spiritual traditions and integrating them into a *sadhana* and thus catapulting the whole nation into the path of *Karmamarga*, transcending greed and hate and establishing the *Regnum Dei – Ramrajya*, Gandhiji led India to achieve emancipation. Thus, he led us to a new multiculturalism, a brand-new secularism that is enshrined in the constitution of India, accepting as chosen by God as an asymptotic openness towards the cross of kenosis and total sacrifice which he experienced from the reading of the Sermon on the Mount. So this prophetic imagination invites us to be otherwise, falling back into the preferential option for God, towards a freedom that liberates one into the truth, energizing one into carrying the cross of poverty, hunger, illiteracy, maladies, just like the servant song given by Isaiah 53.

Prophetic Imagination

Definitely, Prophetic imagination brings in an everlasting hope like that of Isaiah 19, "behold the days are coming when God's promises are fulfilled. Behold the days are coming, when I will bless Assyria, my people of Egypt to my chosen, and Israel, my inheritance" recognizing everyone as chosen and of inheritance. In Acts 10 Peter was shown the vision that there is no impurity, replacing . . . .and the increasing dawning on Peter and Paul that the transformative love of God is not the monopoly of any race, space, tribe, tradition, nation or tongue.

It seems that at present the institutional churches are very weak instruments for this poetic imagination of critical leadership. However, it is the best instrument available at the moment. However, the Churches need to transcend the cultic priesthood and engage themselves in social analysis as Dietrich Bonhoeffer made through his radical life and ultimate sacrifice. Standing with the people to whom he belonged and re-imagining the entire episode and bearing witness to the values he cherished, his life was indeed a prophetic act in our contemporary times. For Dietrich "the Church is the Church only when it exists for others. To make a start, it should give way all its property to those in need. The clergy must live solely on the free will offerings of their congregations, or possibly engage in some secular calling.

The Church must share in the secular problems of ordinary human life, not dominating, but helping and serving. It must tell men of every calling what it means to live in Christ, to exist for others. Church will have to speak of moderation, purity, trust, loyalty, constancy, patience, discipline, humility, contentment and modesty. It must not underestimate the importance of the human; an example of Jesus Christ, it is not an abstract argument but power (Letters and Papers from Prison, P.382-383).

Dietrich continued to state that "the key to everything is the 'in him'. It is certain that our joy is hidden in suffering, and our life in death; it is certain that in all this we are in a fellowship that sustains us. In Jesus, God has said Yes and Amen to it all, and that Yes and Amen is the firm ground on which we stand". (p.391) The prophetic imagination in the Old Testament and in the New Testament according to Dietrich, both bears cross and blessing; only difference is which comes first, and which comes second.

> *Indeed, the only difference between the Old Testament and the New Testament in this respect is that in the Old the blessing includes cross, and in the New the cross includes the blessing. . . In suffering, the deliverance consists in our being allowed to put the matter out of our own hands into God's hands. In this sense death is the crowning of human freedom. (p.374-375).*

As he was continuously discerning the will of God in his life and found that "I'm still discovering right up to this moment, that is it only by living completely in this world that one learns to have faith. One must completely abandon any attempt to make something of oneself, whether it be a saint, or a converted sinner, or a churchman (a so-called priestly type!), a righteous man or an unrighteous one, a sick man or a healthy one. By this –worldliness I mean living unreservedly in life's duties, problems, successes, and failures, experiences and perplexities. In so doing we completely throw ourselves completely into the arms of God, taking seriously, not our own sufferings, but those of God in the world – watching with Christ in Gethsemane. That I think, is faith; that is *metanoia*; and that is how one becomes a man and a Christian." (p.369-370)

According to Dietrich, to be living in this world and involving with the problems and destinies of the world, one discerns with will of God and becomes a saint or a righteous person. Thus, Dietrich emphasized the importance of being relational, taking care of the other and interacting with the other and transforming the world as an instrument in the hand of God. This is exactly what the philosopher Immanuel Levinas in his philosophy highlighted. The other is my alterity and the face speaks to me and transforms me, leading me into responsibility and action. This depth of responsibility is again highlighted by Gabriel Marcel in and through his famous dictum, namely "to exist is to co-exist and to co-exist is to pro-exist". The alterity and responsibility is therefore totally based on the relationality, the fundamental characteristic of humanity.

Alterity as Responsibility

This alterity and responsibility are again expressed by the tragic tone of the individualism that led to the Nazi dictatorship and the lack of standing for the other in communion with the other. Lutheran Pastor and theologian Martin Niemoeller is thus another prophet for our times. The following poem by Martin Niemoeller, written against the lack of relationality of the Germans, who stood in their own individual frames and felt lost when they were all defeated and eliminated one by one. The need of standing for the other, and in communion with the other is very essential for one's own existence.

Martin was a German Submarine (U-boat) commander in the I world war who received the prestigious medal of the Iron Cross for showing extra ordinary valour during the war. Disillusioned by the takeover of the German state by Hitler, Martin later became a Lutheran pastor, fighting against the Nazis, imprisoned and narrowly escaped execution. If we are not standing together in solidarity with the other, what we need to expect is gloom and doom and makes the clarion call as a prophet is what Martin exhorting us today from his depth of experience.

First, they came for the communists
And I did not speak out
Because I was not a communist
Then they came for the trade unionists
And I did not speak out
Because I was not a trade unionist
Then they came for the Jews
And I did not speak out
Because I was not a Jew

> *Then they came for me*
> *And there was no one left to speak for me.*

Thus, the prophetic imagination asks one to live in the world as we are all beings inextricably interwoven in the problems, tribulations and trials and give critical leadership by being a responsible person for the other and taking care of the society and especially the *Anawim* of *Yahweh*. All the prophets could be seen as efficient leaders in transforming the society, either in their times or in later stages. Like Moses, they were with inabilities, fearful like Isaiah, lacking physical abilities like David and formed even from the womb like Jeremiah.

In our contemporary times, timid Gandhi was turned into a firebrand to shake the mighty British empire, Mandela raged with violence to be transformed into a sheep with empathy and *Ahimsa*, Mother Teresa a tiny woman who could pour out love unlimitedly to the depressed suffering poor masses all over the world and like them many and many unsung heroes placed in the international, national and local pedestals. They were all had something in common, a preferential option for God and His people. Touched by God and transformed by God, they did not relay on their merits, talents and vision, they were all being guided and led by this infinite purpose to transform the society. In today's Church leadership this transformational leadership is very essential if the Churches need to be relevant and to be imaginative.

Transformational leadership

Transformational leadership is a new paradigm of leadership which has captured the attention of many. It has been consistently claimed to be more successful than the other leadership styles in "lifting common people to astonishing heights." A transformational leader represents a new paradigm of leadership that may be capable of steering an organization into higher performance. The leaders have a special task to build individuals and organizations. The circumstances, changing lifestyles, values, needs, and attitudes have required the leaders to choose a paradigm in their leadership. Preference has turned from the mechanical approach to a more humanistic approach, in other words, from a transactional to a transformational leadership.

Today's leaders lean on the humanistic or transformational style which centres on enhancing a qualitative relationship with the followers, such as fostering reciprocal trust, considering their personal needs, and freedom, joint decision making, being interaction oriented, consultative, egalitarian, and respecting/ considering the ideas of others. Studies undertaken on leadership say that transformational leadership is positively related to job satisfaction. Transformational leadership is one management practice that has increasingly become dominant in both public and private sector organizations.

Leadership styles have been defined by many scholars, who help us to understand the role of leadership and its impact on organization. Transformational leadership is an enormously accepted image of idyllic practice in all the sectors at the present time. Transformational leaders have a lot of qualities that encourage and motivate their followers. They demonstrate traits like being a role model, understanding the individual differences, creating one to one relation, appreciating and encouraging the individual giftedness/talents, encouraging the personal and professional growth, motivating and creating an atmosphere of interpersonal trust and providing support, and showing concern and consideration to the followers. It is an effective leadership that inspires the co-workers to transcend from self-interest to the organization's interest. They concentrate on the follower's values and slowly help them to merge their values with the organization's values which will help them to accomplish even more.

Transformational leaders have an innate ability to motivate and inspire the workers to get done what they have planned to do. Here the leader's concentration is on each individual's outcome rather than the group. They constantly provoke the followers to a higher form of commitment. Transformational leadership cultivates a close relationship with the employees by encouraging participative management, sharing the information and power in the workplace, promoting reciprocal communication, and encouraging individual development.

Today there is a greater accountability than ever before. With the additional demands fuelled by the government and media, institutions are now forced to improve their performance. It is the co-workers together with the leaders who would maintain their institutions effectiveness and quality. If the transformational leadership in the industries can meet the demands of their customers and shareholders, the same style will show greater performance and commitment in the other sectors as well. Studies of leadership consistently report that leadership ability is directly linked to subordinate performance, organizational citizenship behaviours, and reactions including job satisfaction, affective commitment to the organization, reduced turnover, and pursuit of more challenging goals, as well as goal attainment, individual perseverance and appreciation for the value of work.

Transformational leaders give personal attention to the subordinates, emphasizing the use of their intellect, increasing their level of enthusiasm, and transmitting to them a sense of mission. They influence them in two important areas: directly increasing optimism and indirectly increasing commitment and performance. Many studies have been conducted to understand the components of the transformational leadership and they found that the most important are 1) Idealized influence, 2) Inspirational motivation, 3) Intellectual stimulation, and 4) Individualized consideration.

Idealized Influence

This component refers to the charismatic behaviour of the leaders who act as strong role models for their followers and provide them with a vision and a sense of mission. Followers recognize these leaders as having astonishing capacity, determination and perseverance as well as a high standard of moral and ethical demeanour. They have a special admiration, esteem, and confidence in these leaders, which help them to identify themselves with the leader's beliefs, objectives, interests, and principles.

Intellectual Stimulation

This type of leadership encourages followers' efforts to be creative and innovative. These leaders provide support to their followers by addressing the problems in a new way and demanding them to take chance. They are open to suggestions, ideas and approaches from their followers for the common good of the organization. They expand the interests and ability of their followers. These leaders assist their followers to constancy in their query and cultivate their own beliefs, assumptions, and values. They preserve dignity in their performance and are able to overcome the problems in an innovative way, which then strengthen the followers' organizational commitment.

Inspirational Motivation

This factor describes a leadership that articulates high expectations beyond the original, exhibits optimism and enthusiasm, and communicates the vision to show that it is reachable. Transformational leaders set a behaviour pattern that gives the followers a strong motivation to strive and do better. They stimulate and enthuse the persons around them. Moreover, these leaders involve the followers in envisaging the possibilities of the future and create an affirmative anticipation about their actions. They also set examples of commitment to the common dream and give a direction and meaning to their work. With this kind of motivation, the leaders promote in the followers the affective dedication and enthusiasm to a mission.

Individualized Consideration

This factor is representative of leaders, who are concerned about each follower's needs; support them for their growth; and emphasize employees' aptitude and capacity. Such leader's behaviour plays a part to keep the followers happy. They do this through guiding, supporting, and listening to them effectively. They act as coach and mentor and recognize their followers' individual differences. They foster two way dialogues, offer one-to-one support, and create a personal relationship with their followers. There is a genuine understanding of their followers' individual differences, wants, and ambitions. Such leaders' behaviours are geared toward enhancing the well-being and integrity of the followers. They set aside their own interests and use their vigour and time for the organization or persons within it.

At the highest peak of individualized consideration, the leaders do not only support, understand and satisfy; they also offer helpful comment, confront and inspire them. They also do their part to help them to become conscious of their hidden power, leading to a transformation of both the leader and the follower. Thus individualized consideration enhances commitment and a sense of increased competence in the follower.

According to many research illustrations there is a direct bond between transformational leadership and organizational commitment. They state that the influences of transformational leaders encourage the followers to focus on the common mission rather than their personal interests. Such leaders have a great concern for the individual development and pay much attention to their differing needs and skills. This in turn envelops them with an organizational vision that will lead them to be more committed to the long-term objectives and goals of the organization. These leaders have skills to maintain one-to-one relationship, to solve the old problems in a new way.

Studies establish that transformational leaders and job satisfaction are two significant essentials in producing a healthy organization. It is found that transformational leaders encourage and support their team members for higher performance. They show interest for every person, create a special rapport with each one, convert their basic beliefs and empower them to solve problems in an innovative way. These motivations from the leader inspire the followers to go beyond their personal interest. These leaders do appreciate, trust, and have confidence in their members.

Past studies report that transformational leadership is more effectual, innovative, dynamic, and rewarding to the followers. The attitudes and practices of such leaders make the followers feel that their leaders care for them rather than utilize them to meet their goals. These leaders promote a greater collaboration in vital decision making, share their views and ideas. They are able to give meaning to the environment by adapting to the culture or situations that will draw the concentration and interest of the workers.

The research findings illustrate that when there is a higher purpose for their job and a sense of competence, this will evoke job satisfaction and interest in their profession. The leaders for their part show awe, faithfulness, and admiration for their staff through their communication and other forms of interactions. The leaders constantly induce and develop the interest of their members and give them judicious feedbacks.

Transactional Leadership

This form of leadership is widely practiced by many leaders in different organizations. And their style of function is mostly connected to reward and punishment. In this the leaders' focus is on the behaviour of the followers that must be pursued in order to attain the objectives. They do not care to motivate or inspire them; their focus is only on the result which provides feedback on the followers' performance. They follow a reward-based exchange and encourage the subordinates to comply. So they have a very little personal influence on their followers. They only want to reach their desired target. For them what is important is conformity not higher performance or creative problem solving when confronted with challenges. This type of leadership is built on such extrinsic values as positive and negative reinforcements. This is the way they control everything within the organization.

The transformational and transactional styles of leadership are opposing leadership styles, but sometimes leaders can have both of these qualities. However, transactional leadership seems to be less effective than the former one. According to Burns 1978 and Bass 1985, there are two types of transactional leadership behaviours: 1) contingent reward, and 2) contingent punishment. In the contingent reward type of transactional leadership, the leaders give to the followers' positive feedback, while in the contingent punishment type the followers are given negative feedback or criticisms. Here the leaders are concerned with and prefer a steady atmosphere with a very little competition. Transactional leaders are also good managers as they set goals and distribute tasks. Subordinates are rewarded or punished for their performance of their tasks.

The transactional leaders use the reward method to attract and retain the staff. They see it as the way to improve practice and commitment. This type of leaders' functions from the existing system and closely monitors and takes action on those who make mistakes and deviate from the norms. The ones who fall in line are rewarded and those who don't are.

Passive-Avoidant Leadership

An element of Full Range Leadership Model (FRLM) is referred to as passive-avoidant leadership or non-transactional leadership which entails the avoidance or absence of leadership. Leaders who use this style do not take any action or provide any guidance to their followers. Some characteristics of such leaders are: not engaging in any decision making, neglecting their authority and avoiding responsibilities, overlooking the issues. These so-called leaders do not want to participate in anything, nor do they plan any action or activity for the future.

Other researchers added that these leaders neither enter into any deal with the followers nor steer them to achieve the desired goals. They avoid acting as leaders to their assistants. The authority is given to their subordinates, who then make decisions, plan their programs, and set objectives. There is complete freedom for the members as their supposed leaders do not monitor or control anything. Such freedom makes the individuals place their personal goals above the institutional goals. This kind of leaders has nothing to offer to the subordinates as guidance or support. The Passive-avoidant leadership style is considered as the most unproductive leadership approach. Leaders who use this approach have no effect on their followers and prefer not to do anything with their requirements as well as their interests. It is a passive management style where leaders do nothing to face their problems; rather, they wait for the problems to become more complicated. So, we can see that leadership plays a vital component in a follower's organizational commitment and job satisfaction.

Conclusion

A critical leadership style looks for a transformative leadership. Every pastor and a catechist in a parish and all the more the bishops need to be transformational leaders like Dietrich Bonhoeffer, Gandhiji, Mandela, Mother Teresa and many others. To inspire, to take radical decisions and to transform the people who are given to them in order to create a society which will consider alterity as responsibility. They will be touched by God, fired by a preferential option for God and driven with the purpose of instilling hope, focus and alterity. Discovering alternatives through the imaginative visions evolved from their closeness to God and embarking everyone to these new visions, a new society will be formed with righteousness, justice, empathy, alterity and purposiveness eliminating, vengeance, hatred, materiality etc as envisaged by Paul to be guided by the spirit than by the flesh.

5

Re-claiming Ecclesia in the Context of Empire

Vinayaraj

Introduction

As a student of theology, I am grateful to the honorable Synod of the Church of South India for promoting new discussions in our theological thinking. Of course, no one can deny or disregard the contributions of this church and its theologians in the process of envisaging contextual and significant doctrinal engagements in this country. Now, the effort to re-imagine ecclesiology is going to be yet another significant mark in the contextual theological thinking in this country as it is facing new challenges of neo-liberal economy, culture and spirituality. In the crucial context of marginalization and destitution, as the concept note of this consultation rightly says, it is the high time for the Indian Church to re-construct its ontology (being and becoming), theology (and epistemology), and spirituality (both liturgy and politics) in favor of the victims and the excluded.

The quest for a borderless church is to make the Church open and inclusive. However, the site of border is no more a space of hospitality and difference today. Rather, it has become the site of estrangement, hatred, and violence. The border, whether it is in terms of nationality, re(li)gion, caste and gender, is to be the site of welcoming and conviviality as it envisages a radical space (and time) of deconstruction and reconstruction. It is the site of the divine epiphany where we reconcile, forgive and trans-form each other for a new being, becoming and belonging. It is the eschatological space and messianic time where we de-other 'the other' and de-self 'the self.' As the marginal space of the Cross of Jesus Christ, the border is the site of shared pain and the celebrated hope. Russell Chandran once said, the crucifixion and the resurrection are not two separate events; rather they are concurrent events—the fragments of the Christ Event that determine the redemption of all (Chandran: 1985). We need a theology of border in the crucial context of hatred, violence, violation and segregation that invokes us to envisage a borderless church—an inclusive community of Christ/ Christic community. Church as a borderless community should not be a homogenous community; rather, it is to be a 'community of communities,' as Dyanchand Carr alludes always (Carr, 2007).

Rethinking Church as a borderless community needs to be theologized with caution in the very particular context of Empire. Empire also claims to be an open-global community. It is also a borderless –'imagined community' of Market that operates itself within the logic of neo-liberal economy and culture. Being the ideology of destitution, the claim of the Empire to be an 'inclusive' community is to be interrogated and resisted. It is inclusive and at the same time it is exclusive. The Italian philosopher Giorgio Agamben calls this political dilemma 'the status of exception' in order to expose the inherent problem of inside and outside-ontology and politics in the concept of Empire. Thus, the quest for an open Church in the context of Empire demands a radical ecclesiology of the excluded and the unqualified to be in the 'main-stream.'

Another important issue is all about the question of the de-imperialization of the Church. Assuming the status of Empire, Church in history has had offered the theologies of mission and ministry without de-imperializing its own ontology (being and becoming). Being the structure of patriarchy and hierarchy, many a time in history, Church has claimed its authority and power in terms of administration, but not in ministry. It is here, we realize the imperative to differentiate the logic of Empire and Ecclesia as they differ in their logic of inclusivity and borderless-ness. This paper tries to delineate the epistemological difference between the terms—Empire and Ecclesia and thereby offer a constructive proposal for a contemporary ecclesiology which re-defines Church as a de-imperialized being and becoming. It explores the possibility of envisaging new strategies of mission and ministry in India by initiating significant and relevant theological discourses.

Empire and Ecclesia: Deconstructing the History of an Illegitimate Alliance

Joerg Rieger, while analyzing the relationship between Church and Empire, offers two different responses (Rieger, 2007: 9). On one side, he argues that early Christianity was a critique of the Roman Empire which constituted the context of the early Christianity. The Jesus' movement and the apostolic traditions envisaged counter imperial communities that denied the imperial practices of exclusion and marginalization. At the same time, Rieger points out that Christianity after the Constantine era assumed a hierarchical/ imperial structure. The early ecumenical councils convened by the emperors signify the involvement of the imperial forces in the formulation Christian doctrines and dogmatics. It is really exciting to read Giorgio Agamben, when he investigates the context of the emergence of the theology of *oikoumene* (economic trinity) in the patristic period over against the totalitarianism of the Constantine political power (Agamben, 2011:50). Thus, the relationship between the Empire and Church has always been apprehensive and cryptic. This is true as we go through the historical periods of crusades and the modern mission strategies of the Western Church colluded with the European colonialism.

Exposing the trajectory of the conviviality between Church and Empire, Elizabeth Schussler Fiorenza offers a theological treatise on the anti-imperial ecclesiology in her incredible work—*The Power of the Word: Scripture and the Rhetoric of Empire*. In this book, Fiorenza speaks about Church as a political space—"the radial democracy of equals" (Fiorenza, 2007). The radical democracy of Fiorenza is the *ekklesia of wo/men* which offers the language and space for the imagination to develop a public religious discourse, "wherein justice, participation, difference, freedom, equality and solidarity set the ethical conditions" (Hernandez, 1997: 31). Fiorenza, in contradiction to the kyriarchal model of the Empire, defines Church as a radical political space where the logic of domination and subordination is denied and equality and justice for all is affirmed. Fiorenza articulates Christian community—Church as the radical democratic assembly of all, the *cosmopolis* of God's very different peoples (Fiorenza, 2001: 56).

Alluding to Paul, Alain Badiou signifies the Pauline theology of Christ-Event as the "counter-community of resistance" to envisage a radical ecclesiology in the emerging context of Empire (Badiou, 2003). Richard Horsley's *Paul and Empire* and *Paul and Politics*, offers a convincing case of defining Church as an anti-imperial imagination (Horsley, 1997). In his *Insurrection of the Crucified*, Theodore W. Jennings, Jr., provides another hermeneutical approach for envisaging Church as an anti-imperial community (Jennings, 2003). Engaging with Michel Hardt and Antonio Negri, Joerg Rieger and Kwok Pui-lan embark an "Ecclesia of the Multitude," in their well-read book *Occupy Religion: Theology of the Multitude*. According to them, the Church of the Multitude is the "gathering of diverse people, and it orients them toward service in the world, particularly toward the least among us" (Rieger & Pui-lan, 2011). Here Empire is envisaged as the hegemonic logic of neo-liberal capitalism which legitimizes the ideology of exclusion, the politics of refugization, and the economy of destitution. For them, Church as an anti-imperial imagination which deconstructs its hierarchical ontology and other-centered diakonia, envisages a radical democratic community of justice and equality for all. The task before the Church in the context of Empire is to be the Church of the Multitude.

Church as Coming Community: Giorgio Agamben

It is Giorgio Agamben, the Italian philosopher/ theologian, who rightly analyzes and exposes the imperial inheritance of the Church in the post-Constantine period (Agamben, 2011: 104). Alluding to Paul, Agamben contends that by claiming itself as the kingdom of God or the divinely legitimized Empire, the Church denied its call (*klesis*) to be *paroikousa* (sojourner) and ended up as *katoikein* (to dwell like an empire). When the Church becomes a sovereign power of rule and its liturgies become the celebration of the sovereign God, the calling of the Church is nullified and reversed. Engaging with the Pauline corpus, Giorgio Agamben offers an extended discussion on the "calling" (*kletos)* of the Church. It is a calling that calls back or revokes every other vocation. According to Agamben, the calling of the Church is a call for a messianic vocation that revokes all other vocations in the context of the reign of the emperor. For him, the Church is a "messianic community" that lives in messianic time (Agamben, 1993: 1-2). Messianic time, as it is well explained in the Pauline corpus, is the time that remains—the time in-between the ascension and *parousia.* It is the time that remains in-between Church and kingdom of God—the time the *ekklesia* takes to come to its end. End time, thus is not a futuristic time; rather, it is a qualitative "now"—the time of redemption within the present time (Agamben, 2005: 6-7). Agamben defines Church as a "coming community" that locates itself in a "state of exception"—the site of the marginalized and the excluded and thereby envisages political ontology of the crucified.

By "coming community" or "the community that comes", Agamben means a community of those who have no community. It is a community of people who are being "excluded in" or "included out" in the sovereign political paradigm. It is a community that cannot be co-opted by totalitarian forces. Or it is a community where the sovereign law is being inactivated. It is the community of the de-imperialized subjectivities. Agamben finds this sense of inoperability of the logic of Empire in the kenotic act of Christ on the Cross. First and foremost, the Cross signifies the inoperability of the biopolitics of sovereignty and offers a radical politics of community by replacing himself on the cross in the place of a political victim in the Roman imperial context. In his reading on Paul, Agamben comments that the calling of the Church is to "enslave" itself to this Messiah who becomes weak for the most wretched of the earth (Agamben, 2012): 13-14). For Agamben, Church is called to be the ontology of the marginalized, the tortured—the Multitude.

The Church as a "coming community" embodies the messianic politics through which it takes a turn from liturgy to politics. It is through messianic politics that the Church becomes part of the democratic process that challenges the contemporary socio-political and economic sovereign powers. It is through messianic politics that the Church re-invents its ontology in relation to "social ontology." Defining politics as a "social ontology," Chantal Mouffe says that "the political cannot be restricted to a certain type of institution, or envisioned as constituting a specific sphere or level of society. It must be conceived as a dimension that is inherent to every human society and that determines our very ontological condition (Mouffe, 2005:3)." Church as a "coming community" envisages a "social ontology" that challenges the exclusionary practices of the sovereign power and embodies the agonistic politics of the excluded and exempted in our democratic process. It is the *messianic politics* that signifies Church in the contemporary socio-economic and political context of Empire.

It is the messianic politics that makes redemption happens in the everyday life of the people.

Church as New Humanity: M.M. Thomas

Among the Indian Christian theologians, it was M.M. Thomas who proposed an authentic political ecclesiology in Indian context. Responding to the state of emergency declared at the midnight of June 25-26, 1975, Thomas said: It is nothing but the onslaught on democracy and a betrayal of the nation." Thomas contended that the effort to quell people's revolts for the sake of internal peace, economic progress and self-reliance through a state of emergency was nothing but the repudiation of all human rights envisaged by a welfare state and its democracy. Thomas envisages a participatory democracy where the sovereign power of the state is nullified and the rights of the marginalized are celebrated. Redefining Church as the sign of the secular Koinonia and New Humanity, Thomas envisions radical ecclesiology as it destabilizes the logic of Empire within (Vinayaraj, 2017: 119).

Thomas' theology of state and democracy is founded on his theology of the Cross. According to Thomas, Jesus's cross is a protest against the sovereignty of the Roman Empire and the act of crucifixion was to nullify its logic of domination and marginalization. Replacing a political victim on the cross, Jesus exemplified his political solidarity and identification. Jesus's cross signifies the end of the totalitarian power and the beginning of a new community—kingdom community—a universal community where there is no dichotomies. In the new community, "there is no longer any distinction between gentiles and Jews, circumcised and uncircumcised, barbarians, savages, slaves and free; but Christ is all and in all" (Col.3:11). The new human community is constituted as a single body—the body of the crucified God in history. The crucified body of Christ is not a new thing; rather it is the body of the slain lamb from the creation of the world and it continues to be slain till the end of the world fighting against the totalitarian forces of powers. The mark of crucifixion continues to be the sign of the suffering struggle of God against the principalities and powers till the end of the world. The mission of the Church today is to embody this mark of crucifixion and to reconstitute its ontology in solidarity with the victims of the world.

According to Thomas, the Church is entrusted with a prophetic *diakonia* to discharge its duty based on the servant hood exemplified by the crucified God. Thomas writes: "The church in India is called to proclaim the gospel of the crucified and risen Christ as the source of redemption of all spiritualities underlying religion as well as ideologies, and to demonstrate the Koinonia in Christ around the Eucharist as the nucleus of a movement of the larger Koinonia in Christ uniting peoples of diverse religions, ideologies and cultures—as well as the cosmos with its bio-diversity" (Thomas, 1995: 15). Based on his theology of Cross, M. M. Thomas explains the features of the mission of the church in India: (1) the calling of the church is to resist the idolatry of power and wealth and other gods of death in India's collective life, (2) to be in solidarity with the poor and the oppressed in their struggle for justice, and (3) to give up communal self-interest and self-identity for the sake of creating in India a secular national community in the midst of India's religious and ideological pluralism through manifesting a fellowship in Christ, transcending class, caste, ethnic and religious communal divisions (Thomas, 1990:11).

Thomas's theology of humanization through which he upholds an anti-imperial ecclesiology and missiology, makes him so significant and relevant. Thomas finds the foundation for his eschatological anthropology in the theology of Spirit who raised Jesus from the dead, as the first fruits of the New Creation. Thomas's hope in the future of humanity is incorporated in his understanding of the Risen Christ and His coming. He cites Paul: "We await a Savior, the Lord Jesus Christ who will change our lowly body to be like his glorious body, by the power which enables him even to subject all to himself" (Phil.3:20-21).

Becoming the tortured body of Christ, the Church is being composed and constituted as an open community of all to resist the logic of Empire theologically, liturgically, and hermeneutically. According to Thomas, it is this call and the composition of the Church to be and becoming a messianic community only signifies its relevance in the contemporary context of Empire.

Making Church the Messianic Community Today

Let bring some painful stories here from Kerala. Recently there raised a nun abused case against a Bishop. Some nuns connected with the abused sisters are in hunger strike demanding the arrest of the accused Bishop. However, the church that the Bishop belongs to and the other established churches are observing ether silence or they support the culprit indirectly. The public in India is of the opinion that the illegitimate alliance of the church with the ruling government try to disrupt the police enquiry and save the culprit. It is clear example where the established churches in alliance with the power-centers deny justice to the victim particularly a victim who belongs to the body of church. This is one among the many cases as we see the illegitimate alliance between church and Empire through which it exclude the poor and the weak.

Generally speaking, Empire in India today takes many forms of hegemony in terms of cultural, economic, political, and religious realms. The logic of Empire intrudes into the every aspect of human life. It denies our rights to food, clothing, study and belief. There is no security for a Dalit, woman, transgender in the public spaces. Religion has become the ideology of hatred. The economy of the Empire is nothing but the "economy of suicide" that demands the farmers to sacrifice their life for development. The cultural, religious, and linguistic minorities are in anxiety and fear. Dalits are termed "anti-nationals." The people who stand for human rights are being killed. Intolerance constitutes the public life. On the other hand, the national elites, the multinational corporations, the international nuclear regimes, find home in India. The notions of state, democracy and the people are being transformed in favor of the global Capitalism. The Church in India finds difficulty to respond to this scenario. The silence of the churches is regarded as the conspiracy for Empire.

The challenge before the Church in India today is not just to preach about its inherited salvation to the world around; rather, it is to experience the fragments of salvation in this world by becoming the ontology of the weak. The challenge before the Church is to be the Church of the crucified people. As Agamben opines, it is an act of retreat for the Church to "in operate" its inherent juridical structure and to become a "coming community"—a community which is a community of those who have no community. By becoming the messianic community of the weak, it engages critically with the exploitative systems of our society to make it just and egalitarian. Radical ecclesiology is a call within the call of the Church (*klesis*) to become the "weak church" of the Crucified God by becoming the body of the crucified people "now". Agamben exhorts that the task of the Church today is to find its eschatological moment—the moment when it becomes the open church of all (Agamben, 2012:13):

> Living in this time, experiencing this time, is thus not something that the Church can choose, or choose not, to do. It is only in this time that there is a Church at all.

Bibliography

Agamben, Giorgio. *The Kingdom and Glory: For a Theological Genealogy of Economy and Government.* Stanford: Stanford University Press, 2011.

Agamben, Giorgio. *The Coming Community.* Minneapolis: University of Minnesota Press, 1993.

Agamben, Giorgio. *The Time That Remains: A Commentary on the Letter to the Romans.* Stanford, CA: Stanford University Press, 2005.

Agamben, Giorgio. *The Church and the Kingdom.* London, New York, Calcutta: Seagull Books, 2012.

Badiou, Alain. *Saint Paul: The Foundation of Universalism.* Stanford: Stanford University Press, 2003.

Hernandez, Adriana. *Pedagogy, Democracy, and Feminism: Rethinking the Public Sphere.* New York: State University of New York Press, 1997.

Joerg Rieger and Kwok Pui-lan, *Occupy Religion: Theology of the Multitude* (New York & UK: Rowan & Litlefield Publishers, 2012).

Jennings, Theodore W. *The Insurrection of the Crucified: The "Gospel of Mark" as Theological Manifesto.* Chicago, IL: exploration Press, 2003).

Mouffe, Chantal. *The Return of the Political.* New York: Verso, 2005.

Richard Horsley, ed., *Paul and Empire: Religion and Power in Roman Imperial Society* (Harrisburg, P.A: Trinity Press, 1997).

Schussler Fiorenza, Elizabeth. *The Power of the Word: Scripture and the Rhetoric of Empire.* Minneapolis: Fortress Press, 2007.

Thomas, M.M. *A Diaconal Approach to Indian Ecclesiology.* Rome & Tiruvalla: CIIS & CSS, 1995.

Thomas, M.M. "The Church in India—Witness to the Meaning of the Cross Today," in *Future of the Church in India*, ed. Aruna Gnanadason. Nagpur: NCCI, 1990.

Vinayaraj, Y.T. *Theology after Hardt & Negri: Empire, Church and Multitude.* Delhi: ISPCK, 2017.

Rethinking Ecclesia: Being and Becoming Christ Communities - Towards a Borderless Church from the National Ecumenical Perspective

Empowerment and Educational Perspective

Ella Sonawane

Introduction

The Church of South India has planned seven consultations on the theme "Rethinking Ecclesia: Being and becoming Christ communities – towards a borderless Church".

Being part of this 7th consultation **"Rethinking Ecclesia: Being and Becoming Christ Communities - towards a borderless Church from the National ecumenical perspective"** is an honour. The very fact that I come from the Church of North India speaks about a borderless church. Personally, I do not have any borders when being part of church is concerned. My personal relationship with God is what matters most. Borders today are controlling our lives. Nation against a nation. States fighting over rivers. Neighbors' fighting for their space. We are all caught in many borders whether physical or imaginary thus losing the essence of becoming Christ communities.

I chose to speak on '**Empowerment and Educational perspective**'. And congratulate the leaders who have chosen the topics. I am not going to do any scholarly presentations but will speak out of experience in my working and capacity building with people especially women and children from all sections of the society.

In fact, when we look back at our family's history, most of us present here have come from another place and settled in where you are living now. Or work may have taken you to your place of living. My journey has been one of crossing borders. From Jharkhand to Maharashtra and now to Delhi after a short stint in the Gulf. If there were borders, we would not have had a chance to learn and educate ourselves about other states, people, culture, traditions and communities. It is where we go that we form and build communities and grow.

And strangers who we never met become part of us and those we grew up with are distanced due to the borders we chose to cross. This has only educated and transformed my thinking. Made me inclusive in my thinking and actions. It has made me realize that we are all God's creation and one in Him. Borders are created by humans which only cause discords. Today, the world is suffering because of these borders. To some extent we can say that we are part of this and need to be 'inclusive'.

As a mission worker I can say that my movement enabled my work even more with the under privileged women and children in the villages. They are identified as out castes and looked down upon by the so-called upper castes and wealthy.

We are familiar with the word, ecclesia which means in common language 'a congregation of people called out." Thus, we can say, the church according to the New Testament is a congregation of people called out by God for the special purpose of giving fullness of life to all people in this world, especially to the weak and the poor who live in sub-human conditions in the world today.[1] Recently I joined the Robin Hood family which feeds the hungry. Their aim is to not let anyone sleep hungry. To me this is Church. Where we include those who are thrown out by us from the mainstream of society. Ecclesia today seems to be a popular word, the key words I picked up in the very theme are 'Rethinking' and 'Becoming'. 'Rethinking' and 'Becoming' what and how? Several papers have been presented from various perspectives. We are often talking about Rereading the Bible or Rethinking. The obvious answer is we are to relate to the Bible and its teaching in today's perspective. We are ecumenical in nature and we are to embrace all irrespective of their church affiliation. Not just church communities but also those from other faiths. Does Christ look different in a CSI, Presbyterian, Methodist or a CNI church? Is he different in colour, temperament, nature?

Inclusiveness, equality, justice have become striking issues in today's time when there is so much unrest, turmoil, and injustice not only within homes, churches, communities but also within nations and the world. These always existed but when people became aware of their rights, we have somehow taken this up as contextual. This has created people to think and address these issues. This is a step forward and I congratulate CSI for taking this pertinent question up for discussion and eventually publication of the volumes.

Educating is empowering and vis a vis

They are like two sides of a coin. We see through the New Testament how Jesus empowers people, especially women. He did not do a back-ground check when he chose his disciples but identified those who came from various back grounds but still were going to be in the same mission with him. He chose the lowly, weak, meek, and made him his followers. He asked his disciples to go into the world.

He created a community where there was a sense on building people for His kingdom. He empowered those who were ready to stone the woman brought for adultery thus educating them that they were no one to judge or point fingers at anyone when they themselves were not blameless. He included the Samaritan woman by way of having a conversation with her though his disciples were critical of him. He removed the barrier and became the bridge that broke the wall of discrimination.

In a constantly changing socio-political, economic, cultural, and religious scenario in the world today, our faith is tested and challenged to address the many given realities around us. It is not simply being satisfied with mere increase in knowledge at a cognitive level, but it is also engaging and shaping the whole person-transforming one's beliefs, attitudes, values, behavior and the social realities around him/her.[2]

And let us consider how we may spur one another on toward love and good deeds, not giving up meeting together, as some are in the habit of doing, but encouraging one another—and more as you see the Day approaching (Hebrews 10:24–25 NIV)

In my 15 years of working in the mission, I have worked with people both at the grass root level and urban settings. And it has often been noticed and I have personally experienced their pain of being ostracized and sent out to the periphery.

We have kind of decided who we want within and who we want without the circle we have created. Let us think in terms of the entire community. This is creating a borderless church because people are the church and church are the people. The borderless world of the 21st century is a world in which people keep moving, especially to cities and yet remain connected.

I have identified a few areas where we can empower and educate to create a borderless church

1. Secular Education: If we are convinced that education is a common good, it follows that it should be open to everyone in the community and not to remain the privilege of some segments of the society. The dominant educational policies today, on the other hand, seem to create a deep rift between two social groups; the rich and the well-to-do will be the producers and controllers of knowledge in an information society, whereas the poor will be left to fend for themselves. Such deeply entrenched hierarchical mind-set would think that the poor and the lower castes and classes can be satisfied with literacy and schooling.[3]

Diocesan schools should come with a syllabus that which will be inclusive and be secular in their policies. And also, in their selection of faculty.

2. Ordination of Women as Bishops: Being a woman myself I have strong feelings for my women community. They have always been kept out of the margins.

This is another aspect of being a borderless church. Here comes 'rethinking', Jesus did not create any gender bias. He was inclusive in his teachings. His followers include all . CSI has stood for gender balance not just rhetoric but also in practice. When Jesus said,' Go into the world and preach the gospel,' he did not just instruct the men, but all who were his disciples and to us today. So, when we say rethinking ecclesia, we mean how we can now practice what Jesus said 1000's of years ago. He first appeared to the women and gave them the good news that he had risen. He did not ask them to call the men and then share the news but asked them to go and tell the disciples who were probably hiding somewhere. He created no borders of any discrimination of gender, caste, class, or religion.

We are thus to imitate the character of Jesus when we deal with women and the issues facing them. Be inclusive and give them their share of responsibilities and duties.

3. Educate the Church: It is important that we instill in the minds of our Christian brothers and sisters a spirit of tolerance. We pose as very righteous and 'holier than thou' attitude which has created a boundary. And we like to remain in that comfort zone with our fingers sticking out to point out flaws of others and creating a wall of dissent and disorder. Church leaders are busy with administration than the religious status of the members. Corruption has not only ceased us but chained us and thus we find that we are caught in an enclosure of our own thoughts and practices. Paul Freire in his book, Pedagogy of the Oppressed, talks about the oppressed men and women who are alienated, powerless and poor. They are those who need liberation to become fully human as God intended them to be. He made a point in making education a medium to directly address the existential realities of such people to bring about humanization.[4]

4. HIV/AIDS: HIV/AIDS is an epidemic affecting humanity irrespective of their race, financial or social strata. There is no religion, cultural or gender bias, no age bar, no rich or poor in the eyes of this dreaded disease. As Christian community in the society, to be sensitive to the changing context of the present society and trying to be more effective in addressing problems like HIV/AIDS, to shape the future of humanity and the environment is a priority. The silence and the negative attitude of the church towards human sexuality or making HIV/AIDS a serious moral issue makes things worse. Instead of empathetically standing in solidarity with them and showing Christian compassion and love, we raise our voices to brand them as unclean, scorn, and frown at them thereby adding to their miseries to their world that is already crumbled and shattered.[5] The church needs to include them and cross borders with them. The Church today is called to take the position of the Good Samaritan by identifying with the HIV/AIDS infected persons who are abandoned. To take up the educational ministry of caring for such persons, an attitudinal change of the Church towards persons with HIV/ADIS is called for.[6]

5. Inter-faith: We live today in a globalized world. People of other faiths are no longer in faraway distant countries. The whole world is becoming increasingly multireligious. If believers of one faith community consider themselves superior to others and discriminate against believers of another community, a lasting peaceful solution is impossible. What we need is an open-ended paradigm, a paradigm that does not deny the centrality of Christ for the believer but at the same time is open to accept people of other faiths as children of God with no discrimination.[7] Religious conflicts and tensions have been steadily rising and have exploded into open violence victimizing many people in different parts of the nation. We often see that people when they pass by a holy place bow their heads in respect be, they of any faith . But when Christians go past any of other faiths religious place we do not show the same respect because we have always been taught that we are the righteous ones who will go to heaven. Let us teach our people respect for all faiths and not have the 'Holier than Thou' attitude. [8]Or approach to people of other faiths is very much influenced by our understanding of Jesus Christ,who invited everyone and had no reservations, no boundaries. Theological students especially should have visits and discourses which can broaden their thinking as they are the future shepherds of churches.

6. Denominations: I have met several people who travel the world and when it comes to attending churches will find out the church of their denomination they would like to attend. They even refuse to be part of the eucharist from other denominations. As I asked in the beginning of my talk is Jesus of a different colour in different churches. Is he not the same? Then why do we have certain reservations? Even traditional Christians would like to have inter denominational weddings leave alone inter faith. These are superficial reasons and should not be encouraged in our churches. Today several traditional Christian denominations are in conflict and on the verge of break-up due to internal doctrinal and theological issues such as, question of authority, autonomy of church, admission of women to ordained ministries, abortion, same sex marriage etc.etc.(sic) According to Kuncherai Pathil in his book, *Ecumenical Movement* he says, "I have often asked my ecumenical friends in India, how they would like to be called, 'Roman Catholic', 'Syrian Christian', 'German Lutheran', and 'American Baptist' etc. Their answers are mostly unanimous and unambiguous. They prefer to call themselves Indian Christians". Their answers are a clear indication that today they are no more fanatically attached to their denominational identities as their only specific identity. The denominational identity is only part of their total identity and they would like to emphasize today much more their ecumenical, national and cultural identity.[9]

Conclusion

When we imagine that we, as Christians and humans, can live in total independence and self-sufficiency, we are deluding ourselves. God, from the beginning, never intended that we should go through the world "alone." We simply cannot experience fully the power and delight of life with God without also being drawn into life together with our sisters and brothers in Christ. Without experiencing such life together, we will not discover how wonderful the news about Jesus really is. In our world shaped by multiculturalism and pluralism, it is important that Christ's witnesses become interculturally competent, developing relational skills to bridge and build authentic relationships.

The way we communicate the love of God to the people within our reach is most effective when we understand our contemporary context. Furthermore, witnesses are mandated by Jesus Christ to be "peacemakers" in a world marked by distrust, alienation, and violence.[10]

All churches must move from the center to the peripheries/ margins and prophetically involve in the lives of the poor, oppressed and marginalized and thus become the agents of transformation of society and instruments of unity among the whole humankind irrespective of religion, culture, caste and creed. The target should be not limited simply to the visible unity of all churches, but the focus must be the emergence of the 'Reign of God', a 'New Heaven and Earth', which has radical implications for the whole humankind and the whole creation.[11]

Excerpts from an interview- Tabarrok, author of the forthcoming book "How to Save Humanity," says the world should do away with borders altogether. "We feel now today that it's wrong to discriminate against someone on the basis of race, gender, or sexual preference. And yet, we discriminate against people based upon where they're born," he says. "I think when people realize this is a moral issue, they'll change their feelings about borders"[12]

A beautiful hymn which brings out the meaning of the topic is

For I'm building a people of power
For I'm making a people of praise
That will move through
this land by My Spirit
And will glorify
My precious Name

Build Your church Lord
Make us strong Lord
Join our hearts Lord
Through Your Son
Make us one Lord
In Your body
In the kingdom of Your Son

Let there be borders in unison. A church without borders can only move in the direction of God's kingdom. Thus, bring a positive change in the society. This is Church without borders. Thy kingdom come, thy will be done on earth as it is in heaven. Do we mean this every time we say this, or has it just become a habit?

Endnotes

[1] Gnana Robinson, *Whither the Indian Church* (Delhi: ISPCK 2016), 38.

[2] Akheto Sema, *Understanding the Nature and Purpose of Christian Religious Education* (Delhi: ISPCK,2005), 125.

[3] Felix Wilfred, *Christians for a Better India* (Delhi: ISPCK,2014), 192.

[4] Akheto Sema, *Understanding the Nature and Purpose of Christian Religious Education* (Delhi: ISPCK,2005), 125-126.

[5] Akheto Sema, *Understanding the Nature and Purpose of Christian Religious Education* (Delhi: ISPCK,2005), 186-187

[6] Akheto Sema, *Understanding the Nature and Purpose of Christian Religious Education* (Delhi: ISPCK,2005), 187

[7] Gnana Robinson, *Whither the Indian Church* (Delhi: ISPCK, 2016), 74-75.

[8] A. Maria David, Beyond Boundaries, Hindu-Christian Relationships and Basic Christian Communities (Delhi: ISPCK,2009), xi.

[9] Kuncheria Pathil, *Future of the Ecumenical Movement*, (Delhi: ISPCK, 2017),158.

[10] OCTOBER 31,2016 EVANGELISM& DISCIPLESHIP, SADRI JOY TIRA, Diaspora Missions: People on the Move in the Borderless Worldhttps://www.christianitytoday.com/edstetzer/2016/october/diaspora-missions-people-on-move-in-borderless-world.html (assessed on)

[11] Kuncheria Pathil, *Future of the Ecumenical Movement*, (Delhi: ISPCK, 2017), 183

[12] Published by The Takeaway, The Benefits of a Borderless World Oct 20, 2015.

7

Truly Being Church Beyond Borders
Jung Eun Grace Moon

Firstly, as the Church of South India marks 70 years of its unity in mission and witness, I take this opportunity to extend greetings and best wishes on behalf of the Christian Conference of Asia. While many churches are divided and separated, the churches in India has kept their unique legacy of being a church united and uniting for last seventy years, being constantly engaged in a mission of unity, service and prophetic witness. Also, the churches of CSI have been playing significant roles in the ecumenical movement at the local levels and beyond the borders of their nation. We do believe that the Church of South India will keep this spirit of unity and oneness with the spirit of reformation which is a core nature of truly being church.

1. **"We must go on to the other villages around here."**
    (Mark 1.38/ Good News Translation)

The Gospel Mark starts with a statement, *"the beginning of the gospel about Jesus Christ, the Son of God"* and the Gospel Mark narrates the life of Jesus Christ in a very dramatic way. *"The time has come and the kingdom of God is near. Repent and believe the Good News."* The Gospel Mark tells us how Jesus started his ministerial life, calling his twelve disciples, healing the sick and teaching in the synagogue and on the street. So, the Mark ends with this remark, "then the disciples went out and preached everywhere, and the Lord worked with them." The Gospel Mark starts with the mission of Jesus and ends with the mission of Jesus' disciples.

Many people were so amazed to witness the miraculous powers of Jesus and to hear his teachings and sermons with authority. Even the evil spirit was afraid of Jesus. More people gathered to the city where Jesus was staying. Jesus was the most popular celebrity in the city of Capernaum. One day in the early morning, Jesus went off to a solitary place and hid himself, praying. His disciples, Simon and other disciples started looking for him and when they found him, the disciples exclaimed, "Teacher, everyone is looking for you."

It seems that the disciples wanted to stay in the city with Jesus for some more time to enjoy the authority, power, popularity and glory of Jesus. However, Jesus replied, *"We must go on to the other villages around here, so I can preach there also. That is why I have come."* Jesus was not at all fancy about being a popular and influential celebrity but rather he led his disciples to a new mission field, "other villages" Jesus knew the place where he should be. His disciples wanted to stay back in the city of Capernaum, which has a perfect setting and infrastructure for Jesus' ministry. However, Jesus did not want to settle down in a safe zone. Instead, Jesus started a new journey to new and unknown villages to preach the Gospel. He came to fulfill all that was written in the prophets about the Messiah, which includes and is the essence of preaching the gospel. In his preaching the Gospel, there was no border and no boundary. In Mark 16, the disciples went out to everywhere and preached the Gospel following the way of Jesus.

2.   We are called to go on to "Other Villages" in witnessing the Gospel

Instead of going on to other villages, beyond our safe zone, in witnessing the Gospel, we live today in a world in which we can see more strong boundaries built up in Christian communities, "multiplicity of denominations". This is more as a result of fragmentation within church families. We experience proliferation of churches, para-churches and multiplicity of Christian organizations. Resurgence of denominationalism, confessionalism, freelance evangelism as well as aggressive missionary evangelism strengthen the borders even among Christians and divide the Christians and the Churches all over the world, more specifically in developing countries.

The growth of Pentecostal, evangelical, conservative and charismatic churches have become a new trend that adds more divisions in the churches and families. All these trends ultimately make the church more and more fragmented. Thereby the ecumenical movement becomes more fragile and weaker.[1] It is indeed a fact that, like in many other parts in the world, the ecumenical movement in Asia is in a state of general decline in many ways. Leadership crisis, the proliferation of ecumenical organizations at national and regional levels, increasing denominationalism, lack of ecumenical formation in the younger generation in churches, lack of capacity building efforts, lack of vision and theological thinking. Unlike in the past, the leadership of churches and ecumenical bodies in several Asian countries is not always interested in responding to or addressing the crucial issues in their situations. Secular NGOs or other organizations are more professional in their approach. The other problem we face is the multiplicity of ecumenical organizations addressing the same concerns in almost the same constituencies in Asia; we experience a lack of coherence and co-ordination in our ecumenical work.[2]

The Christian churches are building their dogmatic and hierarchical boundaries more strongly and deepening their divisions rather than uniting, totally ignoring our tasks towards neighbors in "other villages". Then who are our neighbors in "other villages"?

Breaking our borders, we are called to be on a journey, a journey together, following our Lord Jesus, witnessing to God's truth and light, in Asia. We begin our journey in Asia, where we experience the risen Lord, and are related to one another in Jesus Christ. "In him we live and move and have our being." (Acts 17:28). Asia is the home of all major world religions. Majority of the people of Asia are poor, often struggling to get by, due to injustice and exploitation.

> We journey together; ours is not an exclusive path. We walk together, with people of different faiths and no faiths, towards a common goal. As Christians, we journey with our sisters and brothers in churches who join together in communion with one another. We journey with our families and with the people of many nations and cultures who walk the roads, sail the seas and fly the skies, embracing one another and struggling for justice and peace. We journey with the migrants and the excluded as we embrace the stranger (Hebrews 13:2). As religious believers, we journey together with women and men from other religious communities, drawing inspiration from all people who seek the common good amidst the groaning of creation. And as we journey, we know that God will never be far from us, and we will not be overwhelmed or consumed (Isaiah 43:2).

> -(quoted from 'Asia Mission Statement' of 2017 Asia Mission Conference, Yangon, Myanmar)

We are called to be on journey together with all humanity, with all creation, as co-sojourners, and as co-pilgrims on our journey with a sense of oneness, humility and service.

The role of the Church, while journeying together, is to be meaningfully engaged in the mission of prophetic witness to the Truth and Light, in order to make God's love present and effective in all contexts, without any hidden motives. Identifying mission as an instrument for Church growth or expansion of denominational and confessional interests of certain groups should not be the aim of the mission. As a community engaged in mission, the Church should be a living community making visible the presence of God and God's Love.[3]

3.   On the Road to Jerusalem (Luke 24:30-35)

In Luke 24, we find two disciples of Jesus Christ, running away from Jerusalem and walking on the road to Emmaus. They were very much disappointed to see the death of Jesus, who was believed as a Savior and God's Son. And they were so afraid and scared that they would have been arrested and killed on a cross like as Jesus. They could not believe women's witness of seeing the resurrected Jesus. Their faith was not strong enough to believe all the testimonies of Jesus' resurrection. In the middle of their journey to Emmaus, the resurrected Jesus joined and accompanied them. However, these disciples couldn't recognize the risen Jesus. Only when Jesus took bread and broke it and gave it to them at the dinner table, then their eyes were opened, and they recognized him. But when they recognized Jesus, he disappeared from their sight. They asked each other, "Were not our hearts burning within us while he talked with us on the road and opened the Scriptures to us?" Their eyes were opened when they encountered Jesus Christ. Their hearts were burning like a fire when they encountered Jesus Christ. Before they encountered Jesus, they were escaping from Jerusalem to avoid the arrest to be killed on a cross. But after encountering the risen Jesus, they got up at once and turned their way back to Jerusalem. Then in Jerusalem, they boldly witnessed the resurrection of Jesus Christ.

After encountering Jesus,

> the road of sadness was changed to the road of joy,
> the road of despair to the road of hope,
> the road of doubt to the road of faith.

Two disciples would have continued their way to Emmaus where they could find a safe place. However, they turned their way back, with a fire burning in their hearts to Jerusalem where the danger and threats exist, where the conflicts and divisions exist, where their lives could be at stake. Only to witness the risen Jesus! And this is also our given task to be part of God's mission, too.

Endnotes

[1] Mathews George Chunakara, *Called to be Prophetic in the Oikoumene,* (Christava Sahitya Samithi Tiruvalla, 2014) p.14.

[2] Mathews George Chunakara, *Ecumenism in Asia,* (Christava Sahitya Samithi Tiruvalla, 2014) p.37.

[3] For example, how many churches do have any ministry for/with the disabled? Let me share one story of Abraham and Issac.

Whenever I read the words of Genesis Chapter 22, the story of God's test on Abraham to give his only son Issac as a burnt sacrifice to God. I really don't understand how God could test the faith of Abraham with a life of his only child. In this passage, it seems that God is asking too much from Abraham. But one day I read a very persuasive explanation on this story written by one Jewish writer, Kushina who raised a possibility of Isaac's disability. Frankly speaking, Issac was born between very old parents, which can be a very vulnerable environment to be born as a disabled child. In some ways in the bible, Issac showed very strange behaviors. He got married in very old age only with a help of his father Abraham. On his journey to the foreign countries, he introduced his wife as his sister to the King and let her to sleep with a king in a fear of being killed. He behaved cowardly, narrow-mindedly acted and he was not normal in common sense. In the ancient society, the parents took for granted from the community members to abandon their disabled children. In this sense, Abraham could have understood God's order as a grant to kill and abandon his only but disabled child Issac. However, from this story of Abraham and Issac, God wants to affirm that even the disabled children have their own dignities to live their lives by their own wills, their rights to be protected and guided by parents and by the community people and glorify God.

8

On the Road to Jerusalem:
Ecclesiological Reflections from a Reformed Perspective

Matthias Zeindler

Being a theologian from Switzerland – the cradle of the Reformed branch of Reformation churches (Zurich and Geneva), I will approach the topic of this consultation from a decidedly Reformed angle. You may be surprised that this angle will be the *doctrine of election*. But I hope to show that the ancient doctrine of election has a significant potential to give us further perspectives in the pressing questions of our churches.

1.   The doctrine of predestination: its classical shape

The doctrine of election or predestination has a bad reputation. For many it is one of the best examples for theological orthodoxy going wild, generating at its best teachings that have nothing to do with real life, and at its worst doctrines that cause confusion and fears. The doctrine of predestination in its classical shape goes like this: In an eternal decree before creation, God chose a part of humanity to be in his company for ever, at the same time rejecting the other part of humanity to be for ever separated from him. Put simply, he decided who would go to Heaven and who would go to Hell. Of course, this eternal decree doesn't make God the author of sin, on the contrary, he foresaw the fall of humanity, only giving to those condemned what they rightly deserve. While his election of the ones to be saved is a pure act of mercy, of free grace.

Classical doctrine of predestination is usually linked with the name of John Calvin. A fact that does not do justice to historical reality, because the doctrine was to a large extent common sense among Reformation theologians. Luther and Zwingli held it as much as Calvin, and no less the other Reformers all over Europe. We will get to the reason for that in a moment. Before that it important to notice that the doctrine of predestination was in no way new and original in Reformation times. The "father" of the doctrine of predestination is Augustine of Hippo, who developed its string of thought for the first time at the end of the fourth century. And it is most important for the understanding of the logic of the doctrine to identify the context[1] of its development. You probably know that Augustine was one of the great interpreters of St Paul, being part of a so called "renaissance of Paul" in late Antiquity. At the same time, he is one of the great theologians of grace in church history. And the doctrine of predestination is a genuine part of Augustine's reflections on the nature of God's grace. The logic is the following: If grace is God's grace, it must be pure grace, a grace that excludes any possibility of humans to contribute to their salvation. Divine grace can only be grace alone, *sola gratia*. And so, in order to keep grace exclusive grace, Augustine has to go back to God alone, to his eternal decree before creation, where every possibility of human cooperation can be excluded. Only then one can say that God alone has acted. All this taken together makes clear that the doctrine of predestination was originally part of the doctrine of grace. There is no description of the logic of divine grace without predestination.

Augustine was well aware of the fact that his doctrine was horrible. But he was convinced that the Scriptures urge us to face the horror – in the interest of divine grace. In the centuries to come the doctrine could never get rid of its shadow. It could never get over the terrible reality that although Christians confess their God to be a gracious God, he remains a God who has rejected a considerable part of his beloved creation.

The Reformers were also aware of the doctrine of predestination's dimension of horror. Calvin explicitly speaks of God's election as a *decretum horribile*, a horrible decree. But as Augustine, he is convinced that in the first place the doctrine is an interpretation of God's grace. And since the Reformers were theologians of the *sola gratia*, it comes as no surprise that they also resorted to the doctrine in its classical shape. Why then was predestination mainly associated with the Reformed heritage? To make the story short, the Lutherans in the Augsburg Confession found a balanced formulation which intentionally left the question of God's rejection open, while the Reformed, in the train of Calvin's more consequential (or consequentialist) thinking, for centuries kept struggling with the dilemmas of the doctrine.

Why am I telling you all this in a contribution to ecclesiologic questions? Well, we all know that there is no ecclesiology as such, but that our thinking about the church always mirrors our thinking about Christ and God. Ecclesiology is a dimension of Christology and Theology proper. Which means that there is no overcoming of borders within the church without asking what borders the nature and work of Christ or the nature and work of the trinitarian God may constitute or overcome. The only legitimate borders of the church are the ones God himself has set, and the only way to overcome illegitimate borders is to rely on the God who himself conquers barriers. The doctrine of predestination in a very profound sense speaks about borders that are being set by God, namely the ultimate borders between the elect and the reprobate. And we all know that in the history of the church these borders have led to very real separations – e.g. apartheid in South Africa, to name just the worst among them. To deal with the doctrine of predestination is therefore no detour to get to the real questions, but it directs us immediately into the centre of our topic.

2.   The doctrine of election: modern revisions

We don't have the time to thoroughly go into the broad biblical witness on election. It is enough to say that both in the Old and the New Testament there is little support for the classical doctrine of double predestination. While that doctrine deals with eternal election of individuals, the Bible in most cases speaks of election in time or history and of election of social bodies – of Israel in the Old Testament and of the church in the New. In modernity, two major revisions of theological thinking about election took place in the Reformed tradition, and both of them helped to move the doctrine back to the biblical. I am talking about the concepts of Schleiermacher and Barth.

The discomfort with the doctrine of predestination lead to its factual abolition within European churches at the end of the 18th century. There was, therefore, a certain amount of wonder when in 1819 Friedrich Schleiermacher came out with an essay in which he stated that the old doctrine of election needs to be dealt with anew. What he then did in a mature form in his "Glaubenslehre" ("The Christian Faith") of 1830.[2] Schleiermacher's decisive move happens right at the beginning, when he places the doctrine of election within the doctrine of the church, in ecclesiology. The rationale for this structural decision is the following: God – says Schleiermacher – chose to act in the world along the rules of the world.[3] In order to establish his Kingdom, he therefore had to act according to the laws of history. This is why the Son of God became a man within a certain time and in a particular place in history. Jesus called the Apostles to carry on the message of his life, death, and resurrection, and from there the church spread the Good News throughout the world and throughout the ages.

It is this process of historical dissemination of the gospel which Schleiermacher describes with the term "election". We may speak in his case of an *incarnational* logic which steers his ecclesiological thinking. He writes: "It could not be otherwise if the supernatural in Christ is to become nature, and the church to develop as a natural historical phenomenon."[4] To speak of election for Schleiermacher means that God takes the historical character of the world seriously and makes the gospel known along historical lines.

It is easy to recognise a familiar biblical pattern in this concept. Israel was not elected to be a privileged people among the nations, but to make God known to the world. And the church was not elected for its own sake, but in order to witness to Jesus Christ and "to make disciples of all nations" (Mt 28:19). Along these lines Schleiermacher made it possible to think of election as an inner worldly, a historical concept again. It is obvious that with this the doctrine of election has become more biblical.

One may wonder what happened to the governing question of the classical doctrine of predestination, namely the eternal fate of humans. Schleiermacher did not forget that question, but again he gave it a new turn. He notices that in the historical process of spreading the gospel many die without having been reborn. And he goes on with the observation that there could never be a real community of the saved as long as there is a part of humanity that remains excluded from that community.

The beatitude of the Saints, Schleiermacher says, cannot be fully realized without the completion of a universal communion of the Saints – otherwise, it would simply be no beatitude. He therefore concludes that God's salvation will finally be a universal salvation, a salvation of all humanity.[5] The Kingdom of God will be completely borderless, including all humans from all times and places. Those who had the privilege to get acquainted with the gospel and those who did not. With this last move Schleiermacher makes clear that election remains a strictly ecclesiological and therefore a strictly historical term. As there will be no church in the Kingdom, there will be neither elect nor reprobate, but only the one people of God. Or, to put it in more technical terms: There is particularity in God's election, but it is a *relative* particularity. It is a particularity that points to universality.

In Schleiermacher we find a fundamental revision of the doctrine of election, and the same can certainly be said about a concept which was put on paper during World War II, namely the doctrine of God's gracious election in Karl Barth's monumental Church Dogmatic.[6] And while Schleiermacher linked election to history again, Barth linked it to Christology anew. With this he took seriously that in many places in the New Testament it is Jesus Christ who is elect in the first place, most prominently in the Gospel of John.

Other than in Schleiermacher, for Barth the doctrine of election is the cornerstone of his whole theology, the one decisive place in his dogmatic.[7] But let us hear him in his own words: "The doctrine of election is the sum of the Gospel because of all words that can be said or heard it is the best: that God elects man; that God is for man to the One who loves in freedom"[8] This is a very complex sentence, and I am not going to completely unpack it. First of all, it is important to notice that the doctrine of election for Barth clarifies who God is. And the first thing to say about God is: He is the God who elected Jesus Christ to be his beloved Son. Two consequences follow from this initial move. On the one hand with the election of Jesus Christ God has also chosen himself, namely to be the Father of his Son. And therefore, not to be a lonely God, but a God in communion, a covenantal God. On the other hand, in Jesus Christ God has chosen all of humanity. In the decision to be a communitarian God, God decided to be the God of humans and of all creation. There is no other

God behind the God who chose to be the God of Jesus Christ and therefore of all humanity. There is no God behind the loving God for all, a God who maybe could revoke his election, a God who maybe is an unknown abyss about whom we have nothing to say.

We now understand why Barth speaks of the doctrine of election as the "sum of the gospel". There is no more and nothing better to say than this: That God is a loving God for all. Whatever will follow in the Church Dogmatic – there will be more than 6000 pages to come – it will in every paragraph be a detailed explanation of this fundamental insight. The doctrine of election is the gospel in a nutshell. As the Princeton theologian Bruce McCormack has put it, election is "the primal decision of God".[9]

As in Schleiermacher, also in Barth you may wonder what happened to the classical doctrine of predestination. Barth extensively deals with the history of the doctrine, only to admit at the end that in no other context he felt constrained to depart so profoundly from the forefathers whom he otherwise followed whenever possible. Formally he criticizes them for not having thought God's election Christo logically, but to deal with God's eternal decree at the very beginning of dogmatic without ever mentioning Christ. The material consequences are grave, namely that God's decision in Christ to be a merciful God for all plays no role in the eternal decree of predestination. God's mercy becomes limited to the ones elected. The classical shape of the doctrine of predestination corrupts the gospel of God's love so profoundly that it has to be completely revised.

Barth's doctrine of election is extremely rich, in contains sections on Israel, the church as well as the individual elect, along with lengthy exegetical and historical passages. We don't have the time to further develop all that. Before we go on, though, two important aspects have to be mentioned. The first one is Karl Barth's version of double predestination. Yes, there is double predestination in Barth indeed. But it is maybe the best example for what a difference a clear-cut

Christological thinking can make. Election for divine grace or divine rejection does not take place in God's eternal decree, but in the cross of Jesus Christ. And in the cross of Jesus Christ two decisions have occurred. On the one hand, God judged sin and rejected the sinner, but he did so in Christ, freeing humans from eternal condemnation. God, in Barth's words, "was choosing reprobation, perdition and death for himself and mercy, grace and life for human beings".[10] There is double predestination, yes, but because Christ bears the rejection that rightly belongs to humans, there is only the other part left for humanity, to be the people of God's gracious covenant for ever.

And the second aspect: As a young student I had the opportunity to study in the United States for a year (Union Theological Seminary, Richmond/Virginia). I had just read my first three volumes of the Church Dogmatic and was full of excitement about all the discoveries. More than once it happened to me in theological exchanges that other students said: "Oh yes, Karl Barth is great – but he is a universalist!" Up to then I had not felt that there is a problem in Barth's so-called universalist teaching. But I had to realize that in a U.S.-American context it caused quite some unrest to have someone teach that God's grace could be so all-embracing that – in Barth's words – there may well be hell, but it may also well be that hell is empty. Only later I learned that right after the publication of Barth's doctrine of election in 1942 also in Europe there stood up a great cloud of critics who found it highly problematic that in Barth's teaching there was allegedly no room left for a human decision for or against Christ, so that any call for redemption becomes needless.

The discussion hasn't come to an end yet. Barth's defence was always dialectical, e.g. when he said that he does not believe in final redemption but in Jesus Christ the final redeemer. I belong to the ones who think that in his doctrine of election Barth has laid the foundations for a well-founded hope that at the end, in the final consummation of God's works, there will be no-one who will be excluded from divine love, the divine love that is the foundation of the whole universe. In the later volumes of his dogmatic, we find a large amount of passages that unmistakably point in that direction.

But fortunately, we don't have to settle the discussion. For the moment it is enough to realize that after Schleiermacher also the second major revision of the doctrine of divine election within protestant theology includes a strong hope for universal eschatological redemption. And while in the traditional doctrine there always lurked a dark, threatening shadow, in the revised versions of the doctrine of election there is light, light only.

3.   God's borderless covenant

After this sketch of Reformed discussions about election, let us come back to the topic of our consultation and try to draw some conclusions. I have put my reflections under the title "On the road to Jerusalem", and it is now time to provide some explanations for that choice. It is my deep conviction that the church can and will only be the church when she finds herself on the way to Jerusalem. With this I don't say that there should be regular travelling of church groups to the Holy Land, although this is very popular in European and U.S.-American congregations (I don't know about India). You may have guessed from the beginning that the Jerusalem in the title is the New Jerusalem of Revelation 21 and 22. This is the place where the church is bound to, and this is the place where the church should be headed for in all her being and doing.

With this I once more pick up a typically Reformed accent. In the theology of John Calvin, the orientation to the future life, the *meditatio futurae vitae*, plays an important role. In his commentary on the book of Deuteronomy Calvin describes in touching words how the life of Christians is always a life *en route*, a pilgrim existence without a permanent place to stay. Like birds, always ready to leave their tree. And Calvin knew what he was talking about, being a refugee from France himself and Geneva being the host city of thousands of Huguenot migrants. It has been said that the Reformed church always was a church with a migration background. We express the same saying that it is part of the church's existence to steadily be migrating to the Kingdom of God. And it has never been good for the church to forget her ultimate destiny. Where that destiny moves out of sight, there is a great danger that the church becomes an ally of the ruling powers or the ideologies of the age.

This is especially true when we think about the church and its borders. As was said, the only legitimate borders for the church can be those set by God. All other borders are relative, and in many cases have to be overcome. We know that Jesus, in the name of God's borderless love, overstepped a great number of religious and societal borders, one of the main reasons why he had to be eliminated. (In his concept note, Dr. Sadananda has given us an impressive outline of the biblical God's constant will to overcome illegitimate borders.) The Reformed doctrine of God's gratuitous election in its modern shape tries to articulate the same in dogmatical terms. In Jesus Christ God has elected all of humanity to be part of his covenant. There is no part of his creation God does not want to be in eternal communion with him.

The universality of God's covenant is not realized yet. Or in more biblical terms: We are still awaiting its fulfilment. The eschatological fulfilment of God's love will be the universal revelation and publication of his eternal election into his covenant. In the Kingdom of God there will be no limits of God's Love, Peace and Justice, or to be more precise: It will be evident to everybody that there never were limits to God's Love, Peace and Justice, and that any human attempt to put up borders that preclude humans from participating in God's gifts is sinful. We are still awaiting the fulfilling, but we are awaiting it in the firm faith that what is coming is valid already. When it is true that one day all will participate in God's gift, then there is no legitimate reason to even now exclude anyone from that participation. Not only then, but now already the earth is the Lord's, and it is the church's calling to witness to his Lordship in word and deed.

4.   God and the Others

Borders are about inclusion and exclusion. There is Us and there are the Others. You all know sociological theories saying that there can be no cohesion within a group without exclusion of others. We have sufficient evidence for these theories. It is easy both in history and in the presence to point out to what extent groups, whole societies as well as churches work within the logic of exclusion generating internal solidarity. The way the US and Europe – but also Australia and some Asian countries – nowadays deal with refugees is a telling example for that mechanism.

The classical doctrine of predestination is probably the most extreme and problematic solution in Christianity to deal with questions of borders, of inclusion and exclusion, of Us and the Others. There is a good example how the doctrine worked along the aforementioned sociological mechanism. In the Heidelberg Catechism (1563), one of the most important documents of Reformed theology,[11] question 52 goes like this: "How does Christ's return to 'judge the living and the dead' comfort you?" The first part of the answer: "In all distress and persecution, with uplifted head I confidently await the very judge who has already offered himself to the judgment of God in my place and removed the whole curse from me." Important for our question is the second part: "Christ will cast all his enemies and mine into everlasting condemnation but will take me and all his chosen ones to himself into the joy and glory of heaven." You notice, according to the Catechism the fact that God will cast his enemies into everlasting condemnation is part of the comfort Christians supposedly gain from the hope of Christ coming for the Last Judgement.

The doctrine of election in its revised version makes it impossible for church and theology to reproduce the logic of internal solidarity via exclusion of others. Because for God who in Jesus Christ chose all of humanity to be part of his covenant, there are no Others in the sense of the reprobate, in the sense even of his eternal enemies. In the end nobody will be lost because God will win us all to say our grateful yes to his eternal Yes to all creation. And if for God there are no absolute Others, but only present or future partakers in his covenant, then there can be no absolute Others for the church. Whatever Others there may still be, all those Others are future brothers and sisters. So whatever Otherness there may be, it has to be considered as a relative otherness in the perspective of an already existing Unity in Christ.

It is obvious that under these circumstances there is no foundation for a solidarity via exclusion of the Other. Solidarity in the church has to function differently. It has to be an open solidarity founded in God's election of those in the church as well as of those outside the church. It has to be a solidarity that has no need to say no to some in order to be able to say yes to the members of its group. On the contrary, solidarity within the church lives from the great Yes of God to all and will therefore be a solidarity that always goes beyond its borders.

5.   God with the Others

Before we move on with the church, let me at least mention a question which will sooner or later pop up within reflections like the present ones. We have spoken of God's election of all in Jesus Christ, and we have tried to state God's universal election more precisely in eschatological terms, saying that in the coming of the Kingdom God's covenant with all creation, constituted in the eternal election of Jesus Christ, will be manifest to all. But given all this, what can we say about God's presence with the Others not only in his future but in the here and now? What clues, for instance, can the doctrine of election give us for reflections about God's presence with people of other faiths?

It is not my intention to display a full-fletched theology of religions here. All the more because in the last decades there have come enormously important contributions from Asian theologians to that field of reflection.[12] Other than in Europe and the Americas, churches in Asia where always confronted with a majority of people who lived in religious traditions differing from their own. And it is important to add, in traditions that were as rich in their religious practice as they were profound in their theological and philosophical reflections. So, from the beginning churches in Asia were confronted with the existential question as to what extent the God they worshipped is also present in the worship of their neighbours.

It may be, though, that today there are more parallels between Asia and Europe than before. Because in Europe churches also increasingly have to deal with pluralism. This is, on the one hand, a pluralism of religions, because through migration we have a growing presence of other religions than Christianity in the midst of our countries. On the other hand, and more importantly, we have a growing secularism. And although sociologists differ in their estimations, secularism may well be the worldview of the majority in Europe.

It seems important to me to take secularism seriously in theological terms. Whatever hostile secular people may be vis-à-vis religions, their view nevertheless is a worldview, a philosophy that tries to give answers to the crucial questions of life. In addition to that, there has come a lot of good from secular thinking in the last two centuries, thoughts and projects that have contributed to the well-being of our society – not the least a more self-critical attitude of the Christian churches. All this gives us reason enough to ask the question whether God may not also be present in secular approaches to reality. I therefore suggest that we include secular approaches in our reflections about the issue of God's presence with the Others.

Only a few indications coming from a doctrine of election as developed above. To follow the usual, although contested categories of exclusivism, inclusivism and pluralism, there are two solutions that will conflict with that doctrine. One of them is exclusivism in a strict sense, saying that all religion except faith in Jesus Christ is false religion and bound to lead to condemnation. But God's election in Jesus Christ goes beyond explicit faith in Christ. The other solution that will be ruled out by the doctrine of election is a pluralist theology of religion, as it was first presented by the late John Hick.[13] (It is probably better to speak of pluralist philosophies of religion.) Hick presupposes an ultimate religious reality which is intended by all religions and to which all religions point. Hick speaks of the REAL as the central reality which all religions are in different ways symbolizing but none of them will ever fully symbolize.

Other than pluralist theologies of religion, a reflection on other religions and worldviews from the perspective of a theology of election will be highly exclusive, but at the same time thoroughly inclusive. Exclusive to the extent that the unity of humanity is constituted in God's election of his Son Jesus Christ. And inclusive to the extent that in God's election of Christ all of humanity is included.

To get one step further, it is clear to me that the eternal election of all to God's covenant not only constitutes a future fulfilment of God's communion with all, but also a divine presence with the Others in history. And therefore, a presence of Christ also in other religions and worldviews. I am well aware that this is a far-reaching conclusion, which begs for much further explanation both methodologically and materially. Only two remarks: First, the presence of Jesus Christ before his coming for God's Kingdom is realised in the Holy Spirit. The universality of Christ is therefore realised in a universal presence of the Spirit in the world – not only in the church. Inasmuch as Christ works not only within, but also beyond the limits of the church, we may expect the Spirit to work in the world apart from the church.

This gives way for the second remark, namely that we have reasons to hope that God's communicates his truth not exclusively in the church, but also in other religions and worldviews. The rationale for such an assertion can again be found in the Holy Spirit in whom God opens himself for the world and communicates his truth to humanity. Not only in the future, but here and now already the electing God gives participation in his life-giving truth.

6.   Borderless God and borderless church

Let me finish with a few observations on what the aforementioned could contribute to the questions we are dealing with in this consultation. Most of what can be said has already been developed.

First, there will always be *borders* of the church. If there were no defined group which differs from other groups, it would be meaningless to speak of such a thing like the church. There is church, because there is non-church. And this will remain the case short of the Kingdom of God. Only in the New Jerusalem, there will be no temple, no more sacred and profane sphere, but only the Eternal God living with his covenant people. So on the road to Jerusalem, there will always be those who say and live there yes to Jesus Christ, and others who for whatever reason do not say and live such a yes. And normally, those who say and live their yes will be a minority.

But second, there is an important qualification. The borders between church and non-church will always be *relative* borders. If we take seriously what has to be said about God who in Jesus Christ chooses all humanity to eternally be his covenant-people, then there are no borders between saved and reprobate, but only borders between those who by the Holy Spirit were already opened for God's truth, and those who have not yet been elected to discover that truth. The borders between church and non-church are therefore no eternally static borders, but historically dynamic ones. The difference between this and that side of the border is the difference between "already" and "not yet".

Third, the borders between church and non-church have to be drawn in a *differentiated* way. They cannot be identical with the borders between Christianity and other religions or worldviews. There is church and non-church within Christianity itself, and to the extent that God's truth is available in other religions and worldviews, we have to apply the same distinction between abiding by the truth and abiding by untruth to the differing religious and non-religious ways.

Fourth, we again come back to the observation that the *only legitimate borders* in the world are those *set by God*. They are the inscrutable borders of the "already now" and "not yet". Apart from that, is it God who untiringly works on overcoming illegitimate borders, borders with which humans prevent others from participating in God's gifts. So the first thing of a church who wants to be a borderless church is to open herself constantly to God's activity of overcoming borders in the church and the world. The activity of becoming a borderless church starts with the passivity of waiting for God to work upon his church. The borderless church can only be a church that does not stop praying: "Come, Holy Spirit!" In that context let me add a last possible impulse from the Reformed tradition. In the Reformation Jubilee 2017 there was much talk about the phrase *ecclesia reformata semper reformanda* – the reformed church has always to be reformed. It was not easy to make clear what the sentence wanted to say in its original meaning. The phrase in its full meaning reads like this: *ecclesia reformata semper reformanda secundum Evangelium* – the reformed church always needs to be reformed by the word of God. So, the primary activity is not on the side of the church, as it was often misunderstood. The primary activity is on the side of God, of his Word through the Holy Spirit. Which of course does not exclude but include for the church to become seriously active.

Fifth and lastly: To believe in a God who in his Son chose his whole creation to eternally be his covenant-people is a big *relief for the church*. It can be such an excessive demand for a church to feel obliged to save all of humanity or to solve all social problems of the world. Sooner or later such a demand will be destructive. But the church is not called to save the world, it is called to witness to the world that it is already saved. It is therefore a church that is not supposed to be depressed because of its constant shortcomings, but a church that rejoices in the abounding gifts that God has given, still gives and one day will give boundlessly. I may be wrong, but the Asian churches who for centuries have been in a minority position seem to know more than other churches about the church not being responsible for saving the world. But humble witnesses to the riches the eternal God holds ready for the world. And this may be an essential lesson churches in the global North can learn from them.

Endnotes

[1] Fathers of the Church: St. Augustine, Four Anti-Pelagian Writings, Catholic University of America Press: Washington D.C., 1992.

[2] Friedrich Schleiermacher, Christian Faith, Vol. 1 and 2. A New Translation and Critical Edition, Terrence N. Tice/Catherine L. Kelsey (eds.), Westminster Press: Westminster, 2016, §§ 117-20. Cf. Dawn DeVries and B.A. Gerrish, Providence and grace: Schleiermacher on justification and election, in: The Cambridge Companion to Friedrich Schleiermacher, Jacqueline Mariña, Cambridge University Press: Cambridge, 2005, 189-207.

[3] Schleiermacher, Christian Faith § 117.1.

[4] Schleiermacher, Christian Faith § 117.2.

[5] Schleiermacher, Christian Faith § 118.

[6] Karl Barth, Church Dogmatics II.2: The Doctrine of God Part 2. The Election of God. The Command of God, Thomas T. Torrance, Geoffrey W. Bromiley (eds.), T&T Clark: London, 1978.

[7] Bruce L. McCormack, Grace and being: the role of God's gracious election in Karl Barth's theological ontology, in: The Cambridge Companion to Karl Barth, John Webster (ed.), Cambridge University Press: Cambridge, 2000, 92-110; Bruce L. McCormack, The Sum of the Gospel. The Doctrine of Election in the Theologies of Alexander Schweizer and Karl Barth, in: McCormack,

Orthodox and Modern. Studies in the Theology of Karl Barth, Baker Academic: Grand Rapids/Michigan 2008, 41-61; Adam Neder, Participation in Christ. An Entry into Karl Barth's Church Dogmatics, Westminster John Knox Press: Louisville/Kentucky, 2009, 15-28.

[8] Barth, Church Dogmatics II.2, 3.

[9] McCormack, Sum of the Gospel, 59.

[10] Barth, Church Dogmatics II.2, 168.

[11] Lyle D. Bierma, The Theology of the Heidelberg Catechism: A Reformation Synthesis, Westminster John Knox Press: Louisville/Kentucky, 2013.

[12] M. Thomas Thangaraj, Religious pluralism, dialogue and Asian Christian responses, in: Christian Theology in Asia, Sebastian C.H. Kim (ed.), Cambridge University Press: Cambridge, 2008, 157-178.

[13] John Hick, An Interpretation of Religion, Macmillan: London, 1989.

9

Re-membering the Dis-Membered:

Towards a New Body Politics
for a Borderless Church

Peniel Jesudason Rufus Rajkumar

Introduction

Rethinking Ekklesia in terms of 'borderless-ness' is an urgent task in the context of the empire today. Nevertheless one dilemma this enterprise presents concerns the question – How can we speak of borderless-ness in a rigidly bordered context? Taking the Indian context of religious nationalism as a test case my paper argues that the task of moving towards a borderless Church in the Indian context inevitably entails engaging with those forces of discrimination that thrust and thrive upon borders. It is in some ways doing what the concept note for this consultation describes as a first step, "look intently at our borders" and discern ways of dismantling those borders.

Hindutva and Its Politics: Minorities and the Marginalized Caught in the Faultlines of Majoritarian Imagination

If we understand empire as 'massive concentrations of power which permeate all aspects of life' and which "seeks to extend its control as far as possible, beyond the commonly recognized geographical, political and economic spheres, to include the intellectual, emotional, psychological, spiritual, cultural, and religious arenas"[1] then nationalisms across the global are manifestations of the metamorphosis of the empire. In India the empire has resurged in the shape of the Hindutva – a nationalistic ideology based on Hindu majoritarianism.[2] Hindutva seeks to essentialize identities and create imaginary majoritarian fault-lines which thrive through either the politics of co-option or politics of polarization.

Hindutva, Religious Minorities and the Politics of Bordering

At the heart of Hindutva is the accordance of primary status to 'Hindus' – those who consider India as both *Pithrubhumi* (fatherland) and *punyabhumi* (holy land) – as against adherents of other faiths like Muslims and Christians whose 'holy land' is outside India. Therefore, inbuilt to the Hindutva ideology is an inherent religious supremacy which seeks to reinforce a secondary-citizen status to the significant religious minority communities in India namely Indian Christians and Indian Muslims. Various instances in recent years have clearly highlighted this inherent polemic.

In December 2014 *Sadhvi* Niranjan Jyothi, a junior minister (a Hindu female ascetic - therefore *Sadhvi*) in the present Indian government, in a polemical election speech spoke of the need for people to choose between being governed by *Ramzadon* (children of Ram) or *Haramzadon* (illegitimate children), inferring Christians and Muslims as 'illegitimate' children of India.[3] This language of 'children' is potent with dangerous possibilities in the context of the present re-imagination of the Indian nation. Proponents of the Hindutva, like *Sadhvi* Niranjan Jyothi, who transpose the notion of divine motherhood onto the Indian nation, call on Hindus – as the legitimate children of the nation – 'to "save" divine "Mother India" from the contaminating and impure presence of Muslims.'[4] This ascribed devotion towards the divine motherhood of the nation 'morphs into the current virulent politics of Hindutva' whereby the son's devotion to the *deshmata* (mother goddess) is expressed 'by becoming a "demon slayer"... waging war on Muslims.'[5] Such incidents of hostility against the two significant minority communities mirror the convictions expressed by the ideologue of Rashtriya Swayamsevak Sangh (RSS), Madhav Sadashiv Golwalkar, who in 1939 declared, 'The non-Hindu peoples in Hindustan... must... stay in the country wholly subordinated to the Hindu Nation, claiming nothing, deserving no privileges, far less any preferential treatment – not even citizen's rights.'[6]

Hindutva has used both myth and history to fabricate and foster hostility towards Christians and Muslims. Wendy Doniger in her book *Hindus: An Alternative History* brings out how the popular Hindu epic the *Ramayana* is today repressively retold to 'use the mythological moment of Ram-raj (Rama's reign) as an imagined India that is free of Muslims and Christians and any Others, in the hope of restoring India to the Edenic moment of the *Ramayanas*.'[7] In a context where 'a retrospective history of antagonism is not difficult to manufacture,'[8] history has been used to emphasize the 'Hindu' as the native and the Muslim as the 'invader' by Hindutva ideologues like Savarkar through a selective terming of the coming of the Muslims to India as 'invasion' and the coming of the Aryans (forerunners of the Hindus) as 'settling.'[9] While the invader tag is attached to Muslims, Christians are branded with an 'imperial tag' – as foreign agents out to destabilize and divide the Indian nation.[10] Thus the political space is India is one which is forged out of political mythmaking, insidious introduction of negative stereotypes, and the re-fabrication of history, all of which seek to debilitate and disenfranchise Indian Christians and Muslims in India today.

Hindutva, Marginalized Communities and the Politics of Borderlessness

It is not only the religious minorities who are caught in the fault lines of this nationalistic re-imagination. Communities who have been traditionally marginalized on the basis of caste like the Dalits and Adivasis are also caught in these fault lines, however in a different manner – through a politics of inclusion. The Hindutva through its primary political outfit the Bharatiya Janata Party has sought to project itself as a party committed to social inclusion, justice and equality and welfare of the Dalits. The recent efforts of the BJP to lure the Dalits into the Hindu fold have included the election of a Dalit, Ram Nath Kovind, as the President of India; acquiring the London House of Ambedkar with the intention of setting up an 'International Research Centre on Ambedkar'; and Prime Minister Narendra Modi's reference to himself as a 'Bhakt' (devotee) of Ambedkar.[11] Further, Hindutva has actively sought to co-opt anti-caste activists like Phule and Ambedkar as Hindu icons in order to win over the Dalit communities.

However, most ingenuous among its efforts have been its politics of 'Identity-fic(a)tion' which has sought to co-opt the Dalits within the Hindutva fold by forging for them a pan-Hindu identity which simultaneously polarises them against the Muslims and Christians. This was made manifest as early as in 1989 when, during the campaign to construct a Ram Temple in the place of a Mosque in Ayodhya, the Vishwa Hindu Parishad, a Hindutva outfit, ensured that the first brick for the *shilanyas* (foundation) for the proposed Ram temple was laid by a Dalit called Kameshwar Chaupal. In 2016, ahead the elections in the most populous North Indian state of Uttar Pradesh, the national president of the BJP Amit Shah made it a point to pay homage to Raja Suheldev, a 11th century Dalit ruler, from the numerically significant Pasi community, who had apparently defeated a Muslim warrior Salar Masood Ghazi in a battle in Bahraich.[12] This effort to valorise the anti-Muslim identity of the Dalits has long been part of the political myth-making of the Hindutva in its efforts to consolidate the 'hinduness' of the Dalit communities.

Related to this, an important means of containing the Dalits within the Hindutva fold has been through "an idealized scriptural authority cultivated to unify the Hindu community" which is a recent Hindutva tactic. Badri Narayan's book *Fascinating Hindutva: Saffron Politics and Dalit Mobilization* deconstructs how Hindutva forces skillfully reinterpret local and popular myths, memories and legends of Dalit castes as part of a nationalistic agenda, through a Hinduised lens, in order to politically mobilize Dalits. Narayan points out how Hindutva forces depict the protagonists of these local narratives either as protectors of Hindu religion and culture from the Muslim invaders of the medieval period or as reincarnations of the Hindu God Rama thereby effectively linking these local Dalit myths with a unified Hindu meta-narrative and communalizing these characters vis-à-vis the Muslims. Explaining this further Sathinathan Clarke writes:

> *Marginal identities, local myths, and regional divine figures that were important to Shudra and Dalit communities become recognized, rehabilitated and harmonized into "the meta-narrative to form one unified [sacred] narrative of Hindutva."[13] This process of creative, even if calculating, negotiation of scriptural authority brings traditionally outcaste communities back into the Word-vision of Hinduism in order to be part of an all-inclusive sacred narrative.[14]*

In such a context of reification of identities through the polarization of the minorities and co-option of the marginalized, that the Indian church is called to rethink ekklesia.

Rethinking Ekklesia as Ek-Centric With-Ness

Rethinking Ekklessia in the context of the fault lines of religious nationalism in India requires a new theo-politic. Very often in contexts of religious plurality and difference the dominant theological cartography that has been employed has been Trinitarian notion of the *perichoresis*. Meaning mutual interpenetration, the concept of perichoresis has aided the process of referring to the inter-relationship of the three persons of the Trinity. However, such Trinitarian rhetoric where, "Trinity" and "Sociality" are often thought together in such a way that the immanent relational life of God, which is expressed *ad extra* in God's works, toward his creatures, is "imaged" in human relations'[15] needs to be re-visited in the light of challenges which have been posed to it. Such a re-visitation is appropriate if we are to approximate into contemporary ecclesial practice the challenges and the responsibility of re-embodying the Trinity.

The primary challenge is to respond to the critical comment raised by Yale theologian Miroslav Volf in his *After Our Likeness: The Church as the Image of the Trinity*:

> Today the thesis that ecclesial communion should correspond to Trinitarian communion enjoys the status of an almost self-evident position. Yet it is surprising that no one has carefully examined just where such correspondences are to be found, nor expended much effort on determining where ecclesial communion reaches the limits of its capacity for such an analogy. The result is that reconstructions of these correspondences often say nothing more than the platitude that unity cannot exist without multiplicity nor multiplicity without unity, or they demand of human beings in the church the (allegedly) completely selfless love of God. The former is so vague that no one cares to dispute it, and the latter so divine that no one can live it. [16]

Volf does indeed push those of us who sit comfortably in agreement with the Trinitarian analogical argument - to consider what it entails to translate the Trinitarian analogy into contextually relevant practice.

The riches of the Trinitarian analogy for a context like the Indian church can be reaped not by superimposing it as a generic universal model for interreligious relations. Rather this analogy can be used as an internal critique of Christianity – especially of the perspectives from which it has sought to resist discrimination. If we need to press the Trinitarian analogy for rethinking Ek-klessia - the 'Ek-centric' or 'Other-Centred' nature of the Trinity, which makes space for the 'other' – the margins as an important teacher in confronting and subverting borders can offer new methodological possibilities for rethinking ekklesia. It can, in my opinion help rethink of Christian witness in India in terms of With-Ness or solidarity. Let's turn to a note on method.

Ek-Centricity as Method

The striving of the CSI to be a borderless church in the bordered Indian context needs to be realized as prophetic resistance to the borders. In this quest there is need for a rethinking of the method of challenging discrimination and inequality. Despite a proliferation of critical discourses in the public space which have sought to address questions of power and inequality and take up the issues of the "Other"/the subalterns, in several instances such discourses have been implicated in the politics of power as they have often remained elitist in their orientation. Such tacit inclinations towards perspectives emerging from the elites only function to reinforce the asymmetrical status quo rather than change it. This elitist orientation is true of Indian and Western discourses, both theological and secular. A few examples can be cited.

Analyzing the discourses on economic poverty in the Indian context, K.N. Panikkar critically exposes how even "progressive thinking" in colonial India which employed rhetoric and critiqued inequality was clearly entrapped in a bourgeois perspective to such an extent that hierarchy and hegemony were reinforced and reproduced rather than being re-configured and redressed. Critiquing the thinking of people like Keshub Chander Sen, Bakim Chandra Chatterjee and Vivekananda, Panikkar says:

> That the intellectuals in colonial India were concerned with the problem of poverty is in itself not very significant; given the prevalent conditions, they would not have remained insensitive to it. What is important, however, is how they viewed this problem: whether their approach was from the standpoint of the poor or that of the privileged. Generally, it was the latter; therefore, while poverty was decried, the system and structure which decried it was not denounced.[17]

This problem of not approaching transformation and justice from the perspectives of the margins is prompts a subversive methodology for rethinking ekklessia in terms of ek-centricity – or other-centeredness, taking seriously the perspectives of the margins especially in confronting the boundaries in our midst. The journey towards borderlessness – which involves challenging those structures should be done in a way which takes seriously all those efforts undertaken by people from the margins to build life-affirming communities.

This sentiment is strongly echoed in *Together Towards Life* the mission text produced by the WCC. According to TTL:

> *People on the margins have agency, and can often see what, from the centre, is out of view. People on the margins, living in vulnerable positions, often know what exclusionary forces are threatening their survival and can best discern urgency of their struggles; people in positions of privilege have much to learn from the daily struggles of people living in marginal conditions'.* (TTL para 38)

Unless Christian witness is reshaped as With-ness in solidarity with the margins, the church risks losing its identity as an instrument of the divine kin-dom of justice and peace. As Deenabandhu Manchala reminds, 'If the church does not participate in the ongoing revolutionary struggles of the victims of injustice … the church will lose an opportunity to participate in the reign of God unveiling itself among the excluded and despised people of the world'.[18]

In the context of empire, affirmation of the agency of the margins safeguards us from succumbing to the imperialistic framework of the empire because 'we will continue to support empire by default unless we look for those particular and often repressed places where we encounter alternatives'.[19] As liberation theologian and social activist Joerg Reiger reminds us there is need for us to traverse 'the netherworld of truth' which is being 'repressed by empire'. "The truth of empire and the alternative truth of Christ-can only be found if we search below the surface of the powers that be and explore the Christological surplus manifest between the lines of the status quo".[20]

The challenge for rethinking ekklesia is to pursue "Justice in touch with the lives of the marginalized". It is only then that the church can be led to a new awareness and valuation not only of the productivity of the margins – but also to a new awareness of God's own mysterious productivity in places where we least expect it, even on a cross."[21] Can solidarity as with-ness then be the way ahead to becoming a borderless church? What are those aspects of our contemporary life where the church can re-shape its identity and witness as with-ness in critical solidarity with the efforts of the margins to live life in all its abundance?

Endnotes

[1] Jeorg Reiger 'Christian theology and Empires', in Kwok Pui-lan, Don H. Compier and Jeorg Reiger (eds.), *Empire and the Christian Tradition: New Readings of Classical Theologians*, (Minneapolis: Fortress, 2007), (1-13), p.3.

[2] Hindutva, loosely-termed as 'Hindu-ness', is a Hindu nationalistic ideology of religious majoritarianism. It is based on a vision which is 'indigenously religious and inventively political', through which Hindu fundamentalists have "reached inward to reclaim a primordial Hindu essence… and reached outward to reconfigure a religiopolitical nation-space that grew out of this autonomous vision" (Sathianathan Clarke, *Competing Fundamentalisms: Violent Extremism in Christianity, Islam and Hinduism*, Louisville, Kentucky: Westminster John knox Press, 2017, p.99.

The origins of Hindutva can be traced to a book published in 1923 named 'Hindutva' by Vinayak Damodar Savarkar an ideologue of this politics. (Vinayak Damodar Savarkar, *Hindutva*, Nagpur: V.V. Kelkar, 1923). Later several editions were republished. The Hindutva ideology effectively seeks to reduce India to a Hindu nation comprising of Hindus – undermining the pluralistic ethos of the country. Hindutva rests on three pillars of 'geographical unity, racial features and common culture'. It is however with regard to the third pillar that much of the debate on the nationalist ideology of Hindutva has been framed. Hindutva in its definition of Indian culture equates Indian culture with a parochial and selective version of Hindu culture. It introduces a concept of nationalism defined in terms of culture which conflates Indian culture with 'Hindu' culture - a predominantly brahminnical and sanskritised version of Indian culture. This becomes clear if we consider Savarkar's definition of culture:

[W]e Hindus are bound together not only by the ties of love we bear to a common fatherland and by the common blood that courses through our veins and keeps our hearts throbbing and our affections warm, but also by the ties of common homage we pay to our great civilization – our Hindu culture, which could not be better rendered than by the word Sanskriti suggestive as it is of that language Sanskrit, which has been the chosen means of expression and preservation of that culture, of all that was best and worth-preserving in the history of our race. We are one because we are a nation, a race and own a common Sanskriti (civilization). Vinayak Damodar Savarkar, *Hindutva: Who is a Hindu?* (2d ed.; Bombay: Veer Savarkar Prakashan, 1969), pp.91-92.

[3] http://www.ndtv.com/article/india/defiant-bjp-says-minister-of-hate-will-give-more-speeches-630346 http://indianexpress.com/article/india/politics/apology-wont-suffice-sadhvi-niranjan-jyoti-must-resign-opposition-members/

[4] Susan Abraham, 'Strategic Essentialism in Nationalist Discourses: Sketching a Feminist Agenda in the Study of Religion', *Journal of Feminist Studies in Religion*, Vol.25, No.1, (pp.156-161), p.160.

[5] Abraham, 'Strategic Essentialism', p.160.

[6] M.S. Golwalkar, *We, Our Nationhood Defined*, (Nagpur: Bharat Prakashan, 1939), p.48, 49.

[7] Wendy Doniger, *Hindus: An Alternative History*, (London: Penguin, 2009), p.667.

[8] Dipankar Gupta, 'Citizens Versus People: The Politics of Majoritarianism and Marginalization in Democratic India', *Sociology of Religion*, Vol.68, No.1, 2007, (pp.27-44), p.33.

[9] Juli Gittinger, 'Hindutva: From Nationalism to Secularism', *Journal of Theta Alhpa Kappa*, (2007), (pp. 18-37), p.25.

[10] Rajiv Malhotra and Aravindan Neelakantan, *Breaking India: Western Interventions in Dravidian and Dalit Faultlines*, (Amaryllis, 2011)

[11] https://thewire.in/caste/the-two-faces-of-hindutvas-dalit-agenda

[12] Smita Gupta, ' The Dalit-Hindutva paradox' in *The Hindu*, February 09, 2016, http://www.thehindu.com/opinion/op-ed/The-Dalit-Hindutva-paradox/article14068231.ece

[13] Badri Narayan, *Fascinating Hindutva: Saffron Politics and Dalit Mobilisation*, (New Delhi: Sage, 2009), p.112.

[14] Clarke, *Competing Fundamentalisms*, p.117.

[15] John Webster, 'The Human Person', in Kevin J. Vanhoozer (ed.,) *The Cambridge Companion to Postmodern Theology*, (Cambridge: Cambridge University Press, 2003), (pp.219-234), p.232.

[16] Miroslav Volf, *After Our Likeness: The Church as the Image of the Trinity*, (Grand Rapids, Michigan: William B. Eerdmans, 1998), p.191. (***Emphasis** mine*).

[17] K.N. Panikkar, *Colonialism, Culture, and Resistance* (New Delhi: Oxford University Press, 2007), 67–68.

[18] Deenabandhu Manchala's 'Editorial: God of Life and Peace, grant Us Courage to Struggle for Justice', in *Ecumenical Review*, Vol.64, No.4. Dec 2012, (pp.423-426), 426.

[19] Jeorg Reiger, *Christ and Empire: From Paul to Postcolonial Times*, (Augsburg: Fortress, 2007), p.315

[20] Reiger, *Christ and Empire*, p.317.

[21] Ibid., 101.

10

Rethinking the Medical Mission in Today's Context towards a Borderless Church:

Moving Forward

E. V. Suranjan Maben

The medical missionary movement in India is built on the shoulders of foreign missionaries. They sacrificed their entire lives for the cause. Sister Mary Glowrey (founder of Catholic Health Association of India) Dr. Edith Brown (Christian Medical College Ludhiana) Dr. Ida Scudder (Christian Medical College Vellore) to more contemporary examples such as Dr. Paul Brand who pioneered leprosy surgery in India. These doctors were the household names. This period refers to "golden age of medical missions" in India. In the early 20th century by 1932 there were 132 hospitals led by foreign women missionaries and 112 staffed by foreign male missionaries. Hospitals run by the missionaries were the predominant model through independence and till 1960s when national Indian missions became aware of their mission responsibility.

The first challenge was the advent of independence and the formation of welfare states where the state as part of Nehruvian vision assumed the responsibility of providing health care to its citizens. This resulted in establishment of primary health care units and Govt. hospitals throughout the length and breadth of the country. With this, an alternative to mission hospitals had emerged. State run facilities are being funded by the tax payer while mission hospitals had to raise private funds from abroad and local resources. The second challenge happened in 1983 when Apollo hospitals opened in the country and began corporatization of the health care sector. Health care turned into business model level from the clinical level. The third challenge was entry of commercial medical insurance companies who rewrote with some success, the rules about how medicine is to be practiced.

Along with all these things, combined with mushrooming of private medical colleges and medical education becoming very much expensive, the number of young people responding to calling to be a medical missionary are declining. Today medical mission of our churches is at cross roads. It is the right time to rethink and re define our borders. The goal in medical missions is that it is "REAL".

The acronym stands for -
- Right motives,
- Effective partnering,
- Active community participation
- Long- term strategy and planning.

Right Motives

What are the right motives for medical missions?

1. *The example of Christ to love others and to express that love in tangible ways*

Healing was essential to the ministry of Jesus because He had the power to perform miracles. People flowed from different places. He knew it, people sensed it. Jesus welcomed the blind, crippled, leprous, even dead people into His presence. No problem loomed too great for His skill; none intimidated Him into silence. He performed all the healing we would expect since He came as God's Healer.

Healing was essential to the ministry of Jesus. He had compassion equal to His power, as Matthew 8:17 notes; as Matthew 14:14 illustrates. He healed their sick, and then He fed them. Knowing they could receive help if only they could access Him, people responded to that compassion, in bold, ways. The Canaanite woman accepted her state and got her healing through faith (Matthew 16:28). The woman with a hemorrhage crept through the crowd to touch His clothes (Mark 5:28). And the crowds "begged him to let the sick touch the edge of his cloak," (Matthew 14:36), for "all who touched him were healed."

Healing was essential to the ministry of Jesus. He envisioned healing as a physical symbol of forgiveness. The paralytic's restoration is but one of many such examples (Mark 2:1-12). Returning to the miracles recorded in Matthew 9, it is instructive to note the part faith plays in them. In the healing of the paralytic man, Matthew says that Jesus saw his faith (v. 2). To the woman who was healed, Jesus said, "Your faith has made you well" (v. 22). And to the two blind men whom He healed, He said, "According to your faith be it done to you" (v. 29). For the ruler whose daughter Jesus restored to life, his faith is implied in his request to Jesus: "My daughter has died, but come and lay your hand on her, and she will live" (v. 18).

2. *Concern for the varied needs of the community*

India is the second most populous country of the world. Country's changing   socio-political, demographic and morbidity patterns are drawing global attention in recent years. In spite of several growth-orientated policies adopted by the government, the economic, regional and gender disparities are widening. About 75% of health infrastructure, medical man power and other health resources are concentrated in urban areas, where 27% of the population live. Diseases such as diarrhea, amoebiasis, typhoid, infectious hepatitis, worm infestations, measles, malaria, tuberculosis, whooping cough, respiratory infections, pneumonia and reproductive tract infections dominate the morbidity pattern, especially in rural areas. Non-communicable diseases such as cancer, blindness, mental illness, hypertension, diabetes, HIV/AIDS, accidents and injuries are also on the rise.

There is a significant reduction in infant and maternal mortality rate while there is a significant increase in life expectancy of individuals. Over a period of time some progress has been made. To improve the prevailing situation, the problem of rural health is to be addressed at national, state, district and regional levels. This is to be done in a holistic way, with a genuine effort to bring the poorest of the population to the center of the fiscal policies. The current need is to bring a paradigm shift from the current 'biomedical model' to a 'socio cultural model which should bridge the gaps and improve quality of rural life.

3.   *The desire to empower the church to impact it's community*

The WCC's health and healing program facilitates networking and dialogue to promote health and healing for all people. Throughout 2017 and 2018, the WCC is developing a global ecumenical health strategy to meet continuing and new health challenges worldwide. Health is more than physical and mental well-being, and healing is not primarily medical. Health and healing were a central feature of Jesus' ministry and of his call to his followers, and the church has been engaged in health services for centuries.

Effective partnering

Effective Partnering focuses on the relationship between the outsider elements of the NGO (nongovernment organization) and Sponsor, and their integration of planning with the community. Effective partnering involves a clear understanding of the roles of each group. The sponsor clearly has a powerful role in the mission event, but must not take control since the NGO, typically, is the expert in doing the mission (the "How"), while the community is the expert on what is needed (the "What"). The NGO brings the expertise but must also actively run the mission. The local government unit (LGU) and church must learn to work with the outside groups in a manner that is equal, based on mutual respect, and supported with good communication and commonly agreed-upon goals.

Active Community Participation

Active Community Participation is another major component of successful medical missions. It is generally recognized that a medical mission event will fail if the community is not involved, or if it takes on a passive role, in medical missions. The local community must desire the medical mission and believe that it meets a felt need. The local church, local health practitioners and the community in general must find common purpose and be willing to take on their part of the role of the medical mission. They must take on the long-term role of care for the community since the NGO and other outside groups have only a short-term or periodic presence.

The Tübingen consultations in 1964 and 1967 affirmed that the local congregation or Christian community is the primary agent for healing. All basic functions of the local church have a healing dimension which is also for the wider community: Each individual member in a local congregation has a unique gift to contribute to the overall healing ministry of the church.

Long-term Strategy

Long-term Strategy refers to the intention of making the medical mission event part of a long-term process for community improvement.

Long-term strategy does not happen by accident. Medical missions that are not intentionally integrated into a long-term plan will rarely produce long-term results. Medical Mission and the broader long-term ministry in a community is a spiritual work. The ministry is God's ministry, not our own. This dimension of the work must never be forgotten in all of the research, evaluation, goal-setting, strategizing, and training involved in the activity. In fact, proper planning and strategizing should freely and fully incorporate prayer, meditation and seeking God's will. These different activities should be considered not only complementary, but synergistic.

Role of church

Jesus sent His disciples out to preach, teach, and heal. Most churches today preach and teach but have abdicated healing to medical professionals. Yet many ways in which churches can be involved in healing ministry are:

- praying for the sick
- confession and forgiveness
- anointing with oil
- Holy communion
- using creative healing liturgies
- supporting those who are committed to the healing task
- Training healers

Encourage

Involve health care persons "outside mission hospitals". Health professionals are challenged to see themselves as part of a broader network of healing disciplines that include the medical, technical, social and psychological sciences, as well as religions and traditional approaches to healing. This will also encourage the health professionals to share information with and empower the patient to feel responsible and take decisions for their own health.

Medical mission should be included as part of the curriculum in Theological colleges and consultants should be involved as visiting faculty. Stimulate dialogue among faith-based networks and within society, to reflect on the theological basis of medical mission as well as to the development of new concepts of Christian health care.

Empower

A new "toolkit" to empower and enable churches to promote better health in their congregations is in the making. A workshop held 17 – 19 July 2018 in North Carolina, USA, by the World Council of Churches (WCC) prepared the ground for this new resource. The 30 participants included WCC staff, church leaders, health workers, private sector professionals and academicians, from Jamaica, Tonga, the USA, Canada and Switzerland.

In line with its Ecumenical Global Health Strategy, the WCC is mobilizing and supporting churches to take holistic action on health, especially health promotion and prevention of non-communicable diseases (NCDs). The aim of the workshop was to draw from participants' experiences to create a toolkit for churches to use in developing their health-promotion programming. Elements are to include program activities, monitoring and evaluation tools, coordination mechanisms and technological support.

Church bodies and congregations have historically been deeply engaged in healthcare delivery, and participants are already implementing a variety of health promotion activities in their churches. Efforts focus mainly on prevention of non-communicable diseases (NCDs), using different approaches in their respective countries.

Organize health awareness programs in the church/ communities

Churches can engage, for example, in nutrition education; promoting physical exercise; screening for diabetes, hypertension and obesity;

education and support for alcohol and tobacco cessation; growing fruits and vegetables, health education; and linkages and referral to health facilities. The members of a congregation can grow together in health ministry through:

- Bible study on health, healing and wholeness
- Facilitating self-discovery of causes for ill-health
- Practical health education
- Networking of Christian doctors/health care providers
- Studying questions of bio-medical ethics
- Learning to take personal responsibility for health
- supporting EMFI/ other student bible study groups

The global health agenda has changed greatly over the years. Emerging and re-emerging infectious diseases, like Ebola and Dengue, are still a concern. Antimicrobial resistance, neglected tropical diseases and non-communicable diseases, including life-style diseases, have now come to the forefront with a growing global impact. With these continuing and new global challenges, it is time again for the church to reaffirm the role it has played over the centuries as leader in global health and consolidate all efforts towards health and healing for all.

Finally, on order to establish as borderless church with respect to healing ministry we need to have a global vision, rather than be cocooned in our own small narrow worlds. We need to be open to dialogue, experimentation and learning from each other and from global community. We need to explore ways to support each other through our questions, struggles and even failures. We need to share our stories and our resources with others. Let us work with consistency, credibility and continuity in Christ's love.

Bibliography

'Role of Foreigners in the Mission of God in India'-Nathan Grills "On the Wings of Dawn" Published by Evangelical Medical Fellowship of India.2015 Editor Dr. Varghese Philip.

Healthy Medical Missions: Principles for the Church's Role in Effective Community Outreach in the Philippines1 By Robert H. Munson Asia Baptist Graduate Theological Seminary, 2012.

Health, healing and wholenesshttp://www.wcc-coe.org/wcc/what/mission/hhw.html.

"A very sketchy roadmap for Indian Medical Missions"-Dr. Vinod Shah "On the Wings of Dawn" Published by Evangelical Medical Fellowship of India.2015 Editor Dr. Varghese Philip.

11

Christ Community –
Ecclesia - Formation:

A Call to Alternate Church Life and Witness in a Changing Nation

Joseph Daniel

Church's life in a society needs to be a participatory process – a process in which the church participates in the life journey of the community, in the light of the faith revealed to it by the Triune God to attain fullness of life. In this community journey, the culture of the community plays a vital role in facilitating the community to discern and pursue fullness of life. In this sense, the Indian church's life and witness in India's multi religious and cultural context needs to be shared, participatory, dialogical, interactive and conversational with the life and culture of the wider Indian community. The crucial question here is how the church can engage with the forces that rigidly construct and perpetuate boarders as we see in the contemporary Indian context.

In the light of this fact, this paper attempts to deal with questions such as: What is the vocation of the Indian church in the contemporary context of rigidity and borders? How can the Indian church be a true leaven in the Indian society that is multi- religious and multi-ethnic, each of which had developed its own traditional culture, that is the sum of its philosophy, morality, ideology, and corporate life in order to keep India's diversity? The more crucial question is whether the church in India can through inter-faith rational discourse and engagements, create at least a basic framework for a culture and scheme of values for people to build together a new life of love and respect, which is revealed in and through Christ? How can be the church to facilitate, pursue and discern fullness of life in Indian context, which is dominated by "two competing hegemonies of metropolitan elites and of the *Hindutva* movement"?[1] How can the church transcend borders to address the vulnerabilities of human predicaments and to engage with the forces of discrimination in Indian context? Before moving further in exploring answers to these questions we need to delve on the nature of the Indian church. What is the nature of the Indian *Ekklesia*?

Indian *Ekklesia*

Church in India is an integral part of the undivided Church, because it stands in continuity with the universal Church going back through the modern missionary movement and to the medieval period, to the fathers and martyrs of the early Church and to the twelve Apostles and the Jesus movement. *Ecclesia* is movement of disciples who proclaimed Jesus Christ as the historical Christ. It was a movement under Jesus Christ with his disciples and within a short span of time it became a vibrant phenomenon by participating the life journey of the community and embracing others into its fold.

Community emerged from the Jesus movement have aided the *ecclesia* in its life and witness. Later this movement transformed itself into Christianity and Christian church. The connectivity of the church with the Jesus movement opens new vistas of its life and witness in the society including Christ community formation to aid the church in its life, witness and mission. For this, it embodies canon, Nicene Creed, the three-fold ministry, and seven sacraments as well as structures its life and worship by means of them. The church firmly held the undivided church's faith regarding the mysteries of Trinity, the Incarnation and the Eucharist. The Church's life is characterized by its participation in the witness, worship and service. The Indian Church stands in the apostolic succession, of which three-fold apostolic ministry of bishops, priests and deacons is a central expression.

Based on these undivided Church's ecclesiology, the foundation of the faith and practices of the Indian Church is laid. In the light of these it is evident that the Indian church is an extension of the Jesus movement or the creation of the Christian mission and Christian public witness. Christian public witness serves as the key function of the church. Therefore, the main question that we need to address is about the vocation of the Indian church - an extension of the Jesus movement? Since the Indian church is an extension of the Jesus movement it is essential to continue its movement nature in public witness besides reducing the difference between the contemporary reality of the church and nature of the Jesus movement of the first century. This would open new avenues to address the contemporary Indian concerns of human vulnerable predicaments including the church's engagement with those forces that construct and perpetuate discrimination in the Indian society.

History of the Church suggests that when Christian traditions are developed, by their exponents, in to systematic form, they inevitably define themselves in a defensive way over against other Christian traditions. We need to be different and elaborate our differences all along the line. These systems then serve to perpetuate the historic divisions within the Church of Christ. This is not the way to make progress in public witness and particularly to address the forces that perpetuate divisions and discrimination in the society. Without falling into that kind of defensive trap the Indian church have to uphold historic existence, catholic nature, biblical footings, missionary engagements and church unity efforts. However, a critical evaluation of the mainline Indian churches reveal that we have erred from its calling to be a Jesus movement of transforming presence in the Indian public life. The church's historic reasons legitimizes the empire and its effort to excerpt power beyond its geographical, political, economic, religious, intellectual and spiritual spheres and the empires' hegemonic structures.[2] Moreover, the church's reluctance to become an inclusive church made the Indian church a caste church. In this context how do we as a church understand the meaning and content of the vocation of the church.

Vocation of the Indian *Ekklesia*

What is the vocation of the Indian Church in the providence and purpose of God? Does the Church bear witness to vital truths of faith and order in the Christian Church? The vocation of the Indian Church is the same as that of the vocation of the Church of Jesus Christ. First then we have to say that the whole Church is called to conform itself to the four creedal marks or dimensions of the Church namely, Unity, Holiness, Catholicity and Apostolicity. In the context of the Nicene Creed, they are faith affirmations of the Church. They are also statements of truth. There is a unity and holiness that belong to the Church and that can never be taken away. Catholicity and Apostolicity are equally inalienable and indestructible attributes of the Church. Without them the Church would not be the Church.

Catholicity and apostolicity refer to the church's calling to be a witnessing community in the world. For instance, the early church realized that the church is a witnessing community. The church fought against the forms of empire in the Greco-Roman world and its hegemonic structures. To accomplish this task the apostles moved from Jerusalem to other places and formed themselves a part of the wider community and proved themselves as a transforming presence of the Gospel and icons of Jesus Christ through 'martyria, liturgia and koinonia.'

Thus, a real unity, holiness, catholicity and apostolicity are manifested in the Church, amid the world realities, but it is incomplete and often obscured. So, like all Christians and all apostolic Churches, the Indian Church is called to dedicate themselves to work for the fulfillment of its vocation in the public sphere. The church continues to be transforming and empowering agents that aid the lives of the communities, who face vulnerabilities including injustice and oppression. Since the church is the fellowship of love and compassion, it is mandatory to extend its witness to the margins where people experience vulnerabilities.

Simultaneously, the church needs to continue its task of unity and to become a transformative agent in the margins. It demands the church to engage in the task of prophetic and transforming witness in the public sphere. As has often been said in the ecumenical movement, the unity of the Church are a gift and a task, God's gift, our task. It is God's work, but we must strive in God's strength to bring it about. The Church in India is also called to dedicate them to realizing more fully the marks of the Church in order to become an active agent of transformation towards justice and peace in the public life. With this note I would like to go further to bring some historical note on the contemporary Indian context of *Hindutva*, where the church placed for public witness.

Indian *Ekklesia* in the context of the new empire - *Hindutva*

The 'massive concentration of power in all spheres'[3] of Indian life through the ideology of nationalism, religious channels of *sangh parivar* organizations and its political engagements has made the *Hindutva* movement a new form of empire in Indian context. The *Hindutva* movements' contemporary trend to transform the diversity affirmed Indian society into monolithic and homogenous religious cultural entity with a goal of one nation through the banner of nationalism by religiously motivated political and politically motivated religious organizations raise important issues and concerns because its impact on marginalized vulnerable communities, pluralist societies and on the future of democracy is still largely unknown.

Hindutva marginalizes communities on religious lines and caste lines. Dalits and Adivasis are also included in this line of marginalization. This is the immediate context of the Indian church. Since the scope of this paper is not allowing more to delve into this topic, let's move on to the various concerns of Indian nationalism. However, the Indian church cannot ignore these changes in its culture because its mission can never be divorced from her sensitive and responsible engagement with the Indian culture that widens borders.

Ekklesia in the context of Indian nationalism

The root of the Hindutva is related to Indian nationalism. Indian nationalism is a particular religious and political outlook and the movement manifesting it in which traditional Indian society give way to modern notion of a nation.[4] The nation "is an imagined political community - and imagined as both inherently limited and sovereign."[5] Benedict Anderson's definition asserts the imagined nature of nation that seeks complete loyalty to it by its citizens. This definition has implication in understanding Indian nationalism particularly cultural nationalism as its advocates demand ultimate loyalty of all Indians to their motherland and fatherland - India.[6] For instance, "An Indian was defined as one for whom the geographical entity of India was both a *pithri-bhumi*/the land of one's ancestors and the land of *punya-bhumi*/ the land of one's religion."[7] Thus in macro level Indian nationalism was viewed as being anti-colonial with aims of liberating the country from the British colonial rule, and establishing a sovereign rule in India. At the local level, nationalism was perceived to be a form of cultural consciousness that aimed to protect different cultural and religious communities within India.[8]

What is special in Indian context of nationalism is the next question we need to search on. Indian nationalism has cleavage to both religion and ethnicity. Religious consciousness is active on Indian psyche and therefore religion plays a key role in the public domain.[9] It is in this sense the analysis of Eric Lott is special in understanding Indian nationalism. He argues that religion provides the decisive outline and a sacral sense to the origins of particular ethnic groups they confront or encounter it.[10] Secondly, this would lead them to mythologize any threat to their identity and creates a kind of a deep sense of differentiation between 'us' and 'them'. [11]Thirdly, the faith figures have thus got the role of community representative to represent and interpret the faith identity of the community and take a leading role in the affirmation of what a nation means.[12] Fourthly, to generate religious consciousness, religious faiths promote the production of vernacular religious literature that aimed at establishing national identity.[13]

The affinity of ethnicity and religion made Indian nationalism to a form of cultural nationalism. This is somewhat different from the cultural nationalism of Europe. In Europe cultural nationalism was considered to keep the cultural homogeneity by promoting national cultural expressions through activities such as art, literature, music, dance and so on. However, in India, cultural nationalism emerged in a faulty line of thought that try to exclude non- Hindu religions or religious communities – from the Indian national framework'[14] and the sidelining of the broader project of secular, pluralist and inclusive, Indian nationalism in favor of an all-encompassing Hindu solidarity.

From an ideological level, Indian nationalism emerged in India as a political ideology in its colonial setting of the 19th century. However, Indian nationalism allowed itself in mixing with Hindu renaissance forming Hindu nationalism. Hindu nationalism seeks to keep the interest of the one major religion in India and to make India a Hindu nation.[15]

Hindu nationalism: A historical search

What is the difference between Indian nationalism and Hindu nationalism? The Indian nationalism emerged as a political ideology to counter British power and to attain freedom from British rule in India during the 19th century. The Indian nationalistic agenda was to create a unified Indian nation to fight against the British colonial rule in India. However, the *Hindutva* ideology has its roots in the British-sponsored communalism (divide and rule) to counter the Indian nationalism and Indian freedom struggle. The divide and rule strategy of the British power in India aimed at safeguarding the British rule in India. In this pretext, the colonial image of Indian society projected two nations – the Hindu and the Muslim – defined by monolithic religious identities and inherently hostile to each other in order to make the Colonial rule in India easy.[16] Due to the mutual hostility of Hindus and Muslims, a controlling authority from outside was required. The colonial powers considered this as a justification for their rule in India.[17] "The concept of majority and minority communities identified by religion was also introduced by colonial policy. This further consolidated the idea of monolithic religions and these in turn fueled communal politics."[18] "In short the anti-colonial nationalism and both the religious nationalisms build on the colonial construction of Indian religion, though the first borrows much less so whereas the second make it foundational to their ideologies."[19] It was in this context, Hindu nationalism and Muslim nationalism emerged in India with a view to make India a Muslim and Hindu nation.

Thus, the communalism of the 1920s and early 1930s in India was dominated by Hindu-Muslim alienations.[20] Hindu orthodoxy was central to the alienation of Muslims and untouchables (Dalit) in India during this period.[21] The Hindu nationalistic agenda was to create a unified Hindu nation by developing a Hindu cultural and religious consciousness among Indians. With the weakening of liberal nationalism in India's major political party – Indian National Congress – Hindu orthodoxy found organized expression in the *Hindu Mahasabha* and later in the *Rashtriya Swyam Sevak Sangh* (RSS). Thus the Hindu nationalism got an organizational base in India.

The two-nation theory – that of Hindu India and Muslim Pakistan –by Muhammad Ali Jinnah (1876-1948)[22], known in Pakistan as *Quaid-i-Azam* (great leader) and *Baba-i-Quam* (father of the nation), made the Indian freedom struggle more communalistic. Thus, it was in this context, during 1930s and 1940s, that the idea of secular nationalism was proposed as a political ideology under the leadership of Mahatma Gandhi (1869-1948) and Jawaharlal Nehru (1889-1964) to counter the nascent communalistic nationalism and to continue India's age-old heritage of affirming religious and cultural diversities.[23]

Secular nationalism

There are mainly four approaches on religion that have helped India frame its idea of secular nationalism to counter the Hindu nationalism after India's independence in 1947. First, the idea of placing religion in the private realm and a philosophy of secularism that does not allow religious interference in the public life of the state or society. Jawaharlal Nehru (1889-1964) and E.M. Sankaran Nambuthiripad (1909-1998) supported this idea of secular nationalism.[24] The second is the idea of toleration and equality of all religions – that Indian secular nationalism should be an expression of religious tolerance based on the doctrine of equality of all religions.[25] Mahatma Gandhi (1869-1948) and S. Radhakrishnan (1888-1975) advocated this idea. A third view of secular nationalism is that since Indian constitution guarantees freedom of religion and expression, all religious communities have the right to follow their personal religious law. This idea emerged from the minority religious consciousness of the Muslims.[26] Forth idea of nationalism is of subaltern nationalism, that seeks to bring the voices of the people of the land and marginalized sections of the society in India's social, political and cultural realm. B.R. Ambedkar (1891-1956).[27]

Although India's freedom movement was made up of many ideological strands, stretching from Hindu nationalism to socialism, the ideological predisposition of the Indian National Congress, the political party that headed the Indian freedom struggle, has been secular nationalism – the separation of religion from the state. The nationalist (communalistic) inclination was reinforced by the partition of India into Pakistan and the communal violence that followed independence in 1947. The idea of secular nationalism replaced communalist nationalism in 1947, when any idea of having a quota for religious minorities became a political anathema. Secular nationalism was thus "the idea that was supposed to secure social integration and reflect the universal character of human enlightenment."[28] Despite the claims of Indian secular nationalism, India was, and is still dominated by Hindu ethnic groups.[29]

The post-independent Indian political scenario is very complex. With the later socio-political changes of the 1980's and in the aftermath of Emergency rule, a resurgent communalism and the *Hindutva* movement took on a strident tone, and secularism *per se* came under attack. A national political party, BJP, has become a more Hindu communal party. The BJP vote bank political agenda is responsible for the new shift. The party branded Indian secularism as *pseudo-secularism* that pampers religious minorities at the expense of the majority and demanded the withdrawal of minority rights. It engaged in a debate on Indian secularism through two voices – the voice of the *Hindutva* proponents and the liberal voice responding to *Hindutva*.

Hindutva means 'Hindu-ness' – a quality or characteristic that those who are not Hindu by religion may possess, if their culture and lifestyle is Hindu in form and substance. The inherent idea is that there is an innate Hindu quality in the practice of any religion once it makes it home in the Indian sub-continent. Therefore, it is expected that non-Hindus should treat India as their fatherland and motherland. This is a moderate inclusivist position of *Hindutva*. However, the hardline advocates of the *Hindutva* movement have taken a fundamentalist stand and they hold the view that India should declare itself a Hindu nation. From a softer inclusivist stance they manifest the hallmarks of imposition fundamentalism.[30]

In fact, Hindu nationalism has implications Indian Christians inner consciousness in India. It has also the consequence of excluding non-Hindu religions from the national framework, including the dalits and adivasis facilitating their 'othering', and the sidelining of the broader project of secular, pluralist and inclusive Indian nationalism in favor of an all-encompassing Hindu solidarity. It is a strange situation in contemporary India that there have been conscious and deliberate attempts to replace Indian nationalism with Hindu communalism. In this context, there should be a conscious and deliberate line of thought and actions by Indian church to spread the concept of Indian secular culture, keeping in mind the wider goal of reconstructing their national identity. This new self-consciousness would help the church to redefine its witness and their functions in the social and political life in India.

Indian Ekklesia's engagements

Speaking specifically about the church in India and its theological articulation, any theological and hermeneutical expression that we do should seriously consider the ecclesial context. *Hindutva* leaders vehemently attacked the Indian church's dependence on Christo-centrism and its mission activities. Besides, the *Hindutva* advocates attempt to create a corporate identity by assimilating or excluding the minorities with a view to form a monolithic and homogenous Hindu culture. This attempt would benchmark the Christian Indian identity - an identity that would mark them out as permanent *others* and potential enemies either to be driven out or annihilated. To support this view, P.B. Mehta argues,

> Hindu nationalism is not so much about defending a way of life, as it is about creating a litmus tests of true allegiance. These litmus tests are designed in such a way that it is almost over determined that minorities especially Christians and Muslims will fail. They remain the permanent other of Hindu identity that either need to be encompassed by bringing them under the sign of a common ethnicity, or else remain, on this view a permanent threat to Hindu identity and claims.[31]

The *Hindutva* ideologies' *insider* and *outsider* bifurcation of Indians seeks to promote the idea that the *outsider* is entitled to exist in India only at the will and consent of the *insider*. This way of thinking in India is a transition of its earlier conceptual categories – a synthesis of Christian – Hindu models, orientalists' approach to reconstruct of India's glorious past and the indigenous Indian reform movements - to counter colonialism and Christian missionizing. In fact, the Hindu nationalism has implications on Indian church for its own inner consciousness in Hindu India.

Indian church's response

From a theological perspective, the Indian church forms a visible empirical sociological entity in India. They owe this allegiance to the life and work of the Trinity, witnessed in the Bible and the tradition of the one, holy, catholic and apostolic church. Hence the Indian church is committed to their call for the affirmation of the Bible, Church traditions and its participation in the cultural, spiritual, political and social life of the secular Indian state. Backdrop of this context, we need to search for a pattern for Indian church life, which should be open to all sections of the people of God in India. It opens the room for a borderless church.

The knowledge of what the historical Jesus was like can be a potent source of understanding the nature of the Christian church life. Christian life is essentially the task of the church, which stands on the Trinitarian foundation. This foundation provides theological foundation for Christian witnessing and its social relations, modes of dialogue and sharing cultural expressions in India. In this process the task of the Indian church should be the reclaiming of the creative legacies of the past including the European and Indian reformation ideals and to bear witness in the Indian public sphere considering the context and people' struggle for freedom and justice.

Jesus sought the transformation of his public world. Jesus' ministry was for the renewal of the public sphere. "Not only is he witness to the reality of the spirit as an element of experience, but his passionate involvement in the culture of his own time – the social world – connects two realities which Christians have frequently separated."[32] Jesus concerned about creating a new community within his social world, whose corporate life reflected faithfulness to God.[33] Jesus shared much in common with other Jewish charismatics of his time. He also differed from them in several ways. Jesus shared his culture, climaxing in a final journey to Jerusalem, which was the center of their cultural life.[34] Jesus shared the public world of his time.

The social world refers to the total social environment of a people at time in their history, including economic conditions, technology, mixture of population isolation and exposure to foreign culture. Social world also refers to the socially constructed reality of the people that nonmaterial canopy of shared convictions, which every human community erects and within which it lives, and which is sometimes known as culture. It is that world of shared ideas that makes each culture what it is.[35]Culture consists of the shared beliefs, values, meanings and laws, customs institutions, rituals and so forth by which a group orders and maintains its world. The social world of Jesus thus refers to the social world of Judaism within the total social environment of the first century Palestine.[36] Jesus tried to transform this culture by bearing witness relevantly in the public sphere.

Jesus was a transformative sage, but also a subversive sage, who challenged the popular wisdom of the day.[37] Jesus stood in the tradition of subversive wisdom. His teaching involved more than a subverting of conventional wisdom. He affirmed another vision and another way.[38] He taught an alternative way of being and an alternative consciousness shaped by the relationship of spirit and not primarily by the dominant consciousness of culture.[39] Jesus created a sectarian renewal or revitalization movement within Israel – the Jesus movement. The relationship between the renewal movements at the public sphere is of both of an affirmation and advocacy for change. Therefore, the vocation of the Indian church in the contemporary Indian context is to bear witness effectively in the public sphere.

A balance sheet

Having identified the dominant challenges that the Indian church face today, and the need to transform the Indian fundamentalist line of separating the community and culture in to a life affirming culture we need to respond to a few questions that we discussed at the beginning of this study with a view to equip the church meet challenges that it faces.

Perchoresis relation

While addressing the question of how the Christian witness and service through the church be a true leaven in the society to transform it in its fullness in a multi- religious and multi-ethnic Indian context, the Trinitarian understanding provide a key theological basis. *Perechoresis* is the key idea in Trinity. The central message of the Bible is nothing but the revelation of Trinity. The *Perchoresis* relation, relationality or intimacy of the Trinitarian relationship, can be taken as the key hermeneutical principle in exploring the task of Christian witness and service in the Indian multi-religious and cultural context. For instance, the Christian Indians expected to share the people and cultures the new quality of life that Jesus brought to humanity. This message became good news to the unacceptable in the society and culture.

Jesus Christ and his disciples challenged the popular wisdom of the day. Jesus stood in the tradition of subversive wisdom with a view to transform the society – He subverted conventional wisdom. This made Him critically assess the religious and political realm. It provided him wisdom for an alternative life and witness in the public sphere. Jesus' journey was to transform the public sphere of Jesus towards the kingdom of God values. In that journey Jesus travelled with the subaltern community of the time and challenged the empire and its power and constructed a new pathway of compassion to all who seek for reclaiming their lost God given humanity.

Participation and mutuality

Secondly, participation and mutuality are considered central to the understanding of Trinity. Hence Christian witness and service in India should be grounded in the reality of God in Trinity – Unity in Trinity and Trinity in Unity. Based on a Trinitarian model, a new model church can be formed in India. The church can be a witnessing community in the margins by providing its availability accessibility to those who are struggling to reclaim their identity at the margins. On top of it the church can be part of the peoples' struggles in the market place to reinstate their lost humanity, identity and justice.

The Trinitarian basis also helps the Indian church to discern God's will, and challenge and subvert demonic traits that continue its violence by *othering* communities and perpetuating injustice and thwarting the Indian democratic and secular constitutional base. Solidarity and mutuality provide avenue for the church to join with the vulnerable communities' struggle to reclaim their identity and humanity. Regarding the second question on creating at least the basic framework for a culture and scheme of values for people to build together a new life that is revealed through Christ, what should be the

Indian Church's stand? The church needs to be an open community or a borderless community.

Openness

I admit that the Indian cultural context can create a basic framework for India's common culture through ecumenism and inter-religious rational dialogue. Two major ideas, which are common among all religions, need to be mentioned. First, all religions and cultures conceive love as the ultimate moral law of human perfection and profess the formation of a community of love as its final goal. [40] Secondly, all religions are seeking the means to reach that goal. The fundamental idea is that there is a common goal for different religious communities.[41] The Indian culture also provides a unitive vision of human life and in this vision *karma*[42] is the motivating force. In this vision, different religious experiences have their own space. The perfect ethics of *nishkama karma* (unselfish work for the self-realized) and the relative ethics of *artha* (purpose), *kama* (self) and *dharma* (duty) have both been posited in the *sanadhana dharma* concept.[43] There is also space in the Indian culture for plurality in both these ethical contexts for their common existence and growth.

In fact, after the rise of nation states and the upholding of the ideal of secularism in India, some sections in all religions assert a fundamentalist position. If this is what Indian culture speaks, then why did fundamentalism flourish in India? When the majority community perpetuates fundamentalism with a view to gain political power, minority communities feel insecurity. Besides, there is awareness of the destiny of the marginalized communities and their life struggles in India. In this context we need to affirm the plurality of God's creation and consciously create an atmosphere for dialogue and mutual interaction. For this, the church needs to show openness.

Openness to God and openness to the public sphere is needed for a Christian Indians to address this question. The three-ness of the divine persons and the oneness of His essence is the major affirmation of the Trinity. It is in this context that the Nicene-Constantinople creed provides fuel to our journey. The creed never allows the annihilation of the distinction between the Father, Son and the Holy Spirit in the Trinity and the tendency to divide the indivisible essence of the Trinity.

Mystery of the Trinity

Third, how can we be an Indian church to facilitate, pursue and discern fullness of life in the Indian context of *Hindutva*? To address this, we need to affirm the cultural trend of the affirmation of plurality in India. The Indian cultural trend has ever been the affirmation of pluralism – that different religious expressions are valid for some universal reality. "The mystery of the Trinity should be the deepest source, closest inspiration and the brightest illumination of the meaning of life that we can imagine."[44] "God is one, God is three, God is diversity, and God is unity." These are the affirmation of the Trinitarian doctrine. God is relational and he shares the social life and culture of the people. For instance; God made that relationship available to the world in Jesus Christ, who was born in a Jewish cultural setting.

The next task is to address the question of how the Indian church could transcend borders to address the vulnerabilities of human predicaments in Indian context? To Marcus Borg, Jesus is a model for the Christian life. The vision of Jesus movement was a life lived on the boundary of the spirit and culture. This vision is marked by the guidance of the spirit, compassion and dialectical in its relationship to culture. The new birth in the spirit provided identity markers to the apostles and the members of the Jesus movement. Compassion provided room for inclusiveness that makes empathy –a feeling with others and a capacity to be moved by their situation made possible. Consequently, there appeared a relationship defined by radical inclusiveness, free of demarcating boundaries, and undergirded by a new ethos of compassion and hospitality. It was a pathway for the transformation of the public sphere, which was demarcated with boundaries. This model needs to be implemented to address the human vulnerabilities of our times.

Conclusion

The task of the church is not to merely orient its members to imitate Christ on a moral level, it is to become like Him by grace so that church life is a manifestation and revelation of the presence of Christ in the public sphere. Thus the church do not only imitate the *behaviors* of Christ at some external level, but must incorporate His life organically into our own unique personal being, entering into a real union with the divine, and translate that union in the public sphere to achieve fullness of life in the Indian society. Following the model of Jesus' witness the Indian church can stand in the tradition of subversive wisdom with a view to transform the society towards the affirmation of plurality and diversity, democracy and secularism. It can act as a subversive wisdom. This critical wisdom helps the church to be with the subaltern people and to extend its accessibility and availability to the people at the margins and to proclaim the church's solidarity and participation in their struggles to reclaim their God given humanity. This wisdom also helps the Indian church to critically assess the contemporary Indian religious and political realm and provide an alternative life and witness in the society immersed in love that transcend all boundaries. The goal of the church's witness is real transformation towards the fullness of life.

Endnotes

[1] *Ibid.*, 23.

[2] Jeorg Rieger, "Christian Theology and Empire", in: Kwok Pui-Ian, Don H.Compier and Jeorg Reiger,(eds.,) *Empire and Christian Tradition: New Readings of Classical Theologians,*(Minneapolis: Fortress Press, 2007), 3.

[3] *Ibid.*

[4] Joseph Daniel, "Indian secularism affirming religious and cultural diversities", in: *Studies in Interreligious dialogue*, Belgium, 2/26, (February/2016),176-189.

[5] Benedict Anderson, *Imagined Communities: Reflections on the origin and spread of Nationalism,* revised edition (New York, Verso, 2006), 6.

[6] R. Sahayadas, *Hindu nationalism and the Indian Church,* (New Delhi: Christian Word Imprints, 2016), 20-60.

[7] Romila Thapper, *Indian Society and the secular, op.cit.,* 15.

[8] R. Sahayadas, *Hindu nationalism and the Indian Church, op.cit,* 20-60.

[9] Eric Lott, Religious Faith and Human identity: Dangerous Dynamics in Global and Indian Life (Bangalore: ATC-UTC, 2005), 220-236. See., Adrian Hastings, The construction of nationhood; Ethnicity, Religion and Nationalism, (Cambridge: CUP,1997), 188-197.

[10] *Ibid.*

[11] *Ibid.*

[12] *Ibid.*

[13] The theory of 'othering' is originally coined and developed in the post-colonial social theories. Social theories suggest that identities are of social origin. In this sense ethnic minorities are situated always within the specific social contexts. The theoretical concepts offered to explain such process   is otheirng. The process of perceiving or portraying some ethnic or religious minorities as fundamentally different or alien from the dominant religious or ethnic identities are usually called as othering. See, Spikav G.C, The Rani of Sirmur: an essay in reading the archives, In: History and Theory, 24(3), March/1985, 247-272; Diken, B, Strangers, *Ambivalence and Social Theory,* (Aldershot: Ashgate, 1998), 6-22.

[14] M.M Thomas, "Religious Fundamentalism and Indian Secularism – the Present Crisis" in, M.M. Thomas, *The Churches Mission and Post Modern Humanism* (CSS & ISPCK, 1996), 10. See also, Ghanshyam shah, "Caste, Class and the State", Seminar 367, March 1990, in, Gabriele Dietrich and Bas Wielenga, *Towards Understanding Indian Society* (Madurai: Centre for Social Analysis Tamil Nadu Theological Seminary, 1997), 142.

[15] Romila Thaper, *Indian Society and the secular,* (Gurgaon: Three Essays Collective, 2016) 2-20; Romila Thapper, "Indian Society and the secular" in, Sachidanandan ed., *India Facisathilekku,* (Malayalam), (Kottayam: DC Books, 2016) 15-34.

[16] *Ibid.*

[17] *Ibid.*

[18] *Ibid.*

[19] Joseph Daniel, *Ecumenism in Praxis* (Frankfurt: Peter Lang, 2014), 243.

[20] Shabnum Tejani, *Indian Secularism: a Social and Intellectual History,* *op.cit.,*4-5.

[21] Muhammad Ali Jinna was the founder of Pakistan and the first governor general of Pakistan.

[22] M.M Thomas, "Religious Fundamentalism and Indian Secularism – the Present Crisis" in: M.M. Thomas, *The Churches Mission and Post-Modern Humanism; op. cit.,* 10-20.

[23] M.M Thomas, "Meaning of Being a Secular State", in, M.M. Thomas, *The Churches Mission and Post Modern Humanism op.cit.,* 22-23.

[24] *Ibid,* 26-27.

[25] *Ibid,* 27.

[26] B.R Ambedkar was the chairman of the Indian constitution drafting committee and the first law minister of the independent Indian Republic during 1947-1951.

[27] Shabnum Tejani, *Indian Secularism: a Social and Intellectual History, op. cit.;* 5.

[28] *Ibid.*

[29] See Douglas Pratt, 'Fundamentalism, Exclusivism and Religious Extremism', in, David Cheetham, Douglas Pratt and David Thomas (eds), *Understanding Interreligious Relations* (Oxford: Oxford University Press, 2013), 241-261.

[30] Pratab Bhanu Mehta, "Introduction to the omnibus," in: *Hindu nationalism and Indian politics,* Three books in one volume edition, (New Delhi: Oxford University Press, 2004) xiii.

[31] Marcus Borg, *Jesus a new vision,* (London: SPCK, 1993), i.

[32] *Ibid.,* ii.

[33] *Ibid.*

[34] *Ibid.,* 79.

[35] Peter Berger, *The Sacred Canopy,* (New York: Doubleday, 1967).

[36] *Ibid.*

[37] Marcus Borg, *Jesus a new vision, op.cit.,* 115 ff.

[38] *Ibid.,* 116.

[39] *Ibid.*

[40] *Ibid.*

[41] The Sanskrit word, *karma,* means action.

[42] M.M. Thomas, *The Church's Mission and Post-Modern Humanism, op.cit.,* *1-9.*

[43] Leonardo Boff, *Trinity and society,* (London: Burns and Oats/Search Press,1988), 160ff.

Bibliography

Anderson, Benedict. 1996. *Imagined communities,* 7th impressions, New York: Verso.

Borg, Marcus. 1993. *Jesus a new vision.* London: SPCK.

Berger, Peter. 1967. *The Sacred Canopy.* New York: Doubleday

Boff, Leonardo. 1998. *Trinity and society.* London: Burns and Oats/ Search Press.

Cunningham, David S.2000. These Three are One: The Practice of Trinitarian Theology.Massachusetts. Blackwell.

Douglas Pratt. 2013. 'Fundamentalism, Exclusivism and Religious Extremism', In *Understanding Interreligious Relations,* edited by David Cheetham, Douglas Pratt and David Thomas. Oxford: Oxford University Press. 241-261.

Daniel, Joseph. 2014. *Ecumenism in Praxis.* Frankfurt: Peter Lang.

Daniel, Joseph. 2015. "Different expressions, same reality: the Indian religious and culture context as a fertile ground for ecumenism and inter-religiosity", In Internationalle *Kirchliche Zeitschrift,* Bern: Band 2. 127-141.

Daniel, Joseph.2017. "Growing religious fundamentalism and communalism in India today" (Malayalam), In *Spirituality in the Context of Religious Fundamentalism and*

Communalism, Tiruvalla. Mar Thoma Church Council. 29-44.

Gellner, Ernst. 1996. *Nations and nationalism,* Oxford: Blackwell.

Ghanshyam Shah. 1997. "Caste, Class and the State", Seminar 367, March 1990, in *Towards Understanding Indian Society* edited by Gabriele Dietrich and Bas Wielenga. Madurai: Centre for Social Analysis Tamil Nadu Theological Seminary.

Holen, Andrew. 2009. Religious cohesion in times of conflct. London: Contiuum.

Jha, Sumithra. 2008. *Trade Institutions and religious tolerance: Evidence from India.* Stanford University Graduate Business Research School, Research Paper No. 2004.

Kwok Pui-Ian, Don H.Compier and Jeorg Reiger,(eds.,) *Empire and Christian Tradition: New Readings of Classical Theologians.* Minneapolis: Fortress Press, 2007.

Kelley, JND. 1978. Early Christian Doctrines. San Franscisco: Harper and Row.

Mehta, Pratab Bhanu. 2004. "Introduction to the Omnibus,"In. *Hindu nationalism and Indian politics,* Three books in one volume edition. New Delhi: Oxford University Press.

Shethi D.L, Ashis Nandi, eds. 1996. *The multiverse of democracy.* New Delhi: Sage Publications.

Thomas, M M. "Religious Fundamentalism and Indian Secularism – the Present Crisis" In *The Churches Mission and Post Modern Humanism* edited by M.M Thomas. CSS & ISPCK, 1996.

Thaper, Romila. 2016. *Indian Society and the secular.* Gurgaon: Three Essays Collective.

Thaper, Romila. 2016 "Indian Society and the secular" In *India Facisathilekku,* (Malayalam), edited by Sachidanandan. Kottayam: DC Books.

12

"The Idea of 'a Borderless Church' and Its Ecumenical Significance"

Kyo Seong Ahn

I. Introduction: your story and our story

Perhaps it is difficult, if not impossible, to find a theme for this conference more appropriate than "a Borderless Church", which I found timely and contingency-fit for the Church of South India here and now.[1] As the theme of "the unity of the church" of the World Council of Churches (hereafter WCC) has evolved into that of "the unity of humanity" and then to "the renewal of humanity", the topic of the conference, "a Borderless Church", is showing a tendency to expand its interest from an intra-ecclesiastical to an extra-ecclesiastical issue. In short, with the idea of "a Borderless Church", the Church of South India aims to grow from a union church to a borderless church, or from a church 'united among churches' to a church 'uniting between church and society'.[2]

Interestingly, I located similar trends across the world, especially from among the efforts of the ecumenical partner churches such as the Church of Scotland in the West and the Presbyterian Church of Korea in the East: the Church of Scotland proposed a concept of "A Church without Walls" as early as in 2001[3], and the Presbyterian Church of Korea offered a model of "Maeul Mokhoe" (Community Ministry) in 2017.[4] Perhaps we may view this phenomenon as a quickening of the Holy Spirit in this century, who calls the worldwide church to do mission, freshly, efficiently and effectively.

II. The Challenge of the Idea of "a Borderless Church": ecclesiological and missiological

As we have seen briefly, the idea of "a Borderless Church" is national as well as international; and as we shall deal with below, this idea is religious as well as secular. Thus, it is an ecumenical question *par excellence*, in that it covers the issues, intra-, inter-, and extra-ecclesiastical. And it also is related to the being and doing of the church.

1. *A reflection from its own legacy of the Church of South India: from a pilgrim church to a borderless church*

In its early years, the Church of South India tended to emphasize the aspect of a pilgrim church as one of its identity.[5] It was fitting to a new-born church *sui generis* at the time, in that it was a result of the radical amalgamation of different patterns of church polity ranging from episcopal, Presbyterian and congregational, although there emerged other united churches growing out of milder ecumenical experiments in the first half of the last century. Admittedly, this concept of a pilgrim church was necessary for a burgeoning church, since it was important for it to keep balance between past and future and to keep itself from derailing in its journey to fuller unity. However, the concept is basically of a linear paradigm, paying attention to goal rather than process, or its own path rather than the surrounding landscape. Such kind of a goal-oriented church is liable to be a church of focusing on rather than surveying, and at best a church of "Pilgrim's Progress" rather than a church of caring and celebrating.

To be more comprehensive, however, a church needs to grow from a linear to a spatial paradigm of ecclesiology. It is true that to be mature is a multi-dimensional work: "I pray that you and all of God's people will understand what is called wide or long or high or deep." (Eph. 3: 18)[6] We may call a new kind of church a church of a four-dimensional or at least a spatial paradigm. We may also call it an overflowing church, a penetrating church, or a saturating church. Water flows not only downward but also spills over the sides. A newly emerging church can learn from water in this sense. By flowing downward and spilling over the sides, water meets and relates to what it comes to touch. Like water, by flowing downward and spilling over the sides, the church can meet and relate to people, that is, neighbors, the society, and finally the world. It is in this context that we can better understand the idea of "a Borderless Church".

In the past, the Indian church was mainly concerned about 'high and low' or the vertical dimension of the Indian society: for example, the caste system centering around higher Brahman, on the one hand, and low of the lowest, Dalit, on the other. Now, the Indian church including the Church of South India is requested to target at 'in and out' of the Indian church or the horizontal dimension of the Indian society. India, which has already been famous for multiplicity, continues to undergo a tremendous change into a more multi-ethnic, multi-cultural, and multi-religious society. In this new context, the Indian church including the Church of South India has still many to meet and relate to. Indeed, there are still countless neighbors yet to be met.

In this sense, being a borderless church does not mean simply demolishing the boundaries which have safeguarded the identity of the church. Instead, it smooths the church's way out to reach out people; and the church in turn comes to gain a new identity, as it becomes more flourishing through contacts. However, it must be remembered that in outgoing the church requires courage as much as or more than in pilgriming. Thus, to be a new kind of church is to be courageous and even adventurous. To develop this identity issue, it is in order to move to the next section.

2. *A reflection from the ecumenical context: from defining to undefining and to redefining*

Besides the thought-provoking idea of "A Church without Walls" of the Church of Scotland, similar ideas gradually gain popularity in the world, both sacred and secular. For example, research has shown that the new perspective on the relationship between campus and city does "transform urban realities".[7] If the society can do that, why not the church? In this sense, the work of developing a new type of church and society, both of which are changing to be wall-less (Church of Scotland), communal (Presbyterian Church of Korea), borderless (Church of South India) and barrier-free (the disability movement), can be regarded as a genuine ecumenical ministry, in that it encompasses both church and society.

However, to look at freshly the world beyond the church must begin with looking at freshly the church itself. Thus, we need to think differently of what definition is. Traditionally, definition, as its etymology adumbrates, means something cutting off or pinning down. To gain a new way of understanding what definition is, we may apply the well-known educational stages of learning, unlearning and relearning to our discussion: defining, undefining, and redefining. In other words, the new way of defining can be explained as defining through contact and interaction. Furthermore, this kind of definition of the church is expected to be apt to a new cutting-edge theology, for example public theology, which presupposes mutuality between church and public. Now we examine the suggestions of the Church of South India and other ecumenical partner churches.

1. The Church of Scotland's "A Church without Walls" (2001)

If ecumenism is rightly understood as a mutual learning process, we can share our lessons which we have learned from our own ecumenical experiments. To begin with, the report of the Church of Scotland on "A Church without Walls" focuses on the shape of the church. According to the report, four factors to shape the church are as follows: the Gospel, the Locality, Friendship, and the Gifts of God's People. Those factors can neatly be divided into two categories: ecclesiastical and social. The Gospel and the Gifts of God's People can belong to the first category, while the Locality and Friendship to the second. Since we are more familiar with the former, we had better concentrate on the latter. The report says that local[ity] means "identity, diversity, interdependency, creative flexibility, cultural sensitivity, and visionary possibility".[8] And Friendship is to be with "fellow members, the next generation, the searcher, the community, fellow leaders, other churches, rich and poor, the world church, and God's creation ".[9]

Perhaps we may direct our attention to the fact that the word of 'identity' is included in the section of Locality rather than the Gospel. As mentioned above repeatedly, in the new way of being a church such as "a Borderless Church", one needs to think of identity in terms of wider mutual-identity, not narrower self-identity. In other words, identity is not merely something of one-sidedness or givenness. In addition, we may point our fingers at the fact that the section of Friendship of the report leaves much to be desired, since most of the partners dealt with in Friendship belongs to the inner group of the church, while neighbors or people beyond the church are limitedly mentioned. Can the idea of the "a Borderless Church" of the Church of South India fill the gap by developing the genuine and balanced relationship between church and community?

Before leaving the concept of "A Church without Walls", however, it is worth pointing out that the report draws our attention to the question of what gives impetus and creates synergy in the discussions. It is grace. Grace calls, sustains, equips, and sends out the church to be faithful to its tradition and at the same time to dare to be a new church.

2.   The Presbyterian Church of Korea's Maeul Mokhoe (Community Ministry, 2017)

To celebrate the two historical landmark events, the 500th Anniversary of the Reformation in 2017 and the Centennial of the March First Independence Movement in 2019, both of which are very significant for its identity, the Presbyterian Church of Korea chose an overarching theological topic of "The Reformed Church, the Hope of the Nation" for a four-year project starting from 2016. As part of such a grandiose project, the Presbyterian Church of Korea adopted a sub-topic of "The Holy Church, Go into the [Secular] World Again" for the period of 2017-2018 and proposed the concept of Maeul Mokhoe (Community Ministry) to implement this sub-topic. The concept was welcomed as a timely and feasible idea, in that the need for communalism has been strongly felt by both of church and society in Korea; indeed, the former began to collapse facing an unprecedented-scaled church decline, while the latter started to be fragmentized through newly emerging phenomena such as the decrease of birth rate, the increase of single households, and the acceleration of aging society, not to mention drastic urbanization and the impoverishment of rural communities. Significantly, the last decades saw the rise of numerous NGOs targeting at community building projects in Korea.

Putting together two ambitious aims, reformation and resuscitation, the Presbyterian Church of Korea attempted to regain the holiness of the church, especially overcoming the deep-seated false holiness based on the sacred-secular dichotomy and the entrenched myth of church-growth-ism; to flesh out the ideal of Jesus' incarnational ministry, particularly focusing on the minority and the marginalized;

and to flesh out the agenda of the Reformed churches to seek to influence the society.

According to Byeong-ok Lee, one of the expositors of the above-mentioned sub-topic, Jesus was not simply Jesus; but he was Jesus "from Nazareth" (Mat. 26: 71; CEV).[10] In other words, Jesus was Jesus with the name of locality, or Jesus from and for communities. The Presbyterian Church of Korea combines this new idea with the long-standing legacy of 'Missio Dei', and also relates the new attempt to public theology, which is very much *a la mode* in Korea now. Reading the motto of the sub-topic, "[A] Whole Village as a Church, Whole Villagers as Church Members", however, one cannot totally brush away doubts whether this sub-topic shakes off its inveterate church-ism or whether it is no more than a camouflaged rehash of the church-growth agenda.[11] The Maeul Mokhoe (Community Ministry) project continues to look into numerous local-church-based cases in order to concretize this rather slippery concept.[12] In this context, any new idea that claims the cause of the reformation of the church needs to be verified in terms of integrity as well as feasibility.

3.   The Church of South India's "a Borderless Church" (2017-2018)

Then, whence does the idea of "a Borderless Church" of the Church of South India come? Why here and now? Reviewing the history of the Bible and India, the positioning paper of the "a Borderless Church", "Towards a Borderless Church", shows us various roles of borders. In fact, borders appear to be sheer hindrances, ambiguous realities, or precious opportunities in life. Although many borders, both sacred and secular, were previously given, often one-sidedly and even forcedly, now one can and need to take initiative in deciding the borders, employing them constructively and wisely.

Regrettably, even the triple borders which St. Paul dreamt to dissolve in Jesus Christ two thousand years ago, that is, ethnicity, class and gender, still seem to be adamant enough.[13] Nevertheless, the church has tried to be a borderless church throughout its history, although the concept itself is a quite new one and the church cannot claim to have always succeeded in being so. As the Rev. Dr. Rathnakara Sadananda maintains in the positioning paper, to be a borderless church begins with "look[ing] intently at our borders".[14] In order to be authentic, indeed, the church continues to look at the borders within and without the church and in-between, to identify them, and to pull down them, when necessary. In doing so, the church has found that there are many undiscovered and hidden borders such as disability, and that existing borders change into much more complex and hybrid ones through globalization such as 'new ethnic borders on the move' including migrants, refugees, asylum-seekers, the stateless, etc.

India, like any other nations, shows the tendency toward both homogeneity and plurality. For instance, India is renowned for multi-ethnicity, but not exempt from closed communalism. In a similar vein, Dr. Donald McGavran's theology of church growth movement which originally emerged in India as a pioneering missiological theory for people's movement, is liable to end up with the pragmatic church-marketing principle of homogenous unit. Perhaps, it is time for the Indian church to swing from one extreme to the other more passionately.

At any rate, even if one agrees to fell unnecessary and harmful borders, there remain questions of who and how to do so. In other words, one still needs to pay attention to whose borders they are, and who shall take initiative in dealing with the borders.

III. Conclusion: "a Borderless Church", a way of being authentic or a new way of local ecumenism

As Liberation Theology emerged from among various wider liberation movements in the last century, the theology of "a Borderless Church" goes along with similar avantgarde efforts, both sacred and secular. It is no exaggeration that this era is that of people, particularly people with different, multiple, and fluid identities. To bridge the gap between those groups and build up a new community on it, the contemporary church, no matter where it is, is requested to be a borderless church. Although it is an untrodden road, however, one does not need to feel lonely, since there is the cloud of co-pilgrims, like once there was the cloud of witnesses. (Heb. 12: 1)

In a sense, "a Borderless Church" is a brave new phenomenon, and thus the Church of South India as a borderless church is supposed to be a pilgrim church once again just like it was so when it started its journey as an unparalleled united church seven decades ago. In short, a pilgrim church needs to be complemented by a borderless church, and vice versa. In this way, this cycle repeats itself, intertwining those two different identities of the Church of South India at the deep level.

As having been seen above, the idea of "a Borderless Church" raises the question of a new way of being and doing of the church. Through its own experiment and the sharing of experiences with other ecumenical partner churches, the Church of South India will contribute to the growth of church and society in India and beyond. Perhaps the concrete way of implementing the idea will not be applicable to other contexts, and yet the spirit of the idea will ever be. That is what the ecumenical partner churches are all about.

Endnotes

[1] May I suggest an acronym, ABC, to stand for "a Borderless Church", simply for convenience?

[2] To avoid confusion, I use the expression of 'a church uniting' rather than 'a uniting church', the latter of which belongs to the category of the 'united and uniting churches' in the World Council of Churches.

[3] The General Assembly of the Church of Scotland 2001, *The Report of the Special Commission anent Review and Reform: A Church without Walls.* (2001). Sometimes, the title of "A Church without Walls" is used in its abbreviated form, CWW.

[4] The General Assembly of the Presbyterian Church of Korea, *The Commentary to the Theme of the 102nd General Assembly: The Holy Church, Go into the World Again* (Seoul: PCK Book, 2017); The Research Center of the Presbyterian Church of Korea, ed., *The Application Guide to the Theme of the 102nd General Assembly: The Manual for Maeul Mokhoe (Community Ministry)* (Seoul: PCK Book, 2017). Maeul Mokhoe can be translated into English in various ways such as Community Ministry, Village Ministry or the Ministry of Neighborhood. Here I use the term 'Community Ministry' according to the suggestion of the Very Reverend Ki Hak Choi, the Moderator of the 102nd General Assembly, while Dr. Young-sang Ro, the director of the Research Center of the Presbyterian Church of Korea, prefers 'Village Ministry'. See The Research Center of the Presbyterian Church of Korea, *The Application Guide to the Theme of the 102nd General Assembly*, 3.

[5] J. W. Gladstone, ed., *United to Unite: History of the Church of South India, 1947-1997* (Chennai: Church of South India Synod, 1997), passim.

[6] CEV (Contemporary English Version).

[7] Burton Hamfelt, *Campus City Project: The Start-up Campus and the New Education of Things* (n.p.: 2015), [p.5]. https://issuu.com/burtonhamfelt5/docs/campus_city_book_reduced, access date, Oct., 12, 2018.

[8] The General Assembly of the Church of Scotland 2001, *The Report of the Special Commission anent Review and Reform: A Church without Walls*, 17-22.

[9] Ibid., 22-27.

[10] The General Assembly of the Presbyterian Church of Korea, *The Commentary to the Theme of the 102nd General Assembly*, 21.

[11] The wording of this somewhat ambiguous sub-topic can also be translated as follows: "To Transform a Village into a Church, a Villager into a Church Member."

[12] The General Assembly of the Presbyterian Church of Korea, *The Commentary to the Theme of the 102nd General Assembly*, 30-42; The Research Center of the Presbyterian Church of Korea, ed., *The Application Guide to the Theme of the 102nd General Assembly*, 79-170; Young-sang Ro, ed., *The Presbyterian Church of Korea Village Ministry Series 2: Village Church, Village Ministry, Practical Parts* (Seoul: PCK Book, 2018).

[13] "Faith in Christ Jesus is what makes each of you equal with each other, whether you are a Jew or a Greek, a slave or a free person, a man or a woman." (Gal. 3: 28, CEV)

[14] Rathnakara Sadananda, "Towards a Borderless Church", [1].

13

Towards New Forms of Borderless/ Boundaryless Congregations in the Mainland of India

Sunil M. Caleb

Introduction

I don't think I will be exaggerating if I say that the mainline (denominational) Protestant church in mainland India is in bad shape. Instead of being a movement, it has become institutionalized in the worst sense of the term. Instead of there being democracy and equality, there is autocracy and hierarchy. Instead of being a movement that sides with the poor and the marginalized (the Church of the Poor), it's leaders are usually found to be hob-nobbing with the rich and the powerful. As Bishop Sumithra (a former bishop of the CSI) once said a long time ago, "There are three demons of the Church in India, Power, Prestige and Property."[1] And it remains so even today, 60 years after Bishop Sumithra had said this. Nothing, absolutely nothing, has changed (in fact, perhaps things have got worse, just as the state of Indian politics has got worse). The number of congregations and church buildings have increased, the foreign missionaries have long gone, the number of presbyters has increased and have become better educated in terms of theological degrees, but as far as the presence of the three demons goes, they are still dwelling happily and merrily within the church structures and nothing it seems can cast them out.

In the midst of this rather depressing scenario we have been called to envisage the future of the Church in India and especially the need for the Ecclesia (the Assembly of the disciples of Christ) to be border-less or boundary-less. There is the call for the Church to reflect the kind of banquet that our Lord Jesus Christ envisaged, one that was open to all; those who lived on the margins and those who are not usually found in the centres of power (cf. Luke 14:15-24).

Local Congregation as Christ

Since our Lord is the centre of the Christian faith and its founder, all our focus must be on visualizing what is the kind of congregation would be in accordance with the will of Jesus the Christ?

As Dietrich Bonhoeffer has written, "The church is established in reality in and through Christ- not in such a way that we can think of the church without Christ himself, but he himself 'is' the church. He does not represent it, for only what is not present can be represented. But in God's eyes, the church is present in Christ. Christ did not make the church possible, but he realized it for eternity. If this is so, Christ must be accorded central significance in the temporal actualization of the church." [2] In short, for Bonhoeffer, "Christ exists as the congregation"[3] That, I believe, has to be the focus of the new forms of Ecclesia that we need to envision for the future. We cannot speak in terms of the Church as a whole as Christ, for really it is the local congregation that is at the forefront of contact and impact with the masses and it is really the local congregation that is the face of Christ in the community. Thus when we speak of a Border-less Church or a Boundary-less Church we must really focus on the congregation and see how we can think of "Christ existing as the congregation."

It is the congregation that must reveal Christ and that must be our focus and goal.

Borderless/Boundary-less Congregation

Since Christ is the pattern of what a congregation must be like it is just a small step to see that the congregation must be one that does not have rigid boundaries, for our Lord believed in crossing boundaries, be they boundaries of gender, ethnicity, culture, occupation and so on. The gospels are replete with instances of when Jesus crossed over to 'the other side' by engaging with women, tax-collectors, Samaritans, Roman centurions, etc. Jesus was certainly not one to stay within the confines of what the Chief priests and the Pharisees thought should be the boundaries and borders. At the congregational level this must mean that the Christian congregation needs to be open to welcoming people who are different from them in terms of income, ethnicity, culture, language, race, caste, sexual orientation and so on. This is surely a struggle, for we see that congregations have a tendency to very easily and very quickly become 'clubs' where membership is restricted to those who the already existing members like and feel comfortable with. People who are different are rarely, if ever, admitted. As most people prefer and perhaps insist on worshipping in their mother-tongue it is not surprising that Sunday mornings are times when there is the most division within nations which have large Christian populations.

Since bringing the rule of God closer to being established on earth in every realm of life is the ultimate reason for existence of Christian congregations, they need to co-operate with all people of good will who are seeking to challenge situations of injustice, oppression, ignorance, superstition and unnecessary suffering in general. In order to do this, Christian congregations must follow Christ by crossing boundaries of ethnicity, language, race etc. and work together with people of other faith traditions.

Congregations should not only be open to people who are different but also have cordial relations between themselves and other congregations. Borders between denominations are often so rigid that it is like relations between two different religions or two different nations. When this happens marriages across denominations are frowned upon and sometimes people of different denominations settle in different areas of a city or state, as was the case in Northern Ireland for a long time.

However, there are times when there need to be boundaries between congregations. Interestingly, it is here that Bonhoeffer again has something relevant to say to us. At the time of Hitler's rule in Germany, the Nazi party began to try to take over the German Lutheran church. It passed anti-semitic legislation contained in the Aryan clause on 7 April 1933 which required the German church to dismiss those pastors who had Jewish blood. Further, the party installed its candidate as the National bishop. Over this question and others the German Church divided into the National Church or the German Christians and the Confessing Church of which Bonhoeffer was a leader. Later the leadership of the Confessing Church was beginning to go back on the decisions made at the Confessing Church Synods of Barmen (1934) and Dahlem(1935), especially with regard to church order and the rejection of the official state church government. It is then that Bonhoeffer states that there have to be boundaries between the 'church' that has false teaching and the true church. He wrote an article entitled in English, "The Question of the boundaries of the Church and Church Union" in April 1936 which stated, "It must be said again and again that for the church to deny its boundaries is no work of mercy. The true church comes up against boundaries. In recognizing them it does the work of love towards men by honouring the truth. ......True, God is everywhere, 'but it is not his will that you should look for him everywhere.'[4]

How would this practically work out in India today? When we say that there must be strict boundaries/borders between congregations that do not follow the gospel values of Jesus Christ and those that do, how does this work in practice in India today? We have to realize, like Bonhoeffer did, that there are congregations which by their belief and actions have clearly cut themselves off from the True Church of Christ. They are clearly and obviously not following the teaching of Christ and hence cannot be called as part of the True Church. A clear example would be congregations that clearly and unambiguously practice Caste distinctions. There have to be borders and boundaries between such so-called congregations and congregations that can be called as part of the True Church of Christ. Caste in India is a case of *Status confessionis*,[5] as has been pointed out by the National Council of Churches in India.[6] As the practice of Caste is something that is totally antithetical to what Jesus stood for and taught, a stand against Caste is an essential part of the Christian faith and must be thought of as an issue the stand on which defines whether a congregation can be considered to be part of the True Church or whether it is just pretending to be a part of the Church. The presence of caste within the Church and followed by a Congregation is a fit case for being called *status confessionis*.

New forms of Ecclesia

We are now at the stage in India when the old forms of congregational life seem no longer to be the "form of Christ in the world" as they should be. They function too much like secular clubs and worldy institutions. A radical change is needed. Such a radical change happened in the fourth century when after the conversion of emperor Constantine a certain moral decay set in, in church and society and monks began to go into the Egyptian desert and live as hermits or as monks. In Europe in the fifth century St. Benedict of Nursia began a monastic movement that had a great influence on the development of

European civilization and culture and helped Europe to emerge from the "dark night of history" that followed the fall of the Roman empire.[7]

Here again we can turn to Bonhoeffer who said in 1935, " The restoration of the church will surely come only from a new type of monasticism which has nothing in common with the old but an uncompromising allegiance to the Sermon on the Mount. [8] It is this New Monasticism that I believe is the way that the church can be renewed and revived in our current time and such green shoots are coming up in various places in the world. This New Monasticism would have the characteristics of the primitive church who had lived close to one another and had all things in common as described in Acts 2: 43-47 and Acts 4: 32-37. Those associated with the Radical Reformation in Europe took these practices of the primitive church very seriously and added to them a strong following of Jesus' Sermon on the Mount, especially Jesus' call to total non-violence. Intentional Communities of families living together holding property in common emerged at that time and have now taken the form of the Hutterite and Amish communities which are now mostly found in North America (though they are growing in other countries as well). The Bruderhof Community which originated in Germany is a revival of this heritage and has many communities across the world but none so far in India. [9]

As Christians in India we have a double heritage which can be useful for the new expressions of monasticism that I believe are required in India today so that we can clearly make known the abundant life that God wishes to impart to all people. The double heritage is that of the Ashram tradition from the Indian religious tradition and from the Christian side the tradition of communities of believers living together holding all things in common.

In the Ashram tradition the emphasis is upon the deepening of the consciousness of the Divine and a lifestyle that is in tune with nature. As Jules Monchanin and Abhishiktananda, founders of the Shantivanam

Ashram wrote in *An Indian Benedictine Ashram*, 'The ashram life challenges the uncontrolled development of the world's mechanistic industrial complex'. The Ashram tradition[10] which embodies the values of simplicity and renunciation is the ideal way in which we can proclaim a counter-culture to the capitalistic form of development which has captured the minds of the elite and which is having a tremendously negative effect upon human life and upon the environment.

This kind of life-style (found in an ashram or in New monastic communities) would be an ideal way to challenge the destructive pattern of economic development that India is in the midst of. The simplicity of life would challenge the pattern of consumerist consumption which the market ideology very cunningly imposes on us so that the rate of profit of the companies can remain high. Such a life-style would refocus our attention on the fact that there are just some basic needs that we have and which should be met for all people and on the fact that economic equality is something important that makes for greater community. As we are in the midst of an environmental crises with climate change creating extreme weather conditions around the world, from an environmental point of view such a life-style would be extremely beneficial as it would lead to lower carbon emissions. The reduction in consumption would also help reduce the demand for industrial products and electricity which is what is behind a lot of corporate greed that is resulting in the grabbing of the land and resources of our tribal/adivasi brothers and sisters in many parts of India. However, as Jonathan Wilson of the Northumbria Community in England has suggested, this New Monasticism should have the following Twelve marks of New Monasticism.

1.   Relocation to the 'abandoned places of the Empire' (to the margins of society)

2.   Sharing economic resources with fellow community members and the needy among us

3. Hospitality to the stranger.

4. Lament for linguistic/racial/caste divisions within the church and our communities combined with the active pursuit of a just reconciliation

5. Humble submission to Christ's body, the Church

6. Intentional formation in the way of Christ and the rule of the community along the lines of the old novitiate

7. Nurturing common life among members of an intentional community

8. Support for celibate singles alongside monogamous married couples and their children

9. Geographical proximity to community members who share a common life

10. Care for the plot of God's earth given to us along with support of our local communities

11. Peacemaking in the midst of violence and conflict resolution with communities along the lines of Matthew 18.

12. Commitment to a disciplined contemplative life. [11]

In India where Caste is such a problem these Congregational Ashrams need to be ashrams where there is a conscious and deliberate mixing of people from different regions and caste back-grounds with inter-marriage between people between different regions and caste backgrounds given top-most priority. Common kitchens and common property would also be a great witness to Indian society at large. These ashrams need not be in the rural areas as has traditionally been the case in India but can in fact be in cities as well. As new co-operative housing colonies are coming up, it might be possible for Christian families to be able to live in close proximity to one another and practice Ashram life. It might even been possible for a block of flats within a city to become Congregational Ashram.

Conclusion: The time has come for radical change in the way in which the congregation expresses its faith and witness in India. Current forms of congregational life are too infused with the kind of governance and organization that is more likely to be found in the corporate and government world. The church, therefore, brings nothing new to society and is never the Yeast that is leavening the whole dough. As Dietrich Bonhoeffer has suggested, the revival of the Church can come only through some form of new monasticism. This could happen through local congregations turning themselves into Intentional Communities where most things are held in common. In India, these kind of communities have been found in Ashrams, and the conscious formation of Christian ashrams (with perhaps people of other faith traditions also living with them) at the local level is perhaps the way forward for new forms of boundary-less/border-less ecclesia.

Endnotes

[1] Quoted in Michael Hollis, *Paternalism and the Church: A study of South Indian Church History*, London: Oxford University Press, 1962, p. 32.

[2] Dietrich Bonhoeffer, *Sanctorum Communio*, in John de Gruchy (ed.) *Dietrich Bonhoeffer: Witness to Christ* (Selected Writings), London: Collins, Liturgical Publications, 1988, p. 71. This was Bonhoeffer's doctoral dissertation presented to the Faculty of Theology at Berlin University, Germany in 1927 when he was only 21 years old.

[3] Cited in John de Gruchy (ed.) Dietrich Bonhoeffer: Witness to Christ (Selected Writings), London: Collins, Liturgical Publications, 1988, p. 73.

[4] Dietrich Bonhoeffer, *The Question of the Boundaries of the Church and Church union* in John de Gruchy (ed.) *Dietrich Bonhoeffer: Witness to Christ (Selected Writings)*, London: Collins, Liturgical Publications, 1988 p. 155.

[5] *Status Confessionis* is a Latin ecclesiological term in Protestant theology, which refers to an exceptional confession case (denominational emergency). If the *status confessionis is* declared, then the ecclesiastical community's Christian identity at stake.

[6] The NCCI has categorically stated that "Caste and Christ cannot go together". If that is so, then since a Congregation must be "Christ in the world", a congregation that practices Caste attitudes cannot be considered as a Christian congregation. It can only be considered as a Caste association.

[7] The words of Pope Benedict XVI. Cardinal Joseph Ratzinger took the name Benedict on being elected Pope because he admired the contribution that St. Benedict had made to Europe his continent and Cardinal Ratizinger had a special concern for the revival of the church in Europe.

[8] Quoted in www.northumbriacommunity.org (accessed on 21 October 2018)

[9] The Hutterite Communities compose some 50,000 people in the USA which live today in self-contained colonies averaging approximately 100 people for each colony. See James Halteman, "Anabaptist Approaches to Economics" in Paul Oslington (ed) *The Oxford Handbook of Christianity and Economics,* O.U.P., 2014, pp.245-262.

[10] It is unfortunate that the Ashram tradition has within Indian Christianity become associated with the brahmanical Hinduism which is seen as upholding Caste. I believe it is possible to use the good ideas learnt from Ashrams without taking on board the whole concept of brahmanical Hinduism.

[11] www.northumbriacommunity.org (accessed on 19 October 2018).

14

Revisioning Secularization for Inclusive Spirituality:

Downgrading Spirituality for the Downtrodden

Santanu K. Patro

1. Can spirituality be downgraded/ secularized for the people in the margins?

2. Is secularization all about engaging the religion in the public places?

3. Does secularization help Spirituality to be more inclusive and plural?

Throughout the paper I use the term secularization more positively and constructively, though I am aware that the words like secular and secularism have different meanings. To me secularization is a process by which religion is grounded in the world. Therefore, secularization is contextual. This paper does attempt the democratization of religious institutions, for which there is another paper is to be written. My objective in this is only to positively analyze 'secularization' for locating spirituality in the context of pluralism.

According to Nikki Keddie there are three ways to understand "secularization" today: as (a) "an increase in the number of people with secular beliefs and practices"; (b) "a lessening of religious control or influence over major spheres of life"; and (c) "a growth in state separation from religion and in secular regulation of formerly religious institutions and customs." (Nikki Keddie, 2003: 16) Though there are limits to understanding secularization, according to this definition; nevertheless, it makes religion more engaging in public life and enables, the faith practioners to be more accommodative and adaptive.

Introduction

The single most urgent issue that needs to be addressed in spirituality is xenophobia – religious intolerance, caste discrimination, parochial nationalism, male chauvinism, hate-language, hate-crime. The politics to push the Sangh Parivar brand of Religious Nationalism to the fore is nothing but to change the course of history and rewrite the ethos of nationalism from a dominant and majoritarian perspectives. Free speech and voices of dissent on national issues are now considered anti national. The ones who speak for the Kashmiris and similarly for the Dalits and CPI (ML), the Naxalites, are branded as anti-national. In the body politics of today what matters is the vote bank and not the unity and integrity of India.

Francis Fukuyama's thesis on "the End of History" and Samuel P Huntington's "The Class of Civilizations and the Remaking of the Modern World" reinforce the idea how religious ideologies have become inconsistent to the ideals of freedom, justice and equality. There is complete loss of secularized worldviews that otherwise helps religion eases out of mainstream fundamentalism. What we witness from the beginning of this millennium is that the idea of nationalism has attained a very pejorative meaning and produced parochial definitions by conceiving nationalism to race, caste, religion and region. This nationalism today defeats democracy and secularism. India will not be destroyed by the weapons of mass destruction, but weapon of communalism initiated by forces of communalism. What is needed is to liberate religion from religious fundamentalism if we were to towards the unity and integrity of our nation state.

In a new geopolitical divide, religious institutions and communities are facing unprecedented challenges from every quarter. While many religious institutions suffer from spiritual integrity, the masses are torn apart by religious fundamentalism cutting across all religious boundaries. There is a need to address the issues of religiosity and spirituality in the context, appropriating the needs and challenges. On the one hand spirituality is thought to be the best solution for human problem and world's crisis, and deterrent to reconciliation and healings to human community, on the other it has also become an instrument of violence, hatred and exploitation. What then is the relevance of religion for the masses? The world is still not free from political bondage despite the strong civil society. Indian values and ethos have also remained essentially discriminatory, casteist and gendering. The religious masses still suffer from religious discrimination and exploitation. Religion over a period has moved to public places. Instead of building peace and reconciliation, it has become the victim in the hands of the political class. The difference in today's religiosity is that it is in the know of solution yet it does not have the moral conviction and political authority to overcome the impediments of inequality and injustices.

There is another pertinent question, how much spiritual is our religious institutions. I am aware that I may be confronted to define spirituality. I hesitate to define spirituality for the simple reason that I may reduce spirituality to a dominant notions and categories. It is best left to the people to take cue from collective spirituality and profess it. For example, for a religiously plural society, secularization of religion is believed to be the best alternative and it must help promote inclusive spirituality where we not only appreciate the spirituality of our fellow brothers and sisters of other denominations or Christian traditions;

but also the spirituality of our neighbours. The fundamental question that needs to be addressed is: what is place of religion in secular state such as ours? Do Religions promote inclusive spirituality? Today spirituality has become more complex not because of the impact of secularism or secularisation, but because of its refusal to be inclusive.

Secularism in Indian Democracy

Many students of political science think, secularism in India is only 'skin-deep'. It depends on how one defines secularism in India. India is the largest democracy in the world. If the number is the criterion to define majority, then one can say the above statement is true. The success of electoral politics makes India democratic. Does a mere conduct of electoral politics make a state democratic? Since the independence, for nearly 75 years India has been successfully electing its leaders 'democratically' under a strong electoral system from Panchayat Raj to National Parliament. If democracy is defined as 'of the people, by the people and for the people' then India can claim to be a democratic state. Though this minimum definition of democracy does not guarantee equality, freedom and justice to all the people.

Not many in India carry the convictions that the Indian citizens vote with 'free conscience' transcending religion, caste, region, language etc. If democracy is the rule by the majority then it has achieved its objectives. The idea of democracy, the rule of the majority today defeats the very idea of freedom, justice and equality to all citizens. The questions arise, who are the majority? Today in fact those who hold power and exercise power are the majority, not in real sense of the term majority. Numbers are mere vote banks in Indian electoral politics, but ultimately power defines Indian democracy. Therefore, it is not the democracy that in true sense determine the political landscape.

Secularism in the Christian West is evolved in a mono-religious and mono-cultural settings of Europe. When it moved to North America, it carried European religion and social structure, therefore secularism faced many forms of resistance in a monocultural democratic society. The migrants who came later had no choice but to be part of the Christian secular West since there was already in place institutional structures for secularism to function, though in a Christian environment. But that did not take away their religious, cultural and national identity. Today there is a need to redefine secularism in the context of pluralism. Asians with their religious beliefs dominated the discourses on secularism. The relationship between democracy and secularism is factored by the existence and vibrancy of religiousness in all societies and communities. One must understand the different expressions and meaning when we use the term religion, religious etc. The religion was always in the public domain and it has shaped the national history and national identity. It is the religiousness that is now moving into the public spaces and that forces to redefine secularism.

In India the word secularism should not be given any ideological and philosophical overloading that have been uncritically imported from the Western; rather secularism in India must acknowledge religions must coexist and it is the role of secularism to provide ideological foundation and praxiological tools to strengthen democracy. It is not the total separation between 'religion' and 'politics' that will solve all the ails that Indian nation is facing today; but religion while occupying public space, limits its 'religiousness' that are detrimental to the pluralistic society. Democracy is not merely a political system, it is also a social vision, in that, a society in which citizens need to find their identities and make assert their citizen rights. The boundaries and differences are part of the autocratic state. It makes rules by dividing people in line with caste, creed and regions.

Defining Secularization for India

Liberal democracy needs a form of secularism that will counterbalance the influence of religion in politics. If democracy must survive in a religiously plural world, secularism must play a constructive role in shaping and understanding religions. The word secularism has cluster of related terms that have different meanings according to the context. Each of the term refers ostensively, providing altogether different understanding. For examples terms like secular, secularity, secularism and secularization may attribute different meanings. To articulate secularism in the secular age needs analytical distinctions between the 'secular' and its related terms. They all have etymological meanings as well as epistemic functions. What is interesting is that the word secular exists always in relation/contrast to religion.

> There are multiple ways of experiencing the secular – and, indeed, of being secular – and the challenge of social science is to investigate and understand these different forms of secularity. While "the religious" and "the secular" are mutually constitutive, however, and while a good deal of social-scientific effort has been dedicated to the study of religion, the development of reflexive anthropology and sociology of the secular remains in its relative infancy. (Craig Calhoun, 2011:21)

The words secular and secularization are two different concepts and secularism has an ideological tilt. Secular is the one which makes a distinction between religious and that which are non-religious. Secularization is more to do with religion in public places. Religious symbols and practices are interpreted through in the context of secularization of religions. Being religious in public places makes religious people encounter other religious people who are different in faith, and their symbols and practices. They also see that there is a symbiotic relationship between religions. In other words, religion finds its expression in its religiosity in a particular geo-political and socio-economic context. Secularization often is used by some scholars as a concept where a religion is confronted by other religions and other worldviews often challenging one another religious viewpoints and interpretations. This process transforms the inwardly religion and its practices, and exposes to other practices and religious behavior. The boundaries are broken when the religion reaches out other religions. (Cf. Craig Calhoun, 2011:54) Secularization may also transform politics in having constructive and inclusive understanding of religions in the process.

Revisioning Secularisation in a Pluralistic Society

Secularization is an attempt at reducing the influence of religion in public spheres. "The two theory of secularization which is generally understood – "the decline of religion" and "the privatization of religion," have undergone numerous critiques and revisions ..., the core of the thesis, namely, the understanding of secularization as a single process of functional differentiation of the various secular institutional spheres of modern societies from religion, remains relative uncontested." (Craig Calhoun, 2011: 61)

Secularization is a virtue that promotes material culture and committed to develop human welfare and values. It tries to help understand the meaning of life here in this world. The life is not purely other worldly but what and how we live are more important. This is purely utilitarian in nature. Otherwise religion can be extreme in promoting poverty or prosperity depending on how one understands religious worldviews. Secularism rather serves as an antidote to religious conservatism which otherwise become counterproductive in multireligious context. One should not think secularization is an anathema to religious faith and practices. Secularization has to function and identify its role in order to make distinction of what is religious. Rather Secularization makes citizens more responsible transcending religious affiliation and working for common good. Secularization does not necessarily mean anti-religions/ religious. Be it religious or political institution, the role of secularization is to promote the wellbeing, and checkmate any trespasses or overlapping between these two great institutions. (cf. George Jacob Holyoake, 1870: 11)

Religion in secularization

Deficiency in the democratic system is not the root cause of the rise of religious nationalism in India, but the vote bank politics that undermine the democratic norms. The vote bank politics based on religious affiliations divide communities on religious and caste lines. The xenophobic discourses on Hindu Nationalism even in today's world has made the marginalized communities threatened. It may be necessary to do a survey of Indian democracy over a period and study how it has impacted the politics in order to understand the Indian nationalism. Indian nationalism is different in both pre-independence and post-independence eras. While the pre-independence discourses on Nationalism is in the context of the colonial rulers; the post-independent Nationalism is dominated by high castes. While pre-independent nationalism was understood to be the fight against the foreign rule, the post-independence was much about occupying the seat of powers to rule others. This is a home-grown colonialism which dictates on its own term what is nationalism, often preaches the models of Hindu nationalism. For example, the Rama Rajya is nothing but towards an establishment of Hindu Kingdom. This has assumed a dangerous phenomenon.

As much as separation of church and state is a virtue of Western secularism, so much so politics and religions are inseparable virtues of India secularism. There is no doubt that religion cannot be removed from public life, but religion can be exposed to the process of secularization. Secularization should not be construed as opposed to religions, secularism as an ideology may have some reservation about religions. A strict separation between religion and state will only make secularism more arrogant towards religions. Absolute acceptance of religion or secularism will only make one to reject the other, which give rise to fundamentalism in religions, and anti-religion in secularism.

Religion when descended from above, it refuses to go through the process of secularization. If religion were to accept a political system, particularly the systems of democracy, religion has no choice but to conceptualize itself from the perspective of secularization. Unless religion is secularized, there is hardly any scope for religion to constructively contribute to politics. Coexistence is not challenging the supremacy of one institution over the other, rather to make each of these institutions to function in their own place of reference. When religion makes claims to be superior to politics, the space of secularization is defeated by the very ideology of secularism. Therefore, there is a need of secularization that respects religious pluralism than having a secularism that rejects religions.

Secularization and religion are not antithetical, though secularism can be at times. Secularization must remain positive about the function of religions, and religions must also maintain its limits while entering into the arena of secularization. Religion is no more a matter of privacy. Rather religions move to the center of the public domain. Secularization is no longer a threat to religion, rather it helps religion to witness in a very positive and constructive manner in the secularized world.

Secularization provides a good platform to accommodate pluralism. The more contextual reading of religion is done, the better it is perceived by people of other faiths. Secularization does not function to neutralize religions nor play a role to make religions redundant in a secular world. There are many elements that are informed by religion, including, politics and state. If religion is excluded from society, the society may lose its capacity to be conscious of things that are otherwise not found in a society.

Spirituality and Pluralism

While spirituality is always inclusive; at the same time no spiritual experience is same in its manifestations, no matter how textual is our spiritual traditions are. Spiritual experiences by nature are plural and diverse. Its expressions are not limited neither to the texts nor traditions. There is no doubt that today the nation states are shaped by power, wealth and economy but it is also true that culture, religion and language sustain the inclusive and pluralistic nature of a State (cf. Samuel P Huntington, 1997: 21). The nations are trying to articulate their own preferences based on 'cultural and religious differences'. Such preferences are founded on hegemonic culture and religious majoritarianism. The great Jurist Nana Palkhiwala once said, that "the world is witnessing today to two basic splits – one vertical and the other horizontal. The vertical is between the East and the West; the horizontal between the North and the South. The East-West conflict is between tyranny and freedom, just as the North-South confrontation is between affluence and poverty. The solution of the first would release the resources necessary to pave the way for a solution of the second." (Nana A. Palkhivala, 2002:29)

The so-called civilised society is becoming extremely and exclusively mono-cultural, responding monotonously and unilaterally to the religious modes and moulds of the West. The ideals of pluralism, for which East was known, has remained only an academic discourse and theoretical framework meant to be discussed in an intellectual environment. Nevertheless, the humanity belongs to communities that are culturally, religiously and socially plural. When the communities are divested from their basic tenets of pluralism, it is bound to manifest in religious fundamentalism.

V. S. Naipaul's euphoria of "universal civilisation" (V. S. Naipaul, 1990: 20) is an eclectic by-product of Orientalism. He talks about coming together of humanity on shared commonalities of values, beliefs, orientations, manner, practice, behaviour and institution. But what is critical often in such a society is that it lacks a sense of belongingness that holds key to unity. The recognition of the "other" is the only antidote to any form of religious, cultural and social fundamentalism. If one enjoys freedom in a nation when there is no presence of the "other" it is not a real freedom, it is rather a 'mono-dom'. A nation's pluralistic credential can only be measured when the 'other' is present and treated equally with all. The 'other' is downtrodden, always exploited and discriminated because the other is different.

There is another danger. Making religion private promotes individualism. Religious individualism is antithesis to pluralism. There is nothing as 'private religion' in the world of communication revolution and information. In a democratic society all must respect everyone's religious rights. When religion is overemphasised as a matter of individuality, it is evident, that there are growing tensions between individuals within a group and between groups.

The question is who controls religion and religious life? Today religion is not downgraded for the empowerment of the masses, rather it is retained and defined by religious leaders such as priests who dictates from above. Is there a democratic structure that is inclusive? The spurt of religious violence and fundamentalism emanates from individuals who do not tolerate the others. Spirituality today is emphasised more in the context and centrality of the religious institutions. The religion is so institutionalised that it loves to practice within the walls of the churches, temples, mosques. The temple coffers increase their revenue. Church becomes rich and serves the interest of the rich and affluent. The question is, is church shying away in promoting inclusivism and pluralism? Spirituality is today sold as a market commodity by many religious leaders and amassed wealth in the name of religions. People are prescribed easy solutions and healings. Spirituality today has become magic-driven and disease-healing phenomenon.

Most of the major religions are in a way going through a surge of revivalism by which spirituality is defined as individualism. George Wiegal is of the opinion that the "unsecularization" is dominant social factors (George Wiegal, 1991: 27) in promoting such a spirituality. When a democratic state fails to translate the values of secularization, it is bound to have cascading effect on making people to turn to fundamentalism. Samuel P Huntington has rightly observed:

> More broadly, the religious resurgence throughout the world is a reaction against secularism, moral relativism, and self-indulgence, and a reaffirmation of the values of order, discipline, work, mutual help, and human solidarity. Religious groups meet social needs left

untended by state bureaucracies. These include the provision of medical and hospital services, kindergartens and schools, care for the elderly, prompt relief after natural and other catastrophes, and welfare and social support during periods of economic deprivation. The breakdown of order and of civil society creates vacuums which are filled by religious, often fundamentalist, groups. (Samuel P Huntington, 1997: 86)

Religion and Religious Freedom

While democracy and secularism are theoretical construct, democratisation and secularisation are the process of empowerment for political and religious rights and freedom respectively. Similarly, religion is a system of belief, but spirituality is the process by which a believer is empowered. In religion, the faith of the people and the religious experiences when move downward; the empowerment begins at the grassroot with the people in the margins. Religion goes beyond from a system to a process, from an institution to a way of life when it is downgraded.

Spirituality alone will make religion to survive, it is neither the institutions nor the structures. Therefore, people are important. Wilfred Cantwell Smith says if the religion has survived it is not because of the institutions of doctrines and ritual, rather people's expression of faith and practices. If there is any cure for the ailment of religion, it is the spirituality. If religion is moving in opposite direction of fundamentalism it needs to be corrected by secularization of spirituality through empowerment. Strengthen the power of the masses by reducing the power of the so-called religious elites. Empower people more and more and in more secularized ways. This means nobody should be denied of their spiritual freedom including that of the Dalits, Adivasis, women and children. Downgrading spirituality is liberative for it has all the components of plurality meant for the people in the margins.

The limitation of spirituality is when spirituality is confined or held hostage to political/ religious fanaticism. The danger that we face today is that a significant number of people claim to represent the majority when they represent in reality a miniscule number. They are communalists. Communal hatred and religious fanaticism will grow at the cost of national unity and integrity in the absence of genuine secularisation. Nana Palkhiwala says, "to the growing army of terrorists and professional hooligans, caste or clan, creed or tongue, is a sufficient ground to kill their fellow citizens." (2002, 11)

That is why Noam Chomsky says there is a need of conscious and intelligent manipulation of the organized habits and opinions. It is the job of the "intelligent minorities." (Noam Chomsky, 2003: 17) There is a need to offer spirituality to the people by religious class by putting religious teachings in right perspective. The task is to broaden the vision of spirituality to include all. While there is a need to preserve the fundamentals of religions namely scripture, belief systems and traditions, at the same time we ned to build up what I call inbuilt secularization or downgrading spirituality, to make religion descend to the grassroot.

Empowering the masses with spirituality is important but at the same, the religions has to offer diverse and plural spirituality. The faith community cannot become the one 'covenant' people. It should embrace all. Inequality based on caste and gender are the roots of all evils in India. Religion may create institution of equality but unless it practices equality, it becomes mere rhetoric.

Unfortunately, today spirituality is captive to rituals, traditions and constitution. There is no space for freedom of expressing alternative spirituality. In that religion may flourish, but spirituality may not. Spirituality is deterrent to religion and it is not other way. The increase in religious activitism at best may serve as deterrent to religious institution but it may not provide freedom of professing one's faith. At the same time freedom is not always a freedom to choose but freedom to discern what is right, what is common good? Religion functions when all its institutions are downgraded to the point of saturation.

Fundamentalism is historically the weapon of the weak. Those who do not possess power or are powerless in a religious institution, they compensate with intolerant spirituality. Since one cannot fight the power of the day, it seeks to take shelter in the literal interpretations of Scripture and often interpreting it intolerantly. The weapon of intolerance is nothing but making scriptures victim of fanaticism.

Conclusion

Empowering the masses may have some flaws when implemented, nevertheless it should not be set aside for fears of such flaws. It is only when empowerment is put to test it rises and becomes matured over a period of time. Empowerment must take place at all level. It must take place institutionally as well as locally at the congregation level. Secularization should not be a pejorative term considering the strength that it will give to spirituality to locate itself in the world.

Inter-faith harmony and consciousness of the essential unity of all religions is the very heart of our nation. Therefore one might say at the end that there is still hope in our democracy, in the process of secularization. As long as we locate religion within the framework of above elements, it is possible to create a new religious order where all can live in peace, harmony and tolerance.

Bibliography

Keddie, Nikki, (2003), "Secularism and its Discontents," Daedalus 132.

Calhoun, Craig, (2011), "The Secular, Secularisations and Secularisms"

Chomsky, Noam, (2003). *Understanding Power: The Indispensable Chomksy*, ed by Peter R. Mitchell & John Schoeffel, New Delhi: Penguin.

Fakuyama, Francis, (1992), The End of History and the Last Man. New York: Free Press.

Hansen, Thomas Blom, (1999). The Saffron Wave: Democracy and Hindu Nationalism in Modern India, Princeton: Princeton University Press.

Hashemi, Nader, (2009). Islam, Secularism, and Liberal Democracy: Toward a Democratic Theory for Society, New York: Oxford University Press.

Holyoke, George Jacob, (1870). The Principles of Secularism, New York: A K Butts (?).

Huntington, Samuel P, (1997). *The Clash of Civilizations and the Remaking of World Order,* New Delhi: Penguin.

Naipaul, V. S., (1990), "Our Universal Civilisation," The 1990 Wriston Lecture, The Manhatten Institute, New York Review Books.

Palkhivala, Nana A., (2002). *We the Nation: The Lost Decades, New Delhi: UBS.*

Weber, Max. (1930), The Protestant Ethic and the Spirit of Capitalism. London: Unwin Hyman, Translated: Talcott Parsons, Anthony.

Wiegal, George, (1991). "Religion and Peach: An Argument Complexified," *Washington Quarterly,* 14.

15

Building Life Affirming Communities:

Prophetic Diaconal Vocation of Indian Church

Sudipta Singh

Diaconal ministry is the ministry of Word and Service at the intersection of Church and world. Through diaconal ministry the Church happens in the world as healing and transforming presence in the life of God's children who are longing for healing, restoration, justice, and fullness of life. If the mission of the Church is to realize the reign of God in the here and now, then the Church must become a diaconal church, witnessing the in-breaking of the reign of God as it engages in ministries that facilitate the flourishing of life in our communities.

Reimagining *Diakonia*: Biblical Explorations

The term *diaconia* originally referred to those establishments built near a church building for the care and welfare of the poor and other needy people. *Diakonia,* on the other hand, is a Christian theological term derived from the Greek verb *dianonein,* which means to serve. The word *diakonos,* which means male or female servant, also derives from the same root. In the New Testament, *diakonia* is not used in a uniform way. For example, *diakonia* can refer to specific material services to help a person in need (Mk 15:41; 2 Tim 1:18). It also means serving at the tables (Mk 1:3; Acts 6:2). In some cases, it refers to the distribution of funds to people in need (2 Cor 8:19, Rom 15:25). *Diakonia* can also be the vocation of the congregation, alongside other gifts and callings in the church (Rom 12:7). In the story of Jesus washing the feet of his disciples; Bible presents *diakonia* or service to others as an imperative of Christian discipleship (Mk 10:45). For Paul, salvation is God's *diakonia* through Christ (2 Cor 3:7-9) and a *diakonia* of reconciliation through his messengers (2 Cor 5:18-20).

The Bible testifies that Jesus summarized his ministry as being a servant to all. Since the Church is called to continue the ministry of Jesus, diaconal ministry is the vocation of the Church. To understand the implications of this vocation, we need to have a deeper understanding of how Jesus perceived his vocation and engaged in diaconal ministry. For him service was not a passive ministry of care and compassion; rather it was a prophetic ministry of compassionate justice to bring about radical transformation and healing. Jesus reinterpreted *diakonia* through his life as service that transcends borders, seeks justice for the poor and the excluded, and transforms structures that threaten life. In other words, in the paradigm of diaconal ministry set by Jesus, the agenda and the priorities of the ministry of *diakonia* are set by the marginalized and the excluded.

With this alternative meaning of service, let us revisit the biblical witnesses of Jesus' diaconal ministry and vocation. "For the Son of Man came not to be served; but to serve, and to give his life a ransom for many" (Mk 10:45). Here the commitment to embrace and endure suffering and death for the realization of the reign of God is presented as the criterion to engage in diaconal ministry. Remember, for Jesus, service (*diakonia*) was not just one part of his life; rather the very purpose of God becoming human was to serve. "I am among you like a servant" (Lk 22:27). All through his life, he was a deacon, the servant among his disciples. That is the only title that he affirmatively gave himself, even if the church never invokes him as deacon. "The church wants to be the body of a lord, a prophet, a king, a high priest, but which church would really like to be the body of a deacon?" From Christological point of view, *diakonia* is much more than an appendix to the mission and ministry of the church. It is not an adjective, or one expression of the church's life among others, but the expression of the very nature and life of the church itself. From our understanding of the church having deacons as specialized ministers, we need to have an alternative vision of church as deacon. "*Diakonia* is not only about actions or works although they are indispensable. *Diakonia* goes deeper. It is the original destination of the church, her essential characteristic."

As we have already seen, in the New Testament *diakonia* means everything: From the collection for the poor in Jerusalem, widow's service at the table, to the *diakonia* of preaching. It is a comprehensive term which includes the total mission and ministry of the church. We tend to think that *diakonia* is not gospel *per se*; but just the application of the gospel. Bible, in fact, gives us a different understanding. The gospel is proclamation and healing, forgiveness and restoration, word and deed. Bishop Daniel Thiagaraja's words…

> *Diakonia wants to bear living witness to the fact that the power of Jesus is strong in the weak. It seeks and confesses Christ's presence in the powerless, it strives to put its power and privileges at the service of the powerless, to lend them its power, at the price of becoming powerless itself and of sharing the tribulations of the life and the sufferings of the powerless.*[1]

In short, the Church as servant of God in the discipleship of Jesus is called to live out the kenotic Christology of emptying ourselves to become a sacramental community to become authentically diaconal. A diaconal church, following the model of Christ, must denounce the lordship of all prevailing principalities and powers.

Diaconal ministry therefore includes the courage to pronounce God's judgment on ideologies and practices that exclude, stigmatize and criminalize people based on their caste, creed, color, gender and sexual orientation. The diaconal church is not only a voice of critique of the prevailing order, but also the first fruit of the kingdom of God through its alternative existence. *Diakonia* is therefore the very essence and nature of the church so that its very presence will be a "system-threatening presence" of "turning the world upside down."

Reimagining *Diakonia*: Historical Explorations

In the history of Christianity, *diakonia* is understood as "*responsible service of the gospel by deeds and by words performed by Christians in response to the needs of the people.*"[2] It is the ministry of the deacons to translate the love of God into services of assistance, support, solidarity and accompaniment. The ancient churches used to raise funds for *diakonia* from the whole congregation at the *eucharist*. These churches also established the order of diaconate with the special vocation to engage in diaconal ministry. By the 3rd century the church at Rome had over 1500 registered widows and recipients of alms. The city was divided into seven administrative districts, or *diaconiae*, under the care of seven deacons. Instead of the Roman state distributing bread, the deacons looked after it.

Diakonia as an institution to care for the sick and poor, spread from Syria throughout the Byzantine Empire. The deacons of the Eastern churches were involved in social care, liturgical-pastoral care, teaching, administrative-juridical duties and burial *diakonia*. Early church leaders Basil and Benedict developed monastic life in such a way that monks would practice *diakonia*. The monks were expected to receive each guest like Christ. The monasteries used to provide food for the poor at their gates.

When the diaconate came mainly to be a transitional office to the priesthood, the duties of deacons became more limited to the formal liturgical ones. During the middle ages the responsibility for the care of the poor shifted from the bishop to the parish clergy. By the 16th century, the diaconal system was no longer able to cope with the needs. The reformers recalled the role of deacons in the New Testament church: Luther recommended the deacons to keep a register of poor people and care for them; Calvin stressed that the proper function of a deacon was not liturgy but collecting alms from the faithful and distributing them to the poor. This was put into practice in some Reformed churches: male deacons administered the affairs of the poor, while the women cared for the poor themselves. In 1662 the Church of England directed the deacons to search out the sick and poor of the parish and inform the curate, so that "by his exhortation they may be relieved with the alms of the parishioners, or others". In the Roman Catholic Church new religious orders, especially those inspired by St Vincent de Paul, specialized in various aspects of *diakonia*.

With the Industrial Revolution and the rise of capitalism, many people suffered extreme hardship, and churches and secular organizations tried to address these problems. The deacon and deaconess movement emerged during the 19th century with the theological conviction that united the understanding of evangelization and *diakonia* led to the development of institutions to care for the sick, elderly and people with disabilities. At the same time common people became more conscious of their responsibility to their neighbors. Several public charities such as Red Cross came into being during this period. The specialized vocation of care and support also resulted in the development of social work as a professional vocation.

Ecumenical *diakonia* emerged in 1922 with the formation of the European Central Bureau for Inter-Church Aid under the auspices of the Federal Council of the Churches of Christ in America and the Federation of Swiss Protestant Churches, later joined by other European churches. This agency distributed millions of dollars to churches all over the world to engage in relief work. It was during the World War II the ecumenical *diakonia* became more visible in the form of ministry to refugees and prisoners of war. The scope of the refugee service – which focused on the more than 12 million people driven from their homes in Europe – soon extended to work with Palestinians displaced after the founding of the state of Israel in 1948; and from there the WCC broadened its diaconal service to other forms of emergency relief and service worldwide. Further, the ecumenical movement affirmed that the ecumenical *diakonia* is not a temporary engagement that would come to an end with the completion of reconstruction, and that this is a spiritual and not just a material task.

Since then, the WCC has been engaged in contextually reimagining the meaning of *diakonia*. In 1966 the WCC incorporated the idea of social advancement and social action to the prevailing concept of social relief work and service. With the growth of development agencies and government funded aid agencies, there emerged a criticism of the "new missionaries of the interchurch aid empire." The WCC has addressed this criticism and reaffirmed that *diakonia* is "the church's ministry of sharing, healing and reconciliation which is of the very nature of the church. It demands of individuals and churches a giving which comes not out of what they have, but what they are." The 1978 consultation of the Orthodox churches articulated *diakonia* theologically: "Christian *diakonia* is not an optional action... but an indispensable expression of that community, which has its source in the eucharistic and liturgical life of the church. It is a 'liturgy after the Liturgy.'"

A 1986 WCC consultation on *diakonia* discussed issues such as hunger, debt, armaments, and uprooted people, and noted that *diakonia* can exist on various levels – emergency, prevention, rehabilitation, development and change – and that the form it takes should be shaped by local needs. For the future, the Consultation suggested (1) renewal of philanthropic *diakonia*, (2) *diakonia* and development for justice and human rights and dignity, (3) *diakonia* for peace between people, (4) *diakonia* and church unity in the service of society, and (5) *diakonia* and inter-religious understanding for common involvement in justice and peace.

1990s witnessed a shift in the very understanding of ecumenical *diakonia*. Advocacy work for people who face different types of injustice became a major expression of diaconal ministry. Social analysis to understand the root cause of the problem became part and parcel of diaconal ministry. Meanwhile, old problems increased in scope and new ones arose. The plight of the millions of refugees, internally displaced persons and other people living as migrants outside their countries of origin became a major concern for ecumenical *diakonia*. New contexts raised new questions: Would diaconal interventions through financial aid lead to dependency was a major question that ecumenical *diakonia* had to engage with.

The last three decades witnessed the transformation of ecumenical *diakonia* into prophetic *diakonia*. The ecumenical initiatives to combat racism, decade in solidarity with women, advocacy for disabled people, ecumenical accompaniment with people living with HIV and AIDS, economy of life, climate justice, and decade to overcome violence are some of the examples of prophetic *diakonia* that the ecumenical movements have initiated. We see a similar shift in the understanding of *diakonia* of the NCCI.

Diaconal Church: Theological Foundations

As we have seen in our biblical explorations, it is our ministries of *diakonia* that qualify us to be the church. Through *diakonia* the church reaches out to the entire community of creation. This reaching out is an expression of solidarity and service, but it also facilitates transformation in our social relations. Through baptism, we take the allegiance to become part of the body of Christ to continue the diaconal ministry of Christ in our respective contexts. In *diakonia*, those served and those serving are both transformed. The purpose of *diakonia* is not to proselytize. "*Diakonia* is more than the strong serving the weak, which can lead to paternalistic assumptions and practices, and imply that some churches are unable to engage in *diakonia* because of their lack of resources or expertise." Diakonia is part of the calling of all churches and all people of God. In the context of systemic violence and exclusion, breaking the silence and taking the risk of speaking truth to power, even when this threatens the established order and results in hardship or persecution are imperatives of our diaconal vocation.

The church being the sign and sacrament of the expansion of the reign of God, the primary vocation of the church is to engage in diaconal ministry. Kingdom of God is the realization of a new eon inaugurated in and through the prophetic diaconal witness of Jesus Christ. *Diakonia* is a theological concept that presumes an ecclesial structure to be embodied an incarnated. Diaconal work is therefore the praxis, the embodiment of *diakonia*. The church becomes a reality in the life of the community through its diaconal presence and witness. We use different terms to refer to the witness of the diaconal church: social services; deaconry; diaconate; social ministry; justice and advocacy work; the church outside the church; social work; charity; caritas; rehabilitation work; mission activity; urban mission; welfare work; health work; the prophetic action of transformation; the church's face in society; Christ's serving hands here and now. Unfortunately, because of the philosophical and theological tradition of dualism our churches continue to distinguish between *koinonia* and *diakonia*, where the former is the spiritual and theological mission of the church while the latter is our social engagement which is nothing but the application of *koinonia*. The vision of diaconal church is a critique of such dualistic understanding of Christian faith and the mission of the church. Diaconal church is the affirmation that the community experiences the church through its diaconal presence and witness.

Diaconal church, therefore, is a church that is committed to be the visible presence of Jesus, the deacon, proclaiming salvation and liberation to the whole inhabited earth through word and deed. By becoming diaconal church, the church constantly redefines its borders and margins as it strives to become a therapeutic and transforming presence in the world. The diaconal church "follows Christ, its center, to the margins, the hedges and ditches, outside the gates of the city walls, away from the centers of power, away from Jerusalem, to go to the periphery, to the marginalized, to Galilee (Mt 8:7;10), away from the community of a culturally or ethnically defined church to go to the nations (Acts 10:45)."

Prophetic *Diakonia*: Alternative Expressions of becoming the Church

Prophecy, according to biblical narratives, is to discern the justice of God which favors the excluded and oppressed, and to condemn the violations against God's justice. Prophecy today may not differ from that of biblical times in terms of its content, but the methods have changed. One can identify at least three clearly distinguishable dimensions to prophecy: (1) the socio-critical political dimension, concerning the unjust distribution of resources, social injustice and oppressive structures; (2) the dimension critical of cultural, ideological or "religious" values that devalue the intrinsic worth of human beings; and (3) the dimension of the whole of creation.

Diakonia even today is understood as a top-down expression of charity where the haves help the have nots. In this mode of diaconal mission, we are only attending to the victims of the structural evil by offering them ambulance service. The challenge is to find out the root cause of the problem and eliminate it. But it is a costly affair. The Brazilian Arch Bishop Dom Helder Camara categorically addressed this problem by stating that "when I serve the poor, they call me a saint. But when I ask why they are poor, they call me a communist." Dietrich Bonhoeffer's observation is also instructive here: "We are *not* to simply *bandage* the wounds of *victims* beneath the *wheels* of injustice; we are to drive a *spoke* into the *wheel* itself." Doing bandage work will get recognition and applause because we are not disturbing the very systems that create the wounds.

Prophetic *diakonia* is an attempt to reclaim the diaconal mission of Jesus through our disturbing and transforming presence in the world. Drawing from the New Testament motif of the poor, Gustavo Gutiérrez asserted that God is revealed as preferring those people who are 'insignificant', 'marginalized', 'unimportant', 'needy', 'despised' and 'defenceless'. This becomes a core motif in diaconal theory which is strongly influenced by liberation theology.

> *If we are aware of its prophetic nature, and able to integrate diakonia with a prophetic vision, diaconal work moves beyond charity towards social transformation, pointing to the reign of God. As churches become more aware of diakonia' s prophetic dimension, God's mission in the world will be furthered.*[3]

Diakonia is therefore in need of shedding its traditional image. In the tradition of the Old Testament prophets, *diakonia* is committed to unmasking injustice and working for a just, participatory and sustainable society. Prophetic critique of *diakonia* addresses also the church by questioning the latter's conformity to this world. "Thus, while being church in *diakonia* implies the God-given mandate of participating in God's mission to the world, it also means a call to be an incarnated presence, including a radical option with the poor, by following Jesus' example in healing and empowering the excluded." Biblical prophets were defenders of justice. Hence to be engaged in prophetic *diakonia* means to defend and practice justice. A diaconal church is a prophetic community because its vocation includes the task of unmasking injustice and of promoting justice. Prophetic *diakonia* is therefore oriented towards the fringes of society, toward the poorest and their conditions of life. Which means prophetic *diakonia* is informed by the perspectives of those belonging to the periphery. At a Conference in Colombo, Sri Lanka, 2nd-6th June 2012, on 'Theological Perspectives on Diakonia in the 21st Century', it was underlined that *diakonia* has its basic starting-point and perspective from the marginalized.

> The world may tend to see the margins as places of disgrace and powerlessness; however, the biblical witness points towards God who is always present in the struggles of those unjustly pushed to the margins of society. It gives several accounts of God's attention and caring love to people in situations of oppression and consequent deprivation. God hears the cry of the oppressed and responds by sustaining and accompanying them in their journey towards liberation (Ex. 3:7-8). This is the diakonia of God: a diakonia of liberation as well as of restoring dignity and ensuring justice and peace.[4]

Prophetic *diakonia* is at the same committed to engage in self-reflexive examination of the church to see whether we as the body of Christ has lost our saltiness by "conforming to this world" (Rom 12:2). Whether our church structures are inclusive or they are also infested with the plague of domination and exclusion? Have we too easily adopted a lifestyle of religious consumerism and ethical indifference instead of being profoundly provoked by the signs of marginalization and injustice in the world? How do we measure what we are and what we do? Is it done according to the standards of efficiency and professional work as defined in current manuals of development work? Or is it done according to the mandate given by the Lord? In short, without critical prophetic questioning the church and its *diakonia* can easily be trapped by triumphalism, by ecclesio-centrism and other variants of the theology of glory. The church needs constantly to be renewed and reminded of its God-given mandate and to be on the street, even when this is a way of the cross.

Diakonal Engagement of the Indian Churches

The last six decades witnessed different expressions of *diaconal engagement* initiated by the churches and ecumenical organizations. Many churches started their Diaconal wings like CSI SEVA, CNI SBSS. CASA, CMAI etc. facilitated Development and health work of the Protestant and Orthodox churches very efficiently. Hundreds of Hospitals and schools managed by churches have done remarkable service to uplift the poor and marginalized. Catholic churches through their development wings have helped many poor and downtrodden. Many women and men inspired by the Gospel committed their life for strengthening people's movements, whether it is rights of Dalit and Adivasis, Fisherfolks or peasants, Anti-Nuclear Movements, Movements against Corporations and many issues around us. However, a closer look at the diaconal practices of the mainline Indian churches, unfortunately, reveals that we have betrayed our calling to be a transforming presence in the public sphere. Our eagerness to be patriotic and pro-government continues to compel us to support and legitimize the unjust policies of the governments including the colonization of our *jal, jungle,* and *jameen* by corporations. As Christopher Duraisingh observes,

> *The early church appeared as a resistance-movement of folks at the margins, challenging the dichotomy between Jews and gentiles, men and women, sacred and secular etc. At the very DNA of the communities that gathered around in the name of Jesus there was the centrifugal force of a social movement. Our churches today are primarily centripetal and inward looking with very little interest in movement into the world with the message of the gospel.*

Canon Subir Biswas' observations about the church during the 1971 Bangladeshi refugee crisis is still relevant in our times:

> *Some people in India would be quite happy to see the church just keeping to itself, maintaining the beautiful grounds in the midst of violence and tension. Yet we ourselves who are within this feel we can't do it. We have to expose ourselves, to put our property and our church in jeopardy. It is a way of asking repeatedly, what does the incarnation mean in our lives?*

Prophetic *diakonia* is an invitation for the church to incarnate in the here and now.

Arundhati Roy, in her essay "How Deep Shall We Dig?" enables us to understand India from the vantage points of the marginalized.

Shops are overflowing with consumer goods government storehouses are overflowing with food grain. Outside this circle of light, farmers steeped in debt are committing suicide in the hundreds. Reports of starvation and malnutrition come in from across the country. Yet the government allowed sixty-three million tons of grain to rot in the granaries. Twelve million tons were exported and sold at a subsidized price the Indian government was not willing to offer the Indian poor. About 40 per cent of the rural population in India has the same food grain absorption level as sub-Saharan Africa...A relatively small section of people become immensely wealthy by appropriating everything—land, rivers, water, freedom, security, fundamental rights, including the right to protest—from a large group of people. Public infrastructure, productive public assets, water, electricity, transport, telecommunications, health services, education, natural resources, assets that the Indian state supposed to hold in trust for the people it represents, assets that have been built and maintained with public money over decades are sold by the state to private corporations. When victims refuse to be victims, they are called terrorists and are dealt with as such. Anti-Terrorism Act is the broad-spectrum antibiotic for the disease of dissent.[5]

Adivasis of Odisha who lost their ancestral land for the POSCO project lament that, "Our lands, our houses, our rice fields, our betel-vines, our cashew plants, our forest lands, our river, our ponds, our seashore, our fishes will be snatched away from us. They will not only destroy the memories of a grand ma, but also kill the dreams of the village youth."

In the Human Development Index based on life expectancy, health and educational opportunities, India is at 134 out of 187 countries. When it comes to how safe and secure is the ordinary citizen, India is at 96 out of 97 countries. According to International Food Policy Research Institute, India ranks at 65 out of 79 countries in alarming levels of hunger. When it comes to the health of our environment, we are at 125th position out of 132 countries. Peace measured on military expenditure, respect for human rights and transparency, India stands at 142 out of 158 countries. Within the country, 37.7% of households do not have access to a nearby water source, 49% do not have proper shelter, 69.5% do not have access to suitable toilets, 85.2% of our villages do not have a secondary school, and 43% of our villages are not connected to an all-weather road.

We hear similar stories from different parts of the country. The undemocratic repression of people's legitimate rights for self-determination by using draconian laws such as Armed Forces Special Powers Act, violence against women, tribals, adivasis, sexual minorities and religious and ethnic minorities, large scale deforestation and colonization of the commons for corporate plunder. These are all everyday realities of the people of India. It is in the context of this *"impossibility of life"* that we are called to engage in prophetic *diakonia* to proclaim and flourish the gospel of life.

New ways of being: Church as Peoples' Movement

Jesus came to promote a counter-culture. He warned his disciples that their righteousness should exceed the righteousness of the establishment (Matthew 5:20). He promoted the vision of the Church as a Movement for fullness of life for all to be expressed in structures of justice, peace and harmony with nature. But the Church became an institution from the fourth century with royal patronage and followed the Christendom model with crusades, inquisitions, excommunication, and power politics. The Church in India with its close association with the colonial powers is also caught up in this contradiction between the teachings of Christ and the institutional demands. Today the Church could not afford to be quiet, neutral, indifferent, alienated or isolated. To quote Dr. Franklin J. Balasundaram:

> There is a need for Church leadership and others to understand what the members in the pews are faced with in their day-to-day experience. The leadership does not seem to understand the plight of the people in the pews because they are not with the people. The leadership of the Church by and large, is interested

only in its self-preservation, in acquiring more power and wealth, in exercising unlimited authority, in pre-occupying itself with the challenges of maintaining the church structures and raising funds. The preoccupation of the leadership is so intense that they tend to overlook the sufferings of the people. The main challenge today before the Church is of being prophetic and of being relevant in the context of today.[6]

As Tissa Balsuriya, renowned Roman Catholic Theologian from Sri Lanka observes:

We have been too preoccupied with ourselves, with our ghetto concerns. Our social services and institutions have kept us fully occupied. Even the best of the personnel of the Church hardly escaped the stronghold of the Church's institutions which often buttressed the prevailing social system rather uncritically.[7]

The history of the Urban Rural Mission (URM) in India is the history of alternative ecclesial re-imaginations initiated by the people of God, informed by their organic solidarity with the struggling masses at the margins. They launched social action groups and people's movements in different parts of the country among the subaltern communities. At the same time there were attempts to transform local congregations into sites of radical public witness. St. Mark's Cathedral, Bangalore and St. Paul's Cathedral, Kolkata are examples for this. During the 1971 Bangladesh war, Kolkata had to face a huge refugee crisis, and Canon Subir Biswas opened the gates of the St. Paul's Cathedral to welcome the refugees.

The NCCI and the Christian Institute for the Study of Religion and Society and other similar ecumenical organizations also participated in the initiatives to re-imagine Church as a radical public presence in India through consultations and publications, affirming the role of the people of God in the radical transformation of the church and society. One such publication is the book, The Church: A Peoples Movement, published by the NCCI. Mathai Zachariah, in his Introduction of the book observed that,

> *The Church in India has reached a nodal point because of both practical and theological reasons. A nodal point is a point of saturation, a point of no growth, and often a point of stagnation. If we are to survive, we have to take new shoots at this point, and new shoots are always a sign of life.*[8]

The very realization of the Church as stagnant and saturated while it continues to remain as powerful is the starting point for alternative ecclesial and missional re-imaginations.

M.J. Joseph, in his article in the same book, shares the same observation: "*The Church that came into being as a genuine peoples' movement, whenever it got in to an unholy alliance with the powers that be, betrayed its calling and mission.*"[9]

He ends his article with his vision of Church, the peoples' movement:

> *The movement of the Crucified One incorporates the aspirations, longings and the struggle for justice and human expression of two thirds of the masses of this sub-continent. Their involvement in the struggle for better human existence—abundant life as John puts it, is the response to God's act of salvation on the cross. The liberation of the community happens through the liberation of the oppressed. This is the movement of the people—the Church.*[10]

We believe that if the church is to be missional it must be relevant. And for it to be relevant, in today's world, there is need for us to explore new ways of reading scripture, where the Jesus of Nazareth is interpreted as the courageous agitator and advocate for God's liberation in the face of oppression and enslavement; for God's justice in the face of corruption and abuse of power; for God's shalom in the face of social discord and disarray; and for God's hope in the face of disillusionment, cynicism and the temptation for quick fixes while ignoring the bone of contention, the root cause of the problem. For the church to be relevant we must be preparing women and men, for leadership within the church, who are able to make connections between the words of scripture and the world of struggle; who are able to read the signs of the time and relate such reading to the passion of God for *"compassionate justice"* (Allan Boesak), to the call of God for the freedom of the afflicted, and to the plan of God to "give us a hope and a future" (Jeremiah 29). We need leaders with the capacity to resist the temptation to collude with power irrespective of the consequences; to rise above the insatiable appetite for the convenient and the comfortable at the expense of a groaning creation; and to raise a standard, marked by informed understanding of a complicated world and a conscious leader. For the church to be relevant we need worship that is rooted in the spiritualities of a sojourning people, a people who know the struggle they see and the God who walks with them; we need prayers that constitute litanies of hope - the cries of lamentation and discontent and the search for life-giving alternatives; we need new songs – songs reflecting the people's narratives, with theologies that elevate us beyond the boundaries of the cheap prosperity gospel.

Prophetic Diaconal Imagination and Praxis

Rabbi Abraham Heschel, in his celebrated work, *The Prophet*, makes the following observation:

> *The prophet is a person; not a microphone. He (sic) is endowed with a mission... The prophet's task is to convey a divine view, yet as a person, he is a point of view. He speaks from the perspective of God as perceived from the perspective of his own situation.*[11]

There are two affirmations in this observation. Firstly, prophet is a person with an experiential understanding of God as "overwhelmingly real and shatteringly present" in the world. Secondly, prophetic vision is not to proclaim universal and eternal truths from God, rather it is to discern God's perspective from an organic engagement with the contemporary context of death and destruction. Hence Heschel writes:

> *Prophesy is not simply the application of timeless standards to particular human situations, but rather an interpretation of a particular moment in history, a divine understanding of human situation. Prophesy, then, may be described as exegesis of existence from a divine perspective.*[12]

This exegesis of existence from the divine perspective is a call to develop life-affirming communities.

Walter Brueggemann provides us insightful perspectives to understand prophesy and prophetic imagination contextually in our times. According to him, prophesy is *"a persistent voice of dissent, sketching out how differently life is to be lived when YHWH is viewed as the decisive Subject of the public processes of life."*[13]

The prophet being a non-conformist and prophesy a voice of dissent, prophetic vocation in our times challenges us to proclaim divine judgment on the prevailing order and to enable the community to experience the foretaste of alternatives in our midst. Differently said, prophetic diaconal engagement is to expose and reject the sinfulness of the morality of the present, and to strive towards in the company of the victims to realize their vision of salvation in the here and now.

Prophetic Diaconal Vocation as Creating Alternative Consciousness

The tragic reality of our times is the co-option and domestication of our alternative consciousness and vocation. We are told that search for alternative consciousness, practices, and social relations are not only impractical, but also illegitimate. The hegemonic system has got the cultural apparatus to tame and neutralize the prophetic spirit of dissent and its creative energy without using force and coercion. Co-option is the art of emasculating the alternative consciousness by grafting it into the logic and projects of the dominant system. In such a context, the primary task of the prophetic *diakonia* is *"to nurture, nourish, and evoke a consciousness and perception alternative to the consciousness and perception of the dominant culture around us."*[14]

Diaconal churches, therefore, are called to critique and dismantle the prevailing consciousness, and to create counter-cultural imaginations to enable the community to believe that God's future has broken into our midst, and to live out our faith in the anticipation of that hope.

Prophetic Diaconal Vocation as Engaging with the Experience of Numbness

Creative imagination is an existential threat to all hegemonic powers. The audacity to imagine and to believe in the possibility of a beyond of the present is nothing but sedition and incitement to rebellion against the prevailing order. In such situations the dominant system uses its hegemonic power to lead people to numbness by destroying their ability to dream and imagine. Numbness disables our alternative consciousness and moral agency, and leads us to apathy, resignation, and passive acceptance of the regime of death and destruction. In our prophetic engagement with numbness, grief and lament have got an important place. In the prophetic literature, lament and groaning do not represent resignation and despair; rather they articulate the community's public protest against evil, and the unwavering faith in alternatives. *"Grief and mourning, that crying in pathos, is the ultimate form of criticism, for it announces the sure end of the"*[15] powers and principalities of our times. It is only when the church enables the community to come out of their numbness that our diaconal vocation becomes prophetic.

Prophetic Diaconal Vocation as becoming church of the people

The Church ought to remember the fact that she is to live for the ideals and values of the Kingdom, to insert herself in the life and vocation of Jesus of his own historic context, to opt for the poor and the oppressed, to find relevance in the realm of politics, thus going beyond the economics of self-preservation, middle class orientation, neutrality and being rich and triumphalist and to join in the liberative streams of this vast nation.

If the Church wants to be called as '*Church of the people*', they have to be in solidarity with peoples' struggle, to be in solidarity means to put ourselves in a condition where we are equal or at the same level with the people, or one with the people, so that we can feel their despair, pain and sorrow. To struggle in this context means to strive for a better future, free from poverty, oppression, exploitation and degradation of human life and nature and to rejoice in hope in Christ.

Prophetic Diaconal Vocation as becoming Body of Christ among the people

We are called to be the '*Body of Christ among the people*', united by the life-giving Spirit of Christ. The Body of Christ is called to suffer with the suffering and to be in absolute solidarity with the struggling. The body of Christ has to respond to the brokenness of the world. Church needs to be an embodiment of a contemplative and political spirituality. Contemplative is understood not as non-action but as political activity. An active spirituality questions the injustice and suffering of the people and seeks a holistic approach to address injustices around us.

Prophetic Diaconal Vocation as the Audacity of Hope

Our capacity to hope is inextricably intertwined in relationship with God; and it is God in the first instance, and not we, who inspires and enables hope in the human spirit. Prof. Allan Boesak reminds us,

> *Our capacity to hope is truly astonishing; it is something deeply, intimately, uniquely human. It affirms in the most emphatic way our connectedness to the Devine; for God, in whose image we are made, cannot be a God of love and mercy, of justice and peace, or of endless compassion and infinite grace if God is not also, in the most emphatic way, a God of Hope.[16]*

For this reason we can consider ourselves blessed because it is God who first hears the cry of the wounded spirit; it is God who first sees the suffering of the oppressed daughters of the earth; it is God who first agonizes at a groaning creation; it is God who first expresses concern at the broken world in which we find ourselves; it is God whose heart is first broken at Earth's destruction, who weeps at the world's injustice, who is displeased with the excessive greed of human beings; and indeed it is God who calls us to be disturbed and discontented and determined to pray, and struggle, and search, and believe, and imagine, and hope for a different world.

In a context when the community is gripped by numbness, prophetic diaconal vocation demands from us the audacity of hope. Hope is the refusal to accept the present as real and eternal. Hope is subversive. *"It limits the grandiose pretension of the present, daring to announce that the present to which we have all made commitments is now called into question."*[17] For Paul groaning of creation is a labor pain for alternatives. New life is hidden amid death and destruction. This faith instills in us the absurd hope to believe in alternatives. With that hope we are fostered to be an advent community, discerning the partial blossoming of that hope in our communities through our prophetic diaconal ministries of resistance, reconstruction, and healing.

Endnotes

[1] Rt. Rev. Dr. Daniel Thiagaraja, A Biblical Perspective of Diakonia.

[2] Teresa Joan White, "Diakonia, in Dictionary of the Ecumenical Movement, Nicholas Lossky et al (eds), 2nd edition (Geneva: WCC, 2001)

[3] Reinhard Böttcher (ed), Prophetic Diakonia: 'For the Healing of the World', Report Johannesburg: South Africa (Geneva: Lutheran World Federation, November 2002). 16.

[4] Theological Perspectives on Diakonia in 21st Century: from the Conference jointly organized by the Justice and Diakonia, Just and Inclusive Communities, and Mission and Evangelism programmes of the World Council of Churches in Colombo, Sri Lanka, 2nd-6th June 2012 (resource document from the WCC programmes for the WCC Assembly 2013 Busan).

[5] Arundhati Roy, An Ordinary Person's Guide to Empire, (Cambridge, Massachusetts: South End Press)

[6] Franklyn J. Balasundaram, "Being Church in Asia and the Pacific in Partnership with God Today," CTC Bulletin, Vol. XIII

[7] Tissa Balasuriya, Jesus and Human Liberation, Colombo: CSR, 1976

[8] Mathai Zachariah (ed.), The Church: A Peoples' Movement, Nagpur: NCCI, 1975.

[9] M.J. Joseph, "The Church: A Peoples' Movement II" in Mathai Zachariah (ed.), The Church: A Peoples' Movement, Nagpur: NCCI, 1975.

[10] *Ibid.*

[11] Abraham J. Heschel, The Prophets Vol. II, (New York: Harper & Row, 1962), xii.

[12] *Ibid.*, xvi.

[13] Walter Brueggemann, Reverberations of Faith: A Theological Handbook of Old Testament Themes, (Louisville: Westminster John Knox Press, 2002), 161.

[14] Walter Brueggemann, The Prophetic Imagination, (Philadelphia: Fortress Press, 1978), 13.

[15] *Ibid.*, 51.

[16] Boesak, Allan Aubrey, Dare We Speak of Hope? (William B. Eerdmans Publishing Company, 2014), 25.

[17] *Ibid.*, 67.

16

Symbolic Identities and Borders:

Reflections from Church and State

Mark D. Chapman

Remembering and Forging Identity

In the past few years we have had a large number of anniversaries across the world. In Britain this has been a year of remembering – of women getting the vote in 1918, of the founding of the National Health Service in 1948, and of course very shortly we will be concluding four years of remembering the First World War. Last year there was also much reflection on the Independence of India Act of August 1947 which also spawned the Church of South India. The ambiguities of imperialism and colonialism made a rare appearance in the British media – and of course for those of us interested in the history of Christian mission we were able to reflect on the relationship between global empires and the spread of Christianity. Last year also saw the 500th anniversary of the Lutheran Reformation which was remembered across the world. I was present at a conference that tried to connect the remembering of the Reformation with global Christianity. All the varied acts of remembrance allow us to take stock and to reflect on how we came to be and how this might inform the future.

What I think is important to note is that many of our acts of remembering are about moments of identity-shaping: this is obviously clear in the anniversary of the reformation as Christians began to re-forge new identities around what they felt constituted authentic Christianity. Confessional groups were soon established and became focused on a common agreement to fight a foe who stuck to the old religion – the Schmalkadic League required a common faith united around a confession to fight the Emperor's attempt to return the German states to Roman Catholicism. And, of course, the end of the First World War is characterised by the forging of many new national identities as some of the Old Empires collapsed. New lines were drawn on maps and new borders contained people who had never been contained before – a national identity was to replace or at least supplement other identities around clan or tribe or religion. This was obvious in central Europe with new states like Czechoslovakia or Hungary or Yugoslavia. 'National self-determination' often amounted to the creation of new hybrid nations which had never been nations before.

Borders and Conflict

The consequences of such borders and boundaries have been all too apparent in the revived nationalism of the 1990s, especially in the former Yugoslavia. Borders can have an arbitrariness and can be ways of containing peoples whose other identities might be stronger than the lines on a map. Here the example of a hundred years ago is illuminating. The consequences of the collapse of the old Empires during the First World War are still with us. The old Ottoman provinces in the Middle East were carved up between Britain and France following the Conference of San Remo in April 1920 which was attended by the victorious powers. The so-called mandates were created under the League of Nations in order to protect imperial interests. For Britain this involved the supply of oil and adding a further base on the route to India. For France, this was served through close contact with Middle Eastern Christians in Syria, especially in the territory that became the Lebanon. The aftermath of the Conference involved drawing boundaries which divided earlier territories, creating the contemporary divisions between states, including what is now Jordan and Israel/Palestine. The Resolution from the San Remo Conference also enshrined the Balfour declaration of 1917 with its call for a Jewish homeland in Palestine while at the same time paving the way for the Arab states of today. Its vision remained that of co-operation: it claimed, for instance, that 'mindful of the racial kinship and ancient bonds existing between the Arabs and the Jewish people and realizing that the surest means of working out the consummation of their national aspirations, is through the closest possible collaboration in the development of the Arab State and Palestine'. Yet from the very beginning there was conflict and bloodshed: forty-eight Arabs and forty-seven Jews were killed in riots in 1921.[1] It is clear since that time that seemingly arbitrary borders have taken on multiple meanings and have been associated with a range of complex and frequently competing identities that can often erupt in bloodshed.

Another example is closer to home for me. Again, in the aftermath of the First World War a border was drawn between the United Kingdom and the Irish Free State. Six counties in the northern province of Ulster remained part of the United Kingdom while Southern Ireland became a Free State with almost complete independence. The boundary followed historic borders which did not mirror the competing and powerful religious and national identities that had developed over the previous centuries. It is a border that has taken on a powerful symbolic meaning which has frequently had violent consequences. More recently the border between Northern Ireland and the Irish Republic has been almost constantly in the news. It is a key theme in the negotiations over Britain leaving the European Union. A completely permeable border became a central plank of the Good Friday agreement and has taken on a powerful symbolic meaning in the whole peace process. The idea of creating a hard border with customs controls is unthinkable for most of the people in Northern Ireland. And yet, if the United Kingdom leaves the EU without an agreement, this would be an inevitable consequence. The alternative that would see a border redrawn across the Irish Sea would be equally unthinkable for the Democratic Unionist Party for whom union with the United Kingdom is the central pillar of their political ideology: the idea of treating Northern Ireland differently from England, Scotland and Wales is completely anathema.

Both these examples reveal that partition and the creation of borders and boundaries can frequently create more problems than it will ever solve. Examples from the Indian subcontinent are equally obvious – the creation of new borders often led to massive population shifts accompanied by violence, some of which is still with us. The same was true of the Middle East and in Eastern Europe after both World Wars. There are very few Greeks left in what is now Turkey and very few Turks in Greece. Of course, boundary marking and the establishment of borders are probably as old as the first human civilizations and are closely tied up with human identity and belonging, but what is equally important is the fact that boundaries can take on a symbolic force which is almost independent of the lines themselves. They stand for a whole set of cultural and political identities which are frequently formed out of binary oppositions: tensions over disputed territories around which people and nations identify themselves have frequently led to armed conflict. A good recent and apparently intractable example is that of Kosovo, a part of the Balkans around which Serbian identity has been formed since the fourteenth century and is the home of many of the most important cultural monuments and the Serbian patriarch. But it is a territory now populated by a non-Serbian majority and is the home of a strong Albanian nationalist movement. A small landlocked territory has a powerful symbolic force in two competing cultures.

The Politics of Ecclesial Identity

This sort of symbolic power around identities which are defined against other identities bears a close similarity to the sorts of borders that exist between churches and also – and just as often – *within* churches. By way of an example I begin with what might seem like a trivial dispute over ecclesiastical dress which took place in the 1560s. In those days ecclesiastical dress was a matter of the supreme importance.[2] The point at issue was simple: what to wear in church functioned was symbolic of a whole range of identities that related to the role of the reformation in the wholesale clearing away of the clutter of the medieval Church. It was a sign like a flag for a whole set of theological views that distinguished one group from the next. For some, late medieval choir dress embodied in the surplice was the very mark of the beast in much the same way that the Book of Common Prayer was a 'popish dunghill'.[3] Ultimately, questions about what one wore in church were perceived as questions about idolatry, which pointed to far deeper theological and doctrinal tensions.

In my view, these sorts of controversies are symptomatic of the vast bulk of ecclesiastical conflicts: things are seldom what they seem. Just as an arbitrary line on a map means little until it represents the hopes and longings of a group, a clan, a tribe or a nation, so a seemingly unimportant practice can take on a symbolic meaning which acts as a strong dividing line to cut off one group from another. Sometimes it is difficult to grasp the venom with which people promoted or resisted certain practices: later on in the nineteenth century this became true of the controversies where different campaigning groups shaped Victorian perceptions of the identity of the Church of England. Barricades were constructed behind which competing groups established their identity. The Oxford Movement's *Library of the Fathers* was pitted against their opponents' *Parker Society* edition of the works of the Reformers in much the same way as later the mass vestments and credence tables defended by the English Church Union were attacked by the Church Association.[4]

And of course, to take a longer and broader view of the history of the church, it is clear that from the beginnings there was always disagreement and frequently conflict. Boundaries have always separated one group from another. Indeed, it is probably true to say that a proper understanding of the church includes a recognition that conflict has been part of the history of mission since the first mission to the Gentiles. For example, Paul and Peter were sufficiently at odds with each other, with Paul charging Peter and even his friend Barnabas with 'hypocrisy' and rebuking them for not acting in line with the truth of the gospel (Gal 2:11-21). Different views on circumcision were fundamental to Christian identity and symbolic of far deeper differences.

'Condensation Symbols'

Despite these examples, however, what is frequently underplayed in Church history is the *political* nature of ecclesiastical discourse: the borders and boundaries and contested identities that are the bread and butter of politics are found every bit as much in the Church. It is much too easy for all of us – from whatever quarters – to be seduced into what the American theologian H. Richard Niebuhr called a 'closed society' which 'fills the whole horizon of our experience'.[5] It is clear to me that certain issues have functioned as what the political scientist Murray Edelman has called 'condensation symbols'.[6] For St Paul, the issue of 'circumcision' obviously carries with it a whole range of ideas and a whole set of historical presuppositions: it was a sign of a whole way of life. In our own day the slogans of politicians (such as 'gun control', 'family values', 'freedom of choice' in the USA, or in Britain 'tackling unemployment' or 'reducing the deficit') can take on a whole range of associations and become code words for identity politics. This amounts to the erection of a large edifice behind which groups can coalesce. According to Edelman, various historical events (such as 'Remember the Alamo' or 'Remember Pearl Harbor') can become condensation symbols which might later be used to justify wars.[7] Most recently, President Trump's rhetoric with its talk of 'America First' has used one key symbol – the erection of a wall along the Mexican border – to express the fortress conception of the United States. Walls become impregnable and serve to keep out the hostile outsider.

In a similar way, particular theological or ethical positions on a whole range of issues take on a far broader symbolic meaning than the presenting problem. In the Vestiarian Controversy, what one wore in church became a code for whether or not the Church of England should have continued on its journey of the Protestant Reformation. In the twentieth and twenty-first century the presenting issues have been different but have often been just as divisive: for instance, there were times not so long ago when some Anglo-Catholic parish churches in England had notices saying that they were not in communion with the Church of South India because it had 'lost' the Apostolic Succession after union with the non-episcopal churches in 1947.[8] Similarly, during the 1990s cards circulated which were to be given to parishioners in churches opposed to the ordination of women for them to pass on to hospital chaplains to let them know that only male priests should administer the last rites. A whole range of identity questions are involved in such apparently small and sometimes seemingly insignificant gestures which obviously point to far deeper issues. What seems important in trying to understand such symbolic controversies is that there is a sensitivity to language as well as to the contexts – both ecclesiastical and political – in which they emerged.

The mode of theological discourse for much of Church history has been closely related to political discourse with its efforts at the containment of disputes and its frequent eruptions into conflict. Theology is often conducted through the medium of polemics with its distinctive rhetorical strategies and emphasis on the powers of persuasion. It is frequently a profoundly political discipline. The competing theologies of Thomas Cartwright and John Whitgift, Walter Travers and Richard Hooker in the sixteenth century, and later

Laud and Fisher in the seventeenth are all good examples of political theology from my own Church of England: indeed the starting point for Whitgift and Hooker is the series of *Admonitions* or complaints presented to parliament (in which the questions of vestments and the Prayer Book were major presenting issues). Politics and church history became completely inseparable.

Homosexuality, politics, and conflict in the Church

Let me now take a contemporary example of a set of borders and boundaries that are contained in a condensation symbol. Recent Anglican history demonstrates that the realignment of Anglicanism is being promoted around a set of issues that find their focus in approaches to homosexual practice. This gained pace following the Lambeth Conference of Anglican Bishops in 1998 with its Resolution 1.10 which asserted in a subclause that homosexual practice went against scripture. This has taken on a symbolic prominence which its framers could hardly have expected. As Chris Brittain and Andrew McKinnon have written:

> The position one takes on ordaining gay and lesbian bishops and blessing same-sex partnerships has become a symbolic marker around which differing (and competing) interests within the Communion are constructing strategic partnerships, and possibly even forging a new common identity: 'Orthodox Anglicans'. This conflict cannot simply be reduced to the effects of a so-called culture war between liberals and conservatives, terms which do not fit well in a number of the local socio-political cultures discussed here, since these basic poles stem from a U.S. context.[9]

Although this presenting issue might be extremely emotive, I would suggest it is little different in kind from earlier controversies, even if it is being played out on a larger global stage. The rise of the Global Anglican Future Conference (GAFCON) within the Anglican Communion as a rival structure of communion shows that opposition to homosexual practice has become a symbolic focus for a whole range of complex geographical, theological, and ecclesial identities: a distinctive stance on homosexuality is but a part of a range of theological attitudes and approaches. Like earlier disputes, it is framed in terms of identity and boundaries – 'orthodoxy' here is associated with a particular set of symbols which serve to distinguish one group from another. The debates between the different protagonists have been conducted in terms of the manipulation of language and discourse. Much of this involves different models of biblical interpretation or different understandings of natural law. In turn there are sometimes symbolic acts such as refusing to receive communion or to meet with certain people in certain places who have acted in ways which appear to contravene a symbolic code. The borders are being drawn within the Communion and what counts as orthodoxy is being reshaped.[10]

To understand these disputes what seems crucial is that there is a particular sensitivity to language as well as to the contexts – both ecclesiastical and political – in which these conflicts emerge. As with political disputes, there is a vast amount of cultural baggage that is contained in the particular dispute and which might only be loosely connected to the presenting issue. Indeed, I would suggest, the greater the degree of understanding of the nuances of difference and disagreement, the greater the chance that the conflicting parties might begin to understand one another, and the borders will be less impenetrable. Even though this may not lead to resolution it will at least help people to recognize the nature of their differences both at a surface and a deeper level. From my perspective, therefore, understanding the symbolic politics of difference becomes crucial in efforts to live with diversity.

Consequently, in much the same way as the study of politics involves the study of conflict and of the institutions designed to bring about resolution, so in churches it is important to study the mechanisms for handling conflict and dispute. In analyzing ecclesiastical controversy, a study of conflict can thus be extremely important, as Ephraim Radner has pointed out in his call for an analysis of Christian divisions in their relation to political power both inside and outside the church. He writes: 'I would suggest, in fact, that a more proper framework in which to lodge a discussion of Christian division today would be something like "eristology"—from the Greek word associated with the goddess of discord. Eristology, then, is the study of *hostility* in its disordered forms and forces'.[11] Building on this idea, I would suggest that a detailed analysis of the cultural symbolics of theological politics needs to become the key mode for addressing theological controversy both in the past and in the present: the borders between the groups are barriers that have to be defended by rhetorical force which means political discourse analysis is key for understanding. Here, a warning from George Orwell's 1946 essay, 'Politics and the English language', remains particularly relevant: 'In our age there is no such thing as "keeping out of politics". All issues are political issues, and politics itself is a mass of lies, evasions, folly, hatred, and schizophrenia'.[12]

Although in themselves the slogans which function as condensation symbols often have little impact on the daily lives of most people and are quite detached from their everyday experience, they nevertheless instill a sense of identity and security which does not ultimately rely on rational or analytical argument. Indeed personal identity is constructed through the encounters that people have with one another and the ways in which they construct their opponents' views: words like 'traditional' or 'orthodox' take on meanings quite detached from anything theological or rational and can easily be associated with the construction of 'friend' and 'enemy'.[13] As Brittain and McKinnon suggest, 'the construction of effective condensation symbols has been an important component of organizing opponents of the "liberal agenda".'[14] Or, as Edelman puts it more generally, 'people involved in politics are symbols to other observers; they stand for ideologies, values, or moral stances and they become role models, benchmarks, or symbols of threat and evil'.[15] This means that political language exists in part to create rhetorical mechanisms for demonizing opponents and robbing them of personality as well as promoting group solidarity, sometimes by creating a sense of victimhood.

In all this, according to Edelman, there is a degree of the fetishization of the symbolic: 'The political entities that are most influential upon public consciousness and action ... are fetishes: creations of observers that then dominate and mystify their creators'.[16] Consequently, gathering around markers and creating badges or symbols which reinforce group solidarity become the key factors in identity-formation. At the same time, this process of the 'symbolization' of politics can make reasoned discussion difficult, if not impossible. There is no neutral space: instead everything is marked out by clear borders, and strategies are created to ensure that nobody steps over the line. According to Edelman, there is constant re-enforcement and reiteration: 'people in the same social situations use similar language to cope with the problems they face; and that kind of predictability is characteristic of a great deal of political language. Most of it is banal, precisely because it reassures speaker and audience that whatever they think will serve their interests is justifiable'.[17] The use of symbolic language implies that there are wide areas for manipulation and interpretation through careful use of rhetoric, and through networks of persuasion: 'While most political language has little to do with how well people live, it has a great deal to do with the legitimation of regimes and the acquiescence of publics in actions they had no part in initiating'.[18]

All this seems to resonate with the ways in which language can be used in theological controversy: on many matters that will have no direct effect at all on the church member – and here the attitude towards same-sex marriage is probably a good example – there will nevertheless be a manipulation of language to ensure that people feel that they are 'involved in fateful or significant events'.[19] Things become important because people are constantly told that they *are* important, which is how boundaries are erected in the first place.

Symbolic language thereby becomes a form of political persuasion which might be labelled 'heresthetic' (to use a term borrowed from W. H. Riker's book *The Art of Political Manipulation*).[20] Rhetoric moves beyond the simple art of persuasion to a complete redefinition of the terms of the political debate. As the political theorist Iain McLean puts it in relation the catch-phrase became 'There is no alternative' which dominated British economic policy in the 1980s: 'persuading people that it was true, made it true.'[21]

What I am suggesting is that any attempt to analyze and provide a way forward through conflict in the church requires a framing of the issues as widely and as deeply as possible. In particular, there is the need to embrace and understand political rhetoric as this is expressed in highly potent 'condensation symbols'. In all this, much more than ethics and biblical interpretation is at issue. Indeed, it is quite clear from recent history that there is a powerful rhetoric at work across the Anglican Communion that needs to be addressed in detail – and this is equally true of other churches. The more that all those involved are able to analyze and deepen their understanding of these symbols, the more likely it becomes that they will be able to grasp the underlying differences and move towards a perhaps costly peace. It is, however, something inherently risky: peace might only be established by redrawing boundaries through a treaty – as at the end of the First World War – rather than any reconciliation of opponents. In all this, there is a need to be open to the nuances of language and rhetoric, which might perhaps begin with deep facilitated listening.

Remaining open into the future

Ultimately this set of tasks will be about helping people to open themselves up to the 'other', both the transcendental 'other', that is, to the God who always remains distinct from any contextualization and closure, but also to the 'other' whose perception of the Good News and its implications remains different. As Graham Ward puts it (admittedly somewhat provocatively): 'The institutional churches are necessary, but they are not ends in themselves; they are constantly transgressed by … an erotic community … The body of Christ desiring its consummation opens itself to what is outside the institutional Church; offers itself to perform in fields of activity far from chancels and cloisters.'[22] All borders are permeable because God stands beyond all of them. The practice of Christian listening as a means for addressing conflict is highly unlikely to involve reaching uniformity, still less is it about exclusion, but instead it is about trying to express something of the otherness of God as this is recognized in the communities which exist to proclaim the Gospel of his Son. In turn, this requires a listening to the 'other' within that very community. Christian communities exist in an inter-relationality and interdependence, but they do so in a political and highly conflicted world. Of course, there may be splits after listening and there may well be messiness and blurred edges (or in prosaic language, 'impaired communion') but there is unlikely to be complete separation: agreeing to disagree may be a profoundly liberating step and it may well in the end be a way of resisting violence and promoting peace. Agreeing to disagree means that borders remain but are porous and allow for easy visiting.

Whether there is any possibility of reconciliation or acceptance of diversity over the issue of homosexuality or indeed over other condensation symbols is a question that churches and political bodies continue to face. In Britain, for instance, the whole weight of national identity and political frustration was loaded on a referendum that passed by a slim majority to leave the European Union. It has come to dominate discourse – for those who seek to leave the European Union, the issue has come to symbolise a whole range of frequently incompatible foes which set out to destroy national sovereignty and the British way of life. There was very little room for subtlety in the either/or structure of a referendum which means that a clear boundary between two substantial grouping was erected: either in or out became the dominating rhetoric. The more subtle and more complex notion of a negotiated settlement that was prepared to move across boundaries and to make concessions for the sake of continued permeability has been silenced because of internal political squabbles and a popular press that thrives on drawing boundaries between the insider and the outsider. This often leads to (usually implicit) racist and xenophobic rhetoric where the boundary is drawn at the English Channel and all those seeking to come in are treated as 'economic migrants' seeking to scrounge off the state.

Something not dissimilar is happening in the Anglican Communion. The current Archbishop of Canterbury, Justin Welby, an experienced peacemaker, who visited each of the primates within his first year in office, initially expressed a degree of pessimism about the future of the Communion: the boundaries that had been erected around the issue of homosexuality had become impermeable and different groups sought to exclude one another. More recently, however, there seems to have been a change of tone and nuances have been heard across the dividing lines: at the meeting of the Primates held in Canterbury in January 2016 there was a desire expressed to 'walk together', despite differences.[23] Even though relationships with the American Episcopal Church (TEC), which the previous summer had changed its canons to allow for same-sex marriages in church, were particularly strained, and even though there was a request that TEC be removed from doctrinal and ecumenical bodies, it was not to be excluded from the Communion altogether.[24] This policy was upheld at the ACC meeting at Lusaka later in the year. In May 2016 a task group was appointed by the Archbishop of Canterbury to discuss the way forward which notably included participation from the Presiding Bishop of the Episcopal Church, Michael Curry, along with representatives from the Indian sub-continent, Australia, Africa, Canada and England.

Within the Church of England there is significant opposition to changing the teaching on homosexuality, despite the significant number of clergies who have entered into civil partnerships some of whom, since the change of legislation in 2013, have gone on to marry their partners. Facilitated discussions ('shared conversations') to encourage diversity and respect difference have taken place at various levels from bishops to General Synod to groups of Dioceses. There are deliberate efforts to break down the boundaries, and in recent months various commissions have been appointed to investigate the issue of sexuality dispassionately so that the irrational force of the condensation symbol can be properly interrogated, even if this is deeply unsettling to some. Out of all this it is quite likely that legislation will eventually be brought before General Synod within the next few years which will change the policy towards what the Church can offer people living in same-sex relationships: but it is also clear that some will refuse to accept this and will erect new borders and boundaries and possibly even retreat completely behind an impenetrable wall. At the same time, it is also likely that with so many other churches in the Anglican Communion gathered around opposition to homosexual practice as a 'condensation symbol' which has become a badge of orthodoxy that there is little hope that such a method will be exported across all the churches of the Communion. Indeed, if it adopts a pluralist solution the Church of England is likely to be labelled as another of those declining imperialist institutions (like the Episcopal Church) seeking to cast its liberal spell on a hapless Communion. The power of political rhetoric contained in condensation symbols may be too strong for any listening process to overcome. Where condensation symbols have been rendered sacred, there is little chance that there will be the humility enough for the listening process to work, and for any compromises or changes to be made.

Conclusion

My conclusion to these problems is modest but important. To return to borders: in the church as well in politics, they remain the norm. They provide the haven behind which identities can be forged: they might be coterminous with a nationality or a group or in the church with a denomination or a sect. In themselves borders are neutral and might even allow for human identity to flourish. Inevitably an institution, like a building, has walls which protect and keep out the elements. But all borders are in some sense arbitrary: somebody once drew lines on a map. While this was perhaps not always in such an arbitrary way as at the Conference at San Remo in 1920, nevertheless all borders have a beginning, and none is a simple given. In England some of our borders between our administrative districts – the counties – date back well over 1000 years. People identified as Yorkshiremen or Lancastrians. But the boundaries were redrawn in the 1970s as part of a process of trying to ensure that they were all roughly equal. In terms of population. There were no wars, but just a few disgruntled voices. But other borders have not been redrawn with such ease – the symbolic identities are too strong, and the stakes seem to be too high.

As I have already hinted, there is a Christian response to this: while borders cannot be denied and they might be expressed linguistically or culturally, they become problematic as soon as they become all-defining and excluding. However culturally sensitive and however contextual Christian theology might seek to be, it has at the same time to resist hard borders: contexts can exclude other contexts. In Christianity the outsider, the one on the other side of the frontier is equal in the sight of God whatever he or she might look like and whatever language he or she might speak. The reason for this is simple: if God remains transcendent then all borders must be permeable since all are ultimately products of human sin.

The trouble with churches, as with nations, is that it is all too easy for them to become ends in themselves and to forget their fundamental purpose. As the political theorist and theologian David Nicholls put it:

> Christians have often replaced a Trinitarian monotheism by a henotheistic religion which "makes a finite society whether cultural or religious, the object of trust as well as of loyalty" (H. R. Niebuhr). In doing so the Church has transformed itself from being a divinely

chosen and guided instrument of God's purpose in the world into an end in itself.[25]

We find it all too easy to create a 'henotheistic' or tribal deity, and when we do so we forget the disturbing presence of a God who lies outside any boundary, including those of our own churches. The Church is not a closed society, but one constantly provoked and disrupted by the vision of the Kingdom of God which is not contained by any borders. To be an open institution, the Church needs to be able to provoke Christians to risk all, including perhaps the loss of cultural identifiers and the borders which contain them. They are asked to risk all because of the promise of resurrection and hope.

However free, democratic or legitimate our institutions in both church and state, none can claim a finality or absoluteness; both church and state need to be seen as open systems with boundaries that constantly look outwards and upwards. This will force a careful reappraisal of any condensation symbol, and it will mean the norm for Christian politics will be the politics of compromise. Those in authority are always vulnerable to abuses of power and to neglect their finitude – and here the state resembles the Church: unfettered power and state absolutism ought to be constantly questioned and tested.[26] An open and critical approach will be deeply hostile to the elevation of political systems as if they were beyond question, as if their borders were fixed. The logic is simple, as Richard Niebuhr suggested: 'No relative power, be it that of the nation or its people as well as that of tyrants, can claim absolute sovereignty or total loyalty.'[27] That means that borders will always be a problem for Christians whether in the state or the church. The arbitrariness of a line on a map can easily be treated as an absolute truth that can exclude everything else. It will inevitably mean that people will fail to listen and to respond to the other. And that is the tragedy of human politics and, dare I say it, the tragedy of church history. If we look around, we find that new boundaries are constantly being erected and few are prepared to listen to the outsider and to take the risk of compromise.

Endnotes

[1] Eugene Rogan, *The Fall of the Ottomans: The Great War in the Middle East, 1914-1920* (London: Penguin2015), 401.

[2] See Mark Chapman, *Anglican Theology* (London: T & T Clark, 2011), 77-85.

[3] John Field in *An Admonition to Parliament* (1573) in W. H. Frere and C. E. Douglas, *Puritan Manifestoes: A Study of the Origin of the Puritan Revolt* (London: SPCK, 1907), 1-39, here 8.

[4] See Mark Chapman, 'Remembering: living with the legacy of the Reformation', in *One in Christ* 51:2 (2017): 260-75.

[5] H. Richard Niebuhr, *Radical Monotheism and Western Culture* (Louisville: Westminster/John Knox, 1960), 35.

[6] Murray Edelman, *Constructing the Political Spectacle* (Chicago: University of Chicago Press, 1988), 22.

[7] Edelman, *Constructing the Political Spectacle*, 70.

[8] Alan Billings relates an account told him in the late 1960s by Professor Geoffrey Lampe of a notice in an East Anglican church porch which announced: 'Communicants of the Church of South India are not welcome here', see Alan Billings, *Lost Church: Why We Must Find It Again* (London: SPCK, 2013), 103.

[9] Christopher Craig Brittain and Andrew McKinnon, 'Homosexuality and the Construction of "Anglican Orthodoxy": The Symbolic Politics of the Anglican Communion', *Sociology of Religion* 72:3 (2011), 351-73, 352-3.

[10] The Council of Anglican Provinces in Africa meeting on 9-10 March 2015 in South Africa was marked by the absence of some primates of substantial churches – Kenya, Nigeria, Uganda, and Rwanda. They berated the chairman of CAPA, Archbishop Bernard Ntahoruti of Burundi, for attending a meeting in 2014 (along with the Archbishops of Central Africa and West Africa, and Tanzania) with bishops of The Episcopal Church of the USA.

[11] Ephraim Radner, *A Brutal Unity: The Spiritual Politics of the Christian Church* (Waco: Baylor University Press, 2012), 4-5.

[12] 'Politics and the English language', in Sonia Orwell and Ian Angos (eds), *Collected Essays, Journalism and Letters of George Orwell*, 4 vols. (New York: Harcourt, Brace, Javanovich, 1968), vol. 1, 127-40, at 137.

[13] See also Carl Schmitt, *The Concept of the Political* (Chicago: Chicago University Press, 1996), 27; see also *Political Theology: Four Chapters on the Concept of Sovereignty* (Cambridge, MA: MIT Press, 1985).

[14] Brittain and McKinnon, 'Homosexuality and the construction of "Anglican orthodoxy"', 357.

[15] Murray Edelman, *Constructing the Political Spectacle*, p. 2; see also Fred Kniss, *Disquiet in the Land: Cultural Conflict in American Mennonite Communities* (New Brunswick: Rutgers University Press, 1997). For a fascinating account of the use of 'condensation symbols' in American politics, see Colleen Kelley, *The Rhetoric of First Lady Hillary Rodham Clinton: Crisis Management Discourse* (Westport: Prager, 2001), 230.

[16] Edelman, *Constructing the Political Spectacle*, 11.

[17] Murray Edelman, 'Political language and political reality', *Political Studies* 18:1 (1985), 10-19, at 14.

[18] Edelman, 'Political language and political reality', 14.

[19] Edelman, 'Political language and political reality', 14.

[20] W. H. Riker, *The Art of Political Manipulation* (New Haven: Yale University Press, 1986).

[21] Iain McLean, *Rational Choice and British Politics. An Analysis of Rhetoric and Manipulation from Peel to Blair* (Oxford: Oxford University Press, 2001), 225.

[22] Graham Ward, *Cities of God* (London: Routledge, 2000). 180.

[23] Primates' Communiqué at: http://www.anglicancommunion.org/media/206035/Communiqué_from_the_Primates_Meeting_2016.pdf (accessed 4 August 2016).

[24] In the summer of 2016 the Canadian Church also changed its canons to allow for same-sex marriage in church.

[25] David Nicholls, 'Great Expectations: Christian Hope and Marxist Hope' in Kenneth Leech and Rowan Williams (eds), *Essays Catholic and Radical* (London: Bowardean Press, 1983), 278–91, at 290.

[26] Mark D. Chapman, *Blair's Britain: A Christian Critique* (London: Darton, Longman and Todd, 2005), esp. ch. 7.

[27] Niebuhr, *Radical Monotheism and Western Culture*, p. 77.

17

Rethinking Theological Education: Towards a Borderless Church

Rachel Evie Vernon

As Christians, we struggle to follow Jesus; to bring justice, peace and joy to the whole created universe; to create communities that give love and respect to everyone.

But it is indeed a struggle. Too often our churches and church structures are complicit in encouraging injustice rather than in supporting liberation. Too often the vulnerable come to us for help, and we refuse to believe them and turn them away or worse; we promise them help, only to abuse them even more. The tears of those sexually, mentally, physically and spiritually abused in our churches, church schools, charity homes and even our seminaries cry out for justice.

For too long, we have shut our ears, and when complaints have emerged, we have preferred to believe that they pertain to some other community, to some other country, to some other church. And when we have been unable to escape the reality that it touches our own community, our first impulse has been to hush the story up; to silence the complainants; to transfer the perpetrators.

Today we can no longer hide from the truth. There is no church community in the world untouched by the reality that we have all fallen far short of the measure of what we ought to be as a church. And if you think I am overstating the case, let us each take a moment to reflect on our own church situation. What are the cases that we know about, or suspect, that we have been trying to convince ourselves are single isolated incidents, regrettable, but nothing to create a major drama about? Suppose that far from being exceptions, these cases are part of a widespread culture of abuse?

Acknowledging that we have lost our way is a good thing. It allows us to stop, turn around and find a new way to go, i.e. confession and repentance. So how did we get here, and how can we construct new pathways?

I propose that part of our task must be to rethink how we do theological education in its widest sense. How do we prepare Christians to be faithful followers of Christ? We need to look at what and how we teach within our homes, our Sunday Schools, our seminaries and all our church institutions. This root and branch critique is not easy. It must be done humbly, honestly, contextually, and, above all, prayerfully and hopefully. This is a difficult task, but it is by no means impossible. I believe that the God who calls us to this great task of rethinking ecclesia, of rethinking theology, will give us the means and the will to accomplish our part of this mission.

I am going to speak to you from my own experience of theological education and formation, as a woman of faith working, sometimes uncomfortably, I will confess, within the church in Jamaica, in the U.K. and in different parts of the world. I speak no universal truths here, but I hope that the insights I have gained on my journey can inspire your own imagination to look for truths within your own contexts.

I want us to look at how we transmit our Christian faith and values within our Sunday Schools, our youth ministry and church schools, our congregational groups, our seminaries, our training for church leaders, and our synods and church councils. I want to look not so much at the content of our teaching, but at the methodology we use and the value we convey with our attitudes and behaviours, our hidden curricula.

Let me declare myself at this point. If you have not already guessed it, I am a 'nannyish' (term courtesy of the Revd Dr Marjorie Lewis -a womanist theologian dedicated to the struggle for justice, from a Jamaican freedom fighter, Nanny of the Maroons) theologian, with a liberationist bent. I believe passionately the God speaks to all God's people, and that the job of the church and the professional theologian is to discern the wisdom of all, including, perhaps especially, that of the little ones and the excluded ones.

And so to our work with children. How do we ensure that our churches learn as much as we can from these little ones, to whom, according to Jesus, belong the kingdom of heaven? Do we welcome them, or do we banish them into some grubby little corner with moth-eaten books? Do we listen to them, or do we shut them up? Do we let them experience the Christian community as a place of joy and delight, or as a grim, boring torture to be endured until they can escape? Do we love them and protect them, or do we harm them and abuse them?

The stories of the church's treatment of indigenous children in Australia and Canada, of children of unmarried mothers in Ireland, of children accused of witchcraft in parts of Africa, and the many other stories make cruel hearing. The underlying attitude leading to the unspeakable cruelty meted out by some 'good Christians' seemed to be a belief that some children were lesser beings because of their race, class, or perceived sinfulness, and could be subjected to any manner of evil because they did not count. Could the equally troubling silence of those who witness[ed] the atrocities have come from a belief that the children were worth less than 5e good name of the institution?

The children themselves were brainwashed into believing that what they were experiencing was proper Christian behaviour. May God have mercy on us all. (https://www.cbc.ca/news/canada/montreal/resisting-residential-schools-1.3823181; https://www.nytimes.com/interactive/2017/10/28/world/europe/tuam-ireland-babies-children.html; https://www.theguardian.com/society/2017/feb/27/britains-child-migrant-programme-why-130000-children-were-shipped-abroad; https://www.bbc.co.uk/news/world-africa-10671790)

Our approach to children expresses and exposes our theology. We have to be able to relate to them in respectful and, for want of a better word, non- creepy ways. Shutting ourselves away from them in a misguided attempt to protect them just causes more problems.

Fr Aloysius Pieris, a wonderful and wise priest theologian from Sri Lanka, declares that if we cannot communicate our faith to children, we are in the wrong business. He spends quite a bit of his time with the children in his neighbourhood, playing with them, telling them stories and listening to their ideas. If we can think of each child as an icon of Jesus, then we are on the path to wisdom. (http://www.dailymirror.lk/97479/an-epochal-trendsetter-fr-aloysius-pieris-sj)

Now I wish to focus on how we do Christian education and formation of our young people, with particular emphasis on our church schools. One of the church's most important gifts to the world has been its legacy of education. All over the world, churches set up and continue to run institutions of learning at all levels.

In my own country, I went to a Moravian infant school, a Roman Catholic prep school and an Anglican high school. I taught in Anglican, Roman Catholic and Church of God high schools. I have a great appreciation for church led education. I was fortunate to grow up at a time when my society was very open to youth. At St Hilda's, where I was a boarder, we were encouraged to explore ideas. We had full access to a large library, and our sixth form association attended meetings where we cross questioned ministers of government and even Prime Minister Michael Manley on national policy. We were mandated to explore our faith, to plan acts of worship, and occasionally to lead worship at St Mark's church nearby.

We grew up in a time when a very resilient Jamaican culture was beginning to be granted the respect it deserved, so we were taught to be respectful of the support staff, and to use our language for cultural expressions, even if it was not acceptable for classroom conversation.

It was not always thus, and Joyce Gladwell, in 'Brown Face, Big Master' bears witness to an earlier St Hilda's where her yellow-brown face was not respected, and where it is easier to recognise the school as part of global policy of cultural genocide by religious education.

This conscious decision by colonial governments to use Christian education systems to replace so-called local 'superstition' with European culture, in order to make the so-called 'natives' more compliant to European administration, is most clearly delineated in the cases of the Canadian and Australian residential schools mentioned above, but it was part of the policy everywhere.

Church schools were primarily designed not to allow young people to explore how they could best follow Jesus within their own contexts, but to make them into little Europeans, scornful and disrespectful of their own culture. God however has a way of allowing things to get turned upside down. Many activists have used the tools of their European-based education to delve into and bring to public view the treasures from their own heritage. As Joseph told his brothers regarding their selling him into captivity in Egypt, 'You meant it for evil, but God has used it for good,' (Genesis 50:20).

And so what do we do about our wonderful schools? We have to examine them carefully, honestly and prayerfully. How do we refit our curricula and the attitudes of our teachers and administrators so that they encourage our young people to be resilient, questioning and hopeful? How do we ensure that they see the best in themselves, in their family, their culture and the church, while rejecting that which is damaging? That they ask the right questions of their society and its leaders? That they ask the right questions of themselves when they become the leaders?

And what about our congregations, are we preparing people to face the modern world with generosity and compassion, with wisdom and integrity? Do our churches set examples of breaking down the barriers of bigotry and classism, casteism, sexist and other negative 'isms'? Alas, there are too many times when we are the very bastions of oppression. But sometimes churches do indeed walk beside people in their community, part of the struggle for justice. I think, for instance, of work being done by the church in Sri Lanka in tea plantations, and by churches in the Philippines alongside indigenous peoples.

Again we must each take inventory of our own churches and congregations. How do we ensure that our churches are themselves places of equality? What are we doing to challenge the social and political leaders who do and say appalling things under the banner of Christianity?

And now I move on to the seminaries and theological colleges, those places, within most traditions, for the formation and training of the people mainly responsible for the Christian development of the children, the youth and the congregations. Surely it is this part of theological education which must be held accountable for the successes and failures of the Christian ecclesia.

I am an Anglican and I was a student and later taught at the United Theological College of the West Indies, and taught at the Queen's Foundation for Ecumenical Theological Education in Birmingham, UK, so I will mostly use them as my exemplars, but I have visited, discussed, rejoiced in and wept over many other seminaries during my career.

The favoured pattern of Anglican theological education that I have observed calls for two to four years of residential training with regular hours of prayer, preferentially conducted in cassocks. The curriculum differs, but generally includes Biblical Studies, Theology, and a variety of other courses on areas such as Pastoral Studies, Church History, Ethics, Liberation Theology, Interfaith Issues, depending on the faculty and board preferences. The style of teaching tends to favour lectures and occasionally seminars from lecturers and teachers who are definitely 'above' the students.

Students are generally removed from their communities of origin, with little, if any consideration given to their spouses and children, and none at all to their families of origin. Contact with the community nearby the institution is generally limited to participation in Sunday services.

I would venture to say that this method of formation generally continues to be elitist and classist. From my observation, students are prepared so that they can fit most easily into an urban middle-class congregation, which is felt to be the most preferred posting for a clergy person. There is often an underlying assumption that the future minister will go and 'take charge' of their future church assignment.

I posit that this type of formation tends to foster a culture of clergy entitlement and tolerates the type of molestation which has been exposed in the last few decades. John Monaco has written an indictment of his experience in a Roman Catholic seminary, but much of the abuse he describes is unfortunately common in too many other theological institutions. This type of training and formation, has also encouraged an 'old boy' (mostly) network which serves to protect its members from complaints by outsiders. It values the institution of the church above the people, and upholds the culture of impunity.

(https://medium.com/@johnmonaco/i-love-the-catholic-church-which-is-why-i-say-churchtoo-8490704fc020)

The only salvation for the church is frank and open confession, apology, restitution and reparation, and repentance. We have to approach theological formation very differently. First we have to acknowledge that clergy are just people, called from within their communities to serve the church, not to govern it.

This means that their communities and families need to be, as far as possible, part of their formation and training. I pay homage to programmes such as those I have been told of at Tamil Nadu Theological Seminary (TTS) in Madurai and Carlile College in Nairobi which immerse students in rural, urban and inner city communities. These represent steps in the right direction. Whether they go far enough is for the people at those institutions to say.

Traditional theological colleges are costly both emotionally and financially, for the students and for their communities and their families. Even when the tuition and boarding costs are met by the church, the candidate still has to find clothing, travel and other incidental expenses, as well as negotiate their loss of income from the employment they could have had if they had not enrolled in theological education. If they have to leave their family behind, they still have to cope with the upheaval of being away from their chief sources of emotional support, while if they are accompanied by their nuclear family - I have never heard of a seminary supporting any extended family members- the whole family have to adjust to a new and confusing lifestyle. Some institutions do provide some kind of training and support for spouses, but I have never heard of one providing preparation for children. Their church communities are often at a loss as to how to replace their most active member.

Many churches have established various types of distance education and training for clergy and church workers, quite often with intense formation periods when all the students come together for intensive residential sessions. This type of training certainly addresses some of the issues related to costs and the removal of the student from their family and community for the training period. When it is embarked upon merely as a cost-saving venture, it often fails to increase community involvement in ministerial formation, and pays even less attention to the needs of the student's family. If it operates alongside a residential programme, it runs the risk of being viewed as a lesser, second-tiered approach to ministry.

Where do we need to go from here? We need to, within our own contexts, to explore theological formation and training that is respectful of the community's wisdom and experience. We need to recognise that candidates' families, both nuclear and extended are intimately bound up with their ministry, and need support and preparation, quite as much as the candidate. There are some promising ventures which we can explore and build on.

And finally, what of preparation and training for clergy and laity in leadership positions. If they are not engaged, then the most wonderful programmes at other levels will be entirely for nothing. Again there are promising attempts to engage with church leaders in different ways. The Asian Theological Academy, for instance, is a tries to engage theologically with church leaders across Asia, with visitors from other regions; and the Diocese of Harare engages the clergy in annual refresher schools.

The church in the twenty-first century faces a major time of challenge, when it needs to rethink its whole way of being. It has much to repent of, if it is to restore its credibility. It needs to rethink its way of being ecclesia, but to do this, it must rethink its way of theological education and formation, in order to more faithfully follow the simple teacher of Galilee.

18

Borderless Church –
An Inclusive Church

Scripture Passages: (i) Isaiah 52.13 – 53.12
(ii) John 9. 1-7; 24-41

Daniel S. Thiagarajah

As our Church of South India marks 70 years journeying from our formation to the present with guests from global partners, I am reminded that we owe our formation to the great missionary enterprises of previous centuries. Our diocesan cathedral in Jaffna will soon celebrate 400 years since its construction by Portuguese missionaries. It is just over 200 years since American missionaries adopted the cathedral as their own, and it is 70 years since the cathedral became the central church of the Jaffna Diocese of CSI. Our diocese shares with many of the dioceses of southern India a historical connection with the American missionaries. This historic connection gives the Jaffna Diocese the unique perspective of being both a member diocese of CSI and - as a separate national church in Sri Lanka - we are something of a global or international partner within CSI. It is this history of colonialism, changing international mission theology, and the reality of political upheaval that today stands under the judgement and mercy of God's saving word, which informs my response to our theme of 'towards a borderless church'.

The borders that provided a measure of security for our diocese in Sri Lanka's long-running civil war were largely obliterated in the final years of civil war and the years immediately after. At first the state over-ran our borders, with diocesan land confiscated by the military, churches destroyed by the fighting, pastors and their families' innocent victims of war, and countless thousands of Tamil civilians in our towns and villages massacred. We suffered daily as a borderless church, made borderless by the evils of war. And to our immense distress, we found that some of those we had previously relied upon distanced themselves from us, with some global partners withdrawing their support and friendship. Being a borderless church through this time was a disturbingly lonely, anxious, and heart-breaking journey.

Throughout these traumatic years, I, and many in our Jaffna Diocese identified with the servant of Isaiah's great poetic testimony to the traumatised Israelites in Babylonian captivity and exile. 'For he grew up before him like a young plant, and like a root out of dry ground; he had no form or majesty that we should look at him, nothing in his appearance that we should desire him. He was despised and rejected by others; a man of suffering and acquainted with infirmity; and as one from whom others hide their faces, he was despised, and we held him of no account' (Isa. 53:²⁻³). When the borders of Tamil identity in Sri Lanka were obliterated by the ruthless dictates of war, we knew what it was as a Tamil people to have 'no form or majesty', to be 'despised and rejected', to be overwhelmed with suffering and disability, and to be held to be 'people of no account'.

Isaiah's use of the past tense to describe the servant's suffering reminds us that Isaiah is recalling Babylon's historic and brutal oppression of Israel to understand the present plight of his people's depressed captivity to Babylon's borderless ambitions. Isaiah will declare that the borders Israel had constructed to protect its identity were destroyed as an act of God's judgement because Israel had turned from God's justice and mercy to sustain its life as God's people. Are we in Sri Lanka then to witness in the destruction of our borders as a Tamil church, a similar judgment by God on 'identity-markers' we inherited from our missionary forebears?

Consider these seeds of the devastation we endure. Nineteenth century Christian evangelists erected a rigid border with Hinduism and Buddhism through their despising of other faiths as 'the moral darkness of Asia'. Evangelical piety feared the evil it saw in these faiths, causing a strong fundamentalist reaction from these faiths that still echoes today. Missionary education in the English medium that advantaged higher caste Tamil men became the gate-way to a career path in British colonial administration and businesses. An unintentional consequence of this elitism was to help foster fear amongst the Singhalese majority against the Tamil people, which in turn led to our rejection and oppression in post-independence Ceylon.

This reality mirrors the trauma that Israel experienced under the colonialist administration of the expanding Babylonian Empire. I suggest that Isaiah's song of God's suffering servant has similarities to Tamil suffering, where the victims of expansionist Empires share a common experience of life. Victims of injustice are created when identity-marking borders are forcibly shattered by a merciless exercise of power.

And yet here, when the servant's suffering and powerlessness are at their lowest point, when the disfigurement of the servant is 'astonishing', 'his appearance, beyond human semblance', and 'his form' inhuman, the prophet Isaiah's poetry takes an unexpected and profound turn. The kings experience a sudden insight, enough to 'startle' them to the point of bringing them to 'contemplating' what is the real truth behind their exercise of power. Suddenly Isaiah sees something in the plight of the servant that no-one else could see. For this poem is really about the exercise of power, and more particularly, about the way that God exercises power: 'Who has believed what we have heard? And to whom has the arm (or power) of the Lord been revealed?' (53:¹).

This insight leads me to ask – what is at stake for the Church of South India in our relationship with ecumenical global partners when we consider the possibilities for being a borderless church for our future formation of Christian communities? At stake is our whole understanding of the nature and effect of the power of God in relation to the worship and mission of the church. And this comes to the forefront for those who look upon the servant with a sense of revulsion, for the truth that Isaiah reveals is that God's power is actually shown in God's solidarity with the servant's suffering. God's power to be in solidarity with the very persons that God's people had despised and rejected radically undermines their previous certainty of faith. This is a profound turn towards a radical re-reading of God's purpose, to which Isaiah calls us with his prophetic re-framing of what divine justice requires of God's people.

It is quite incongruous that the preeminent herald of justice (Isa. 42:¹⁻⁴), God's servant, is brought to a state of abject suffering by the way justice is carried out by those who see themselves as God's people.

'He was oppressed, and he was afflicted, yet he did not open his mouth; like a lamb that is led to the slaughter, and like a sheep that before its shearers is silent, so he did not open his mouth. By a perversion of justice he was taken away. Who could have imagined his future? For he was cut off from the land of the living, stricken for the transgression of my people' (53:⁷⁻⁸).

The very person who God called to have a vocation to bring about justice according to God's will, is subjected to a perversion of justice by others who claim for themselves the privileged status of being God's people. Isaiah's stark poetry exposes the gulf between the just reign of God and the ungodly and unjust practices of some of those who see themselves as God's people.

In the years after my consecration as bishop of Jaffna Diocese, I experienced a personal measure of the servant's rejection and powerlessness and - after the war's end - of being identified with a people who were seen by the victorious powers to be 'of no account' to Sri Lanka's future. Then one day I was approached by a Singhalese Christian man, a member of that very ethnic community with whom the Tamil Tigers had been at war for three decades. He asked me if he could become a pastor in the Jaffna Diocese, a church that had been exclusively Tamil for nearly 200 years. What did he see in me that prompted this request? I don't know, but God knows. All my life I had viewed being a Christian Tamil in terms of our people's yearning for a national Tamil identity. This was the 'border' I had grown up with that had surrounded my identity for a life-time. This Singhalese pastor's question caused me to query the previous certainty of my faith. The just reign of God was calling me to a life-changing turn towards God's borderless purpose.

As I pondered and wondered about his request, I sensed that this man too, knew something of suffering as a Singhalese Christian pastor in a nation of predominately Singhalese Buddhists. Perhaps for the first time, I identified with the 'we' in Isaiah's poem, and I saw my questioner with new eyes. As I reflected on my awareness of the border between Tamil and Singhalese communities, and my part in the collective 'blaming' of the other for our fractured relationships, I accepted that this border had also trapped me in an identity of Tamil nationalism that was captive to the ideological strategy of the state for preserving its own power. As Isaiah's poetic imagination declared, this new awareness was 'startling'. It brought me to 'contemplate' what the truth was about my exercise of power as a Tamil bishop. Suddenly I began to see something in the question of this 'other' Singhalese man that I had not seen before. **'Who can believe what I have heard? And to whom has the arm (or power) of the Lord been revealed?'** (53:[1]).

By the grace of God a new possibility was being opened up for me, the possibility of being liberated from my own personal borders of Tamil nationalist identity. By the grace of God, this new possibility was renewing my Tamil identity as one who was in solidarity with members of the Singhalese community. By the power of God's love, today the Jaffna Diocese is becoming a reconciling national church committed to forming our people into a community who finally understand what God has already declared: 'All we like sheep have gone astray; we have all turned to our own way' (53:[6a]).

When you open your heart to the pain of the 'other', you may be open to the power or 'arm' of God that breaks through the borders that sustain identities captive to the powers of Empire. When 'we' who believe ourselves to be God's people too easily justify our distance from the suffering of the other, it is God's power that disturbs our assumptions and teaches us to speak with a contrite heart and in a confessional voice. As the perception of the 'we' in Isaiah is transformed by what God reveals in those we have judged to be godless, so may we acknowledge how our spiritual blindness not only traps us in a past without hope but it also prevents us from seeing the human reality within the feared 'other'. Then we may renew CSI's historic vocation for unity, not in being borderless, but by God's grace, through our diversity.

I trust that as we are renewed by the power of God's grace, we may attend to all of our historic and current relationships with an open and contrite heart as we learn to speak truthfully to one another in a humble and confessional voice. Then we may hear God's prophetic word spoken to us to direct our worship and mission: **'See, my servant shall prosper; he shall be exalted and lifted up, and shall be very high'** (52:[12]). May it be so. Amen.

Contributors

1. Rev. Dr. K. Jesurathnam, Professor of the Old Testament, The United Theological College

2. Dr. George Zachariah, Trinity Methodist Theological College

3. Felix Weise, Youth Minister and member of EMS Youth Network

4. Fr. Mathew Chandran Kunnel, Director, Ecumenical Christian Centre, Bangalore

5. Rev. Dr. Y.T. Vinayaraj, PhD, Professor of Systematic Theology, Mar Thoma Theological Seminary, Kottayam

6. Mrs Ella Sonawane, Associate General Secretary, Publishing & Mission, ISPCK

7. Rev. Jung Eun Moon Grace, Christian Conference of Asia

8. Prof. Dr. Matthias Zeindler, Professor of Dogmatics at the Institute for Systematic Theology, University of Bern, Schwitzerland

9. Rev Dr Peniel Jesudason Rufus Rajkumar, Programme Coordinator - Interreligious Dialogue and Cooperation, Professor - Ecumenical Institute, Château de Bossey, World Council of Churches,

10. Dr. E.V. Suranjan Maben, Consultant Physician, Professor and Head, AJ Institute of Medical science

11. Dr. Joseph Daniel, Professor of History of Christianity, Mar Thoma Theological Seminary, Kottayam, Visiting faculty at the University of Bern, Schwitzerland

12. Rev. Prof. Kyo Seong Ahn, Presbyterian University and Theological Seminary (PUTS), South Korea

13. The Revd. Dr. Sunil M. Caleb, Principal, Bishop's College, Calcutta, W.B.

14. Rev. Dr. Santanu K. Patro, Professor of Religious Studies, Registrar, Senate of Serampore College

15. Sudipta Singh, Mission Secretary, Research and Capacity Development at Council for World Mission, Council for World Mission

16. The Revd Canon Professor Mark D. Chapman, Vice-Principal and Academic Dean, Ripon College, Cuddesdon, Professor of the History of Modern Theology, University of Oxford, Canon Theologian of Truro

17. Rachele (Evie) Vernon O'Brien, Theological Adviser at USPG

18. Bishop Daniel S. Thiagarajah Ph.D., Bishop of the CSI in the Jaffna Diocese